Muslim Women's Quest for Justice

Muslim Women's Quest for Justice is an urban ethnographic study of several Muslim women's organisations in northern India. These organisations work to carve out spaces that allow for the articulation of alternative experiences and conceptions of religion and justice that challenge Islamic orthodoxy as well as the monopoly of the Indian state in the domain of family law. While most analyses on reform efforts within Muslim family law in India have focused on women's protection within the state legal system, this book offers the rare opportunity to understand how organised groups of Muslim women's rights activists contest marginalising forces present in the family and criminal courts, Shariat courts, local mosques, workplace, legislature and legal documents. In doing so, the author pushes against troubling assumptions that Islam is incompatible with ideas of women's rights and that the State is the only dispenser of justice. This book offers new directions for studies on the dispersed nature of women's identities in Islamic family law. It suggests the ways in which non-state regulated legal bodies can assist in upholding the rights, dignity, and freedom of Muslim women. This book will help scholars in exploring the intricate realities of socio-legal reform within contested local, national and transnational settings. It is especially valuable to those in the field of feminist legal studies, law and society, sociology, anthropology, Islamic studies and post colonialism. It is further of interest to policy-makers, legal advocates, and human and women's rights groups dedicated to finding integrated grassroots solutions toward the realisation of gender justice.

Mengia Hong Tschalaer teaches at the John Jay College of Criminal Justice, City University of New York. She is a legal anthropologist with a focus on the relationship between politics of knowledge production, women's subjectivities, law, and Islam in contemporary India. Her scholarship specifically examines the micro-realities that shape people's understanding of women's rights and religion. She was a Visiting Scholar and Research Fellow at the Center for Gender and Sexuality Law, Columbia Law School and has also taught undergraduate courses on intersectionality, gender and sexuality, law and society, and culture and identity at the City University of New York and Columbia University.

Cambridge Studies in Law and Society

Cambridge Studies in Law and Society aims to publish the best scholarly work on legal discourse and practice in its social and institutional contexts, combining theoretical insights and empirical research.

The fields that it covers are: studies of law in action, the sociology of law; the anthropology of law; cultural studies of law, including the role of legal discourses in social formations; law and economics; law and politics; and studies of governance. The books consider all forms of legal discourse across societies, rather than being limited to lawyers' discourses alone.

The series editors come from a range of disciplines: academic law; socio-legal studies; sociology; and anthropology. All have been actively involved in teaching and writing about law in context.

Muslim Women's Quest for Justice

Gender, Law and Activism in India

Mengia Hong Tschalaer

CAMBRIDGE
UNIVERSITY PRESS

CAMBRIDGE
UNIVERSITY PRESS

University Printing House, Cambridge CB2 8BS, United Kingdom
One Liberty Plaza, 20th Floor, New York, NY 10006, USA
477 Williamstown Road, Port Melbourne, vic 3207, Australia
4843/24, 2nd Floor, Ansari Road, Daryaganj, Delhi – 110002, India
79 Anson Road, #06–04/06, Singapore 079906

Cambridge University Press is part of the University of Cambridge.

It furthers the University's mission by disseminating knowledge in the pursuit of education, learning and research at the highest international levels of excellence.

www.cambridge.org
Information on this title: www.cambridge.org/9781107155770

First published 2017

Printed in India by Nutech Print Services, New Delhi

A catalogue record for this publication is available from the British Library

ISBN 978-1-107-15577-0 Hardback

To
all the Muslim women
who have so generously shared their stories with me

To
my children Anaïs Faye and Jasper Soon
who had to relinquish their time with me to the writing of this book

To
my parents
who taught me to pursue my goals and aspirations and never give up

Contents

Preface

Muslim Women's Quest for Justice marks an important milestone of a long journey. A journey that begun in 2005. Back then, in November, I set off to commence fieldwork for my master thesis in rural south Rajasthan, near Udaipur. There, I examined the ways women of the Meena community (re)negotiate patriarchal gender norms and women's identities within an unusual tribal women's court. Presided over by women, this court offered room for impoverished tribal women to articulate novel ideas of women's rights in the areas of marriage and the family within a women-friendly environment. During the six months of fieldwork, I learned that for many tribal women, this informal court was the only place where their concerns about domestic violence, marital rejection, polygamy, child custody, property, and maintenance were taken seriously. Then in contemporary India the sluggish and expensive state courts as well as the men-reserved community assemblies are generally more concerned with upholding patriarchal values than with the socio-economic needs of tribal women as mothers, daughters, and wives. My research evinces that such a female legal space could be particularly valuable for tribal women who are confronted with a predominantly men-dominated patriarchal legal context.

However, the possibilities for the realisation of gender justice on the ground that are opened up by informal legal institutions, such as this tribal women's court in Rajasthan, have been little acknowledged in the scholarship concerned with women's rights in contemporary India. Instead, legal, political, and feminist scholarship on issues of gender and law tends to posit non-state law and accompanying social forums as diametrically opposed to the modern state-legal system and to classical liberal-legal ideology in general. From such a perspective, informal institutions and laws – and especially Islam – are disparaged as illiberal obstacles to justice and citizenship rights and progress.

This book challenges such simplified modernist accounts that stress the dichotomy of non-state law versus state law. Instead, it highlights the recently renewed endeavours of Muslim women's rights activists to re-articulate gender justice and Muslim women's rights outside of the state legal system. There has been a highly polarised and politicised debate on the reform of Muslim family law in the Indian subcontinent. All too often, the relationship between gender justice and religion is reduced to one of conflict between Muslim women's rights activists and the state and/or the Muslim leadership. In the context of South Asia, the continuing controversy has thus been long on polemic and ideological positions, but often short on facts. *Muslim Women's Quest for Justice* addresses this contentious issue through a careful empirical scrutiny of the ongoing initiatives of sociolegal reform from below. How do progressive and secular Muslim women organisations currently negotiate space – from where to articulate their claims for gender justice within the framework of Islam? What legal and moral borders do these interpretations of Muslim women's rights reveal and, in so doing, transgress?

Muslim Women's Quest for Justice is an urban ethnographic study of several Muslim women organisations rooted in the city of Lucknow, India, which articulate ideas of Islamic gender justice within a complex patriarchal and polycentric legal landscape. Such complex landscape includes state-run Family Courts, the conservative men-dominated All Indian Muslim Personal Law Board that claims to represent the entire Muslim community at the national level, and the equally men-dominated, more recently, formed All India Shia Personal Law Board. This book highlights the *opportunities* – rather than restrictions – that such legal and ideological heterogeneity offers for marginalised Muslim women to negotiate participation and inclusion beyond the politics of identity and monolithic ideology. Paying close attention to the micro-level institutional interaction, discursive complexity, and everyday understanding of justice and equality, *Muslim Women's Quest for Justice* aims at evincing a more nuanced understanding of the categories of gender and justice within contested local and national settings. In so doing, the book reveals that the production of ideas and discourses of women's rights is not restricted to the state and its legal system. In this manner, I argue, Muslim women's rights activists contribute to the pluralisation of the meaning of gender and sexuality in Islam. This renders visible the unevenness and complexity of the categories of women's rights and gender justice within an increasingly politically, ideologically, and economically fragmented world.

The book begins with a brief discussion of the current Muslim women's rights activism in postcolonial India against the background of the contested political debates on personal laws. The Introduction discusses Muslim women's rights activism in South Asia in relation to national and transnational scholarly debates on human rights, feminism, legal pluralism, and Islam. Chapter 2 of the book clarifies methodology. It makes a case for the necessity of multi sited ethnography (Marcus 1995) and outlines the study's research design, which combines nonparticipant observation, narrative interviews, case studies, and the analysis of legal documents. The second part of Chapter 2 sketches a vivid image of the institutional landscape within which Muslim women's activism in the city of Lucknow is given meaning. The empirically rich Chapters 3, 4, and 5 offer examples of how Muslim women activists both fragment and pluralise the categories of Islam and gender justice. The substantive Chapter 3 asks how Muslim women's rights activists in Lucknow shape and contest institutional relations, equations of power, and precepts of Islam and gender – revealing the lines of fragmentation that run through the Muslim communities in postcolonial India. Chapter 4 exposes how Muslim women's rights activists in Lucknow publicly contest the parameters of women's subjectivity within marriage under Islamic law through the release of their own Islamic marriage contracts (*nikahnama*). Based on a close analysis of these documents, this chapter asks about the instability of the categories of law and gender in current political struggles on gender justice in Islam. Chapter 5 steps back from the elite discursive space as created by Muslim women's rights activists. It gives voice to litigants in the *Shariat*-courts, the Family Court, and in the office of Muslim women's rights organisations. Based on these narratives, Chapter 5 probes the meaning and analytical purchase of liberal categories of women's rights and justice in a context where women's legal subjectivity is bound up to the social networks of their kin and community rather than classical liberal ideas of individual freedom, autonomy, and choice. The concluding Chapter 6 reiterates the book's main argument: The interplay of religious ideology and women's rights is diverse – and research at the grassroots level thus is crucial. In closing, Chapter 6 identifies key lessons for policymakers, legal advocates, and human and women's rights groups on how to advance processes of gender reform within an institutionally and ideologically pluralistic legal landscape.

Muslim Women's Quest for Justice adds to the expanding legal, political, feminist, and anthropological scholarship that engages critically with questions surrounding legal reform in the context of a polycentric legal sphere. Drawing on methodologies that allow for a rigorous attention to micro-level processes of legal and social reform, this book is dedicated to let those women (and men) speak whose lives are inextricably tied up in the intricacy of the legal reality on the ground . Where will I go and who will feed my children after a divorce? How would a divorce affect my reputation and that of my family? What is my relationship with the police, judges, and advocates, and how does this influence my possibilities of a fair trial under the law? How can I obtain justice if neither the advocates nor the judges are interested in my case and I don't have the money to pay for a good lawyer? What are my chances to win a case in a men-dominated world of law and justice? These, and others, are questions that influence (Muslim) women's course of action under the law. The voices of the Muslim women from various socio-economic and ideological backgrounds featured in this book render visible the complexity of the categories of gender and equality as well as the unevenness of the process of lawmaking and adjudication on the grassroots level. Thus, I consider this book especially valuable for feminists, sociologists, anthropologists, and scholars of law, Islamic religion, and postcolonialism interested in exploring the dense realities of legal and social reform from below. They will be most attracted by the book's focus on how individual micro-realities combined with the multi-scale reality of the legally pluralistic landscape contribute to a more comprehensive understanding of the women's rights situations of Muslims on the ground.

This study furthermore speaks to the most recent trend in international development. In an era of globalisation, questions about gender justice within a multicultural legally pluralistic context are pressing issues. Currently, a number of international organisations, such as the United Nations Development Programme (UNDP), the World Bank, United Nations (UN) Women, or the International Human Rights Council, as well as governmental bodies, are engaged in the development of legal strategies and intervention mechanisms for the protection of social and gender equality apart from the state and state law. However, the complexity of legal pluralism at the practical level has so far remained under-researched. *Muslim Women's Quest for Justice* will, hopefully, also interest policymakers, legal advocates, and human and women's rights groups dedicated to finding integrated grassroots solutions toward the realisation of gender justice within the contested local, national, and transnational settings. It is my vision and hope that the arguments made and the insights gained in the book will effectively contribute to the vigorous debates on the realisation of human and women's rights within the real context of shared legal authority between the state and various societal bodies and organisations at the ground level in India and elsewhere.

Acknowledgements

This book is not only the result of countless hours, days, weeks, and months of intensive writing, reading, analysing, and researching, but also of carefully forged relationships with Muslim women's activists, lawyers, litigants, the clergy, and everyday people in the field. Further, this book is the product of the vigorous support of my family, friends, and academics in Zurich, India, and the United States. The list of people who have contributed and made this project possible is long.

First of all, I would like to acknowledge those Muslim women and men in Lucknow who have so generously shared their life stories with me. Litigants at the Family Court and the *Darul Qaza*, members of Muslim women organisations in Lucknow as well as a number of randomly approached Muslims in the city have patiently answered my many questions in regard to their legal cases, marital lives, family, and their knowledge about Islamic norms and practices. Some of them invited me to their homes where I became familiarised with the everyday life in Muslim Lucknow. Without the openness, trust, and friendship of Naish Hasan, Shaista Amber, and Shehnaz Sidrat, this book would not have been possible. These presidents and founding members of the three largest Muslim women rights organisations in Lucknow have always taken out time from their busy schedules to talk about their activism and their ideas of a better future for Muslim women in India. I also would like to thank Begum Naseem Ali Ikhtedar Khan, who has facilitated my access to the Sunni clergy at the *Firangi Mahal* and the *Darul Uloom Nadwatul*. I especially express my acknowledgement to Ateeq Ahmad Qasmi, *qazi* at the *Darul Qaza* in Lucknow, for giving me permission to access the case records and observe at a dispute settlement. I thank *maulana* Abdul Kayum and *maulana* Mirza Mohammed Athar for providing me with valuable information on Islamic law and ideology. I would like to acknowledge the feminist lawyers Risha Syedi and Tulika Srivastava and the women's activist Kamla Bhasin, who have generously shared their critical views on the legal and social realities of Muslim Personal Law in India. I am very grateful to

Saleem Kidwai, Ram Advani, Madhavi Kuckreja, Runa Banerjee, and Veena Talwar Oldenburg for facilitating valuable contacts with Muslim women and men in the city of Lucknow. I also thank Saroj Kumar and Nashat Ansari for transcribing and translating the recorded interviews in Hindi and Urdu to English, and Shalini Kumar for accompanying me on my many field visits as an interpreter, research assistant, and friend. I thank Rajat and Jayshree Dhesi and Pinky Devi, who made sure that my little daughter and I were well looked after during our stay in Lucknow.

At the University of Zurich, I owe my first thanks to my PhD supervisor Shalini Randeria. Her relentless support, mentoring, and constructive comments have been of immense value for the successful completion of this book. I also thank Bettina Dennerlein, my second PhD supervisor, for her academic support. I greatly acknowledge Therese Steffen, who has always believed in my capability and encouraged me to complete this undertaking despite having two young children. I am grateful to University of Zurich and the Swiss National Science Foundation for their generous financial support. In the United States, I gratefully acknowledge Suzanne Goldberg and Katherine Franke, the Directors of the Center for Gender and Sexuality Law, for offering me first a position as a Visiting Scholar and later as a Research Fellow at Columbia Law School. I have benefited immensely from the opportunity to participate in the academic life at Columbia Law School. My findings in this study were shared at various conferences and I have profited from the suggestions of Sylvia Vatuk, Katherine Lemons, Nandini Gooptu, Sandria Freitag, Livia Holden, Rohit Jain, Yüksel Sezgin, Gopika Solanki, Kaiama L. Glover, and Latif Tas. Parts of this book were published in the *Journal of Law and Social Research* and the *South Asia Multidisciplinary Academic Journal*, and I am very grateful to the anonymous reviewers for their comments. I also owe a debt of gratitude to the editor Qudsiya Ahmed and her team at Cambridge University Press India, who were a great catalyst within the publication process of this book. I acknowledge the three anonymous reviewers at Cambridge University Press for their constructive comments, criticism, and suggestions, which greatly improved the manuscript.

Finally, I wish to extend my gratitude to my friends who supported me with their love, care, empathy, and stimulating conversations. My family has been a source of strength in many ways. Jhipo Hong encouraged me with his strong believe in my capability to complete this book. I am grateful to my parents Claudine and Hansjürg Tschalär, who put me back on track during the rough phases of this project. I also thank my sister Annina Tschalär for her unwavering support. My daughter Anaïs Faye and son Jasper Soon were a source of true inspiration. I hope that by the time they are able to read and understand this book, the endeavour of Muslim women's rights activists to establish gender justice has successfully penetrated the everyday realities of Muslim women in postcolonial India and elsewhere.

Abbreviations

AALI	Association for Advocacy and Legal Initiatives
AIMPLB	All India Muslim Personal Law Board
AISPLB	All India Shia Personal Law Board
AIMWPLB	All India Muslim Women's Personal Law Board
BJP	*Bharatiya Janata Party* (India's People Party)
BMMA	*Bharatiya Muslim Mahila Andolan* (Indian Muslim Women's Movement)
CEDAW	Convention on the Elimination of all Forms of Discrimination Against Women
CrPC	Criminal Procedure Code
CSSS	Centre for Study of Society and Secularism
DMMA	Dissolution of the Muslim Marriage Act, 1939
DPA	The Dowry Prohibition Act, 1961
FIR	First Information Report
IPC	Indian Penal Code
MPL	Muslim Personal Law
MWA	Muslim Women (Protection of Rights on Divorce) Act, 1986
NGO	Non-Governmental Organisation
OXFAM	Oxford Committee for Famine Relief
RSS	*Rashtriya Swayamsevak Sangh*
UCC	Uniform Civil Code
UN	United Nations
UNDP	United Nations Development Programme
UNICEF	United Nations Children's Emergency Fund
UNIFEM	United Nations Fund for Women
UN Women	United Nations Women
UP	Uttar Pradesh
UPA	United Progressive Alliance
USAID	United States Agency for International Development

Chapter 1

From Legal Binaries to Configurations

Muslim Women's Rights Activism in South Asia

There are many misunderstandings about the Quran in regard to women's rights. Islam is not an obstacle toward the realisation of women's rights. The conservative clergy is!

– Shaista Amber, AIMWPLB

The postcolonial state needs to codify the Quran from a secular point of view so as to undermine misogynist interpretations of Muslim Family Law in the courts.

– Naish Hasan, BMMA

Once women understand their Islamic rights, they will also understand their rights as citizens.

– Shehnaz Sidrat, *Bazme Khawateen*

These voices belong to three prominent Muslim women activists based in the city of Lucknow. Lucknow is the capital of the north Indian state Uttar Pradesh, not far from the Nepal border, and home to a sizeable Muslim minority. Within the last decade, the city has – like no other Indian city – witnessed a proliferation of Muslim women's rights activists and accompanying women-led networks. These diverse groups are demanding gender justice from various religious perspectives within the framework of Islam. In their endeavour for justice, they reference both the Indian Constitution and the authority of the *Quran* in order to claim their rights as Muslim women and as citizens of India – home to the world's second-largest Muslim population.[1] Their bold readings of the sacred texts challenge the dominant monolithic orthodox interpretations of women's rights concerning property, inheritance, education, divorce, and bodily integrity. According to these activists, the orthodox interpretations that were traditionally endorsed by Muslim India's powerful religious authorities, especially those affiliated with the all-national All India Muslim Personal Law Board, are directly linked to much of the dire economic, political, legal, and social realities faced by Muslim women in South Asia. Employing women-friendly interpretations of Muslim doctrine and tradition – derived from both secular and non-secular sources – these women are proactively stretching the boundaries of *gender-appropriate* activities within the public space. These innovative activists are leading rallies in major cities, drafting their own Muslim marriage contracts (*nikahnama*), solemnising weddings, dissolving marriages, engaging in dispute settlements, and participating in political debates. Employing the many types of local and national media to promote their agenda, these women's rights workers have acquired unprecedented public visibility in the highly male-dominated legal and political landscape. In short, Muslim women's rights activists in the city of Lucknow have carved out unique sociolegal spaces of semi-autonomy from which they publicly make their voices heard and their bodies seen.

Although Lucknow has long been a political and cultural crucible for India's diverse Muslim community, looking back to a rich colonial-*Nawabi* past and boasting several of India's major Shia and Sunni seminaries, it is by far not the only South Asian region where Muslim women's activism is currently flourishing. Muslim women's rights organisations and networks are gaining foothold in major cities such as Mumbai and Delhi. They have found their way into rural areas of Tamil Nadu too. Therefore, the activists featured in this study are not unique, but they do reflect the increasing endeavour of Muslim women in contemporary India, as elsewhere, to engage in political struggles over misogynist interpretations of the Islamic scripts – offered by the Muslim religious authorities – and the monopoly of the clergy over these interpretations.

The remarkable ways in which ideologically and politically different Muslim women's rights activists in India currently destabilise and transform patriarchal notions of gender and justice in the public space produces alternative discourses on women's subjectivity in Islam. This further points to the following three issues addressed by the book. Firstly, the production of ideas and discourses of women's rights is not restricted to the state and its legal system. Rather, issues of Muslim women's rights in the context of contemporary India, with its complex history of modernisation and nation building are, as Deniz Kandiyoti has so succinctly put it for the Muslim world, 'a hotly contested terrain' (1991a, 4).[2] Like most postcolonial states, the Indian state acknowledges *de facto* the legal authority of non-state bodies, from caste and community mosque councils to neighbourhood associations and women's organisations. Such legal heterogeneity is susceptible to internal power struggles over 'what' constitutes law and 'who' may participate in its making and in its adjudication. In this respect, I contend that Muslim women's rights activism in north India renders valuable insight into complex negotiations of gender relations at the intersection of state and civil society. Secondly, in the context of these current power struggles on political, religious, and legal authority, I argue that Muslim women's rights activists contribute to the pluralisation of the meaning of gender and sexuality in Islam.[3] Mixing formal and informal legal discourses, these activists produce alternative formulations of women's rights that take into consideration their rights as citizens (for example, right to equality, right to political participation, freedom of speech and expression, right against exploitation) as well as their intricate daily realities on the ground. Muslim women's activism in Lucknow, thus, evinces law and religion as fragmented rather than unitary and social normative orders as overlapping rather than distinct. To this end, this study challenges tendencies in the scholarship on Islam, gender, and law in South Asia, which tends to posit Islam as a fixed and hence unchangeable religious ideology – seen as obstructive to the realisation of women's rights. Thirdly, the ways in which Muslim women's activists vigorously participate in debates and struggles on women's rights, using Islamic history and ideology as an explanatory framework, shows that subjectivities predicated on a discursive Islamic tradition do not necessarily strip women of their agency. Rather, I suggest, it constitutes a different form thereof.

Muslim Women's Quest for Justice offers a critical analysis of the state as the champion of justice and of Islam as an impediment to the realisation of women's rights. Based on empirical material collected over the course of nine months of fieldwork on several state and non-state legal institutions, this book explores current attempts by three ideologically different informal Muslim women's organisations in Lucknow to create a space for claims regarding Muslim women's rights and gender equality within the framework of Islam. These are the reformist All India Muslim Women's Personal Law Board (AIMWPLB), the secular Indian Muslim Women's Movement or *Bhartiya Muslim Mahila Andolan* (BMMA), and the rather conservative Women's Club (*Bazme Khawateen*). Whereas the last mentioned was founded in 1937 under British colonial rule, the former two organisations are new, having only been established in 2005 and 2007 respectively. These forums are neither part of the formal state legal system nor of the informal *Shariat*-courts manned by the *Qazi*. However, the well-educated middle-class women, quoted at the beginning of this chapter, who preside over these Muslim women's organisations in Lucknow, cooperate to a different extent with the men-dominated religious institutions on the one hand and the state on the other. This study maps these newly emerging female legal spaces and unravels the diversity of how contemporary Muslim women's activists understand and represent Muslim women's rights and justice within these spaces.

The presidents and founding members of the AIMWPLB, the BMMA, and *Bazme Khawateen,* all belonging to Lucknow's middle and upper-middle class, are amongst the most vocal Muslim women's activists in the city. Within the last decade these women have established an unprecedented presence within the community and the English, Hindi, and Urdu language press. The growing visibility of these three activists, namely Shaista Amber, Naish Hasan, and Shehnaz Sidrat, facilitated a multi sited research enterprise in which I could potentially identify and follow discourses on gender justice in Islam as they travelled across media and sociopolitical spaces in Lucknow and beyond. Moreover, they use different ideological and political strategies to vie for the support of Muslim women (and men) and, not surprisingly, cultivate unique relationships with the state and with the Muslim leadership. This provides a good comparative lens for the study of the diversity of Muslim women's activism on the ground. Lastly, their distinct and ideologically differing interpretations of the religious texts offer an ideal vantage point for an analysis of the plurality of voices and ideological and political perspectives that shape contemporary grassroots struggles on Islamic gender justice.

The questions that motivate such inquiry are: How do these ideologically different Muslim women's activists engage with state and non-state legal institutions, and discourses in their struggles for just laws in the areas of the family, marriage, and women's rights? What legal and moral borders do these interpretations of Muslim women's rights reveal and, in so doing, transgress? And in what specific ways do these legal interventions of Muslim women's rights activists destabilise constitutional as well as orthodox-conservative assumptions of religion, law, and gender?

Muslim Women's Rights in Colonial India

The contemporary condition of semi-autonomy within the state, wherein the above-mentioned women's organisations and activists currently play an active role in the production and adjudication of Muslim Personal Law, can only be explained by looking at the ways in which the colonial (ca. 1858–1947) and postcolonial state has negotiated, framed, and administered religion-based family laws.

Contextualising the legal history of Muslim Personal Law in precolonial and colonial India is crucial as much of the debate on Muslim Personal Law tends to be tangled in generalising assumptions of Muslim Personal Law as homogenous, rigid, and unchangeable. In fact, there is a tendency in the scholarship concerned with Islam and law in the subcontinent to narrate the development of what is today known as Muslim Personal Laws as somewhat counterproductive to – or even a failure of – endeavours of democratisation and modernisation. However, as postcolonial scholars such as David Scott (1995) or Partha Chatterjee (1993) suggest, such simplified and orientalist portrayals of Islam and the law – and ultimately legal subjectivities – need to be revised. Instead of thinking about the colonial project of legal reform as a unilinear and teleological process intended to ultimately result in the creation of abstract (and emancipatory) citizenship, freeing the individual from communitarian affiliations, there is a need to think about the transformation of law in colonial India through the political rationalities of colonial power. This includes an analysis of the political rationale of various sections of the Muslim communities in India to reframe their identity through discourses of the 'Muslim family' in the context of democratisation. I will show that Islamic jurisprudence in India grew out of political struggles around the interpretation of the 'true' Islamic laws as well as the colonial encounter.

In precolonial India, the legal and social codes that were observed by Muslim communities in different parts of India were diffused and its sources were varied. Like Hindu, or *Smirti* law, Islamic law in India is the result of various interpretations offered by representatives of various schools that differ in their positioning of the Islamic law and practice (Agnes 1999, 12).[4] As a result, the laws that developed in various parts in Muslim India differ greatly in terms of their textual sources, mode of interpretation (*ijtihad)*, and manners of adjudication. In fact, the boundaries between the equally diverse Hindu laws and Muslim laws were at times fluid, or, 'fuzzy' as Kaviraj (1992, 20–1) terms it. For example, there were instances where converted Muslims followed their earlier non–Islamic customs and practices (for example, joint family property system – coparcenary), and some Muslim communities, such as the Khojas, the Sunni Bhora, and Molesalam Girasias were governed by the Hindu law so far as inheritance and succession were concerned (Fyzee 1964, 63). Law as interpreted by Shia scholars of the rank of a *mujtahid*, the only ones authorised to interpret the law in Shia Islam, consists of customary practices, interpretations of the *Quran* and the *Sunnah*, and the decisions of the *Imam* (ibid., 46). In short, a single and coherent Islamic framework did not exist. Instead, the textual sources of Islam were subject to interpretation, flexible, and often hybridised with customary laws and practices (Pearl and Menski 1998, 32).

While such flexibility in the interpretation and application of law might have allowed for the 'fluid construction of the self' in precolonial South Asian cultures, as Ashis Nandy (1990) puts it, it has nevertheless marginalised people from lower castes, women, and other stigmatised groups who found themselves excluded from the possibility to renegotiate identities and subjectivities (Menon 1998, 4). A central element in the ideological justification of British colonialism was then the emphasis on the 'barbaric' and 'cruel' religious traditions that subjected especially women to violent practices such as *sati* – a Hindu widow's self-immolation by burning on the funeral pyre of her husband (Mani 1987). Taking a sympathetic stance towards the unfree and oppressed Indian woman, the British administration justified its 'civilising' mission in the subcontinent with their goal to free women from despotism, anarchy, and lawlessness (Chatterjee 1989, 623). The postcolonial scholar Gayatri Chakravorty Spivak (1988) theorised this very relationship between the colonised and the coloniser through a feminist lens arguing that the idea of 'white men saving brown women from brown men' not only justified colonialisation, but also reflects the manner in which Western imperialism is produced and ultimately naturalised.

So, in order to enhance the position of women within marriage and the family, the British administration deemed it necessary to transform the legal system in the area of the family as according to the path of Western Enlightenment (Chatterjee 1989). However, because of this diversity of ideological and religious sources by which family and personal matters were regulated at that time, the colonial administration did not succeed in formulating a uniform set of regulations pertaining to issues of personal and family laws. So, in order to systematise as much as possible the existing legal realities, the colonial administration transformed non-state arbitration systems into state regulated and state-controlled adjudicative systems, and an official body of Muslim and Hindu personal law was established (Agnes 1999, 41; Pearl and Menski 1998, 33).[5] In so doing, the British subjected the so-called 'general Muslim law' to codification. The idea was to formalise Muslim laws and apply them through a uniform criminal and civil justice system modelled after the British legal system.[6] For this purpose, the British administration worked closely with legal experts and advisors from different sections of the Muslim clergy to establish good precedents based on which a body of law, called Anglo-Muhammadan law, was developed. Anglo-Mohammedan law, as the British called it, was a case law system which, although providing room for interpretation, came to rely more and more heavily on law reporting and legislative activities (Pearl and Menski 1998, 33). In so doing, the colonial state heavily contributed to the creation of the legal and political categories of 'the Hindus' and 'the Muslims' (ibid., 37).

In the nineteenth century, the authority of Islamic judges and scholars in the area of lawmaking and adjudication was dwindling. This prompted representatives of the influential Deoband Sunni-school to set up their own Islamic courts, or *darul qazas*, for the administration of the family. This was deemed as necessary in order to 'preserve' and 'protect' Islamic laws from the ideological onslaught of the colonisers. More importantly, such measure was deemed as important in order to 'protect' Muslim women from Westernisation (Chatterjee 1989).[7] So, in order to establish and preserve the 'pure Muslim family' and 'the pure Muslim woman', the Muslim League,[8] with the support of religious leaders, the *ulema*,[9] initiated a legislation that made it mandatory for all Muslims to be governed under *Shariat* law (Agnes 1999, 69). The introduction of the Personal Law (Shariat) Application Act in 1937 by the colonial administration then signalled the colonial state's acceptance that Muslim Personal Law is henceforth considered as the basis for the legal regulation of all personal matters regarding divorce, marriage, maintenance, inheritance, and custody (Agnes 1999, 69; Narain 1998, 48). The *ulema*, moreover, justified such political agenda with their intent to improve women's position under customary laws.

The Dissolution of the Muslim Marriage Act (DMMA), 1939, was another effort by the *ulema* to strengthen their political and legal authority over Muslims, and over Muslim women in particular. Although the DMMA grants Muslim women the right to petition for judicial divorce on certain grounds, it denies women's – and not men's – relatively easy option to reach a divorce by apostatising as granted under *Hanafi* law.[10] Moreover, this Act does not provide for spousal support for divorced women (Narain 1998, 48). The government gave in to the *ulema's* request that this law applies to all Muslim women regardless of their school, but refused to comply with the *ulema's* demand that only Muslim judges will have the authority to administer Muslim divorces. This refusal resulted in the *ulema's* withdrawal of support from the Act and led them to later decry the Act as 'un-Islamic' (ibid., 49). This Act, nevertheless, mirrors the willingness of the colonial government to maintain separate personal laws for Hindus and Muslims *within* the formal legal system.

Apart from this piecemeal reform on divorce, no attempts toward the codification and reformation of Islamic laws were undertaken during colonial times. So, what is known today as Muslim Personal Law, as the eminent religious scholar and reformist Asghar Ali Engineer notes,[11] is not as divine as it is claimed to be. Muslim Personal Law is a combination of substantive law based on the *Hidayah* (Guidance, the classic *Hanafi* juridical text of the twelfth century authored by Burhan-ud-din Ali ben Bakr al-Marghilani) and Anglo-Saxon law as administered in the British courts during colonial times. What is known today as Muslim Personal Law is therefore, according to Engineer, far from being God-given, but a colonial construct that reflects the political struggles between the British administration and various sections of the Muslim communities in the subcontinent.

'Modernising' the Muslim Family: The Debate on a Uniform Civil Code

After independence in 1947, the postcolonial state envisioned the creation of individual citizens by replacing the plurality of religiously based personal laws with a Uniform Civil Code (UCC). The Indian leadership under Prime Minister Jawaharlal Nehru at the time of independence envisioned a secular Constitution based on the model of a Western democracy. The aim was to bring the 'family' under state control and institute a particular family norm (Chhachhi 2005, 229). Prime Minister Jawaharlal Nehru's idea was to introduce a secular UCC on the basis of the principles of social equality and the strict separation of state and religion. Article 15 of the Constitution prohibits discrimination against any citizen on the grounds of religion, race, caste, sex, or place of birth and Article 14 guarantees equality before law to all citizens. So, on the level of the state, the identity of the citizen was to supersede all other identities. Nehru saw this shift from particularism to universalism on the state level as a crucial aspect in the process of democratisation and modernisation. However, as noted by critical and postcolonial scholars, the liberal universalism project as envisaged by Nehru after partition has not followed the evolutionary path of rationalisation and individuation as envisaged in stereotype Western conceptualisation of political modernisation. Instead, such a political project has created dynamics of in- and exclusion based on race, ethnicity, and class and thus ultimately produced segregation.

In the context of postcolonial India, the liberal project of equality, freedom, and autonomy, in fact, engendered fierce opposition especially by minority groups who felt that they were excluded from such a project due to their cultural, ethnic, and racial difference vis-à-vis the governing upper-caste Hindu elite. *Dalit* and Muslim groups, especially, have resisted the increasing advancement of ideological ideas of Hinduness in the guise of liberalism and secularism, by demanding their right to be protected as a minority group under Article 29 and to religious freedom under Article 25 of the Indian Constitution. While the Indian Constitution with its rights guarantees is a liberal document, the adaptation of such document in the Indian context, however, has more often than not been used to further minority claims rather than the rights of individual citizens. Let me explain. Articles 25–29 provide religious freedom and protection of minority rights. In so doing, the Indian state provides for special protection of minority groups as a means to address the ongoing marginalisation of (especially religious) minority groups vis-à-vis the Hindu majoritarian government in the process of democratisation. However, unlike an authoritarian model of secularism that envisages the neutral and indifferent state to ensure freedom of religion to all citizens, the Indian state subscribed to the concept of secularism that has emerged in the context of religious pluralism.[12] Such approach to secularism, as Ratna Kapur (2014b, 110) has pointed out, stresses the toleration and equal protection of all religious communities rather than the protection of the individual – especially in the area of the family.

The basic contradiction inherent in Articles 14 and 15 (providing for formal equality) and 25–29 (providing for religious freedom and protection of minority rights) offered fertile soil for heated debates on the very meaning of secularism and the place of religion in politics. Within these debates the rhetoric of the Muslim clergy was geared towards the avoidance of state intervention into religion-based family laws and towards the creation of a homogenised Muslim identity. The Muslim clergy has strongly opposed a UCC in the area of family law. In their view, a UCC would bring the Muslim community into the Hindu fold and deny their separate cultural and religious identity (Hasan 1998, 74).

Hindu right-wing political movements and parties such as the Rashtriya Swayamsevak Sangh (RSS) and the Bharatiya Janata Party (BJP), on the other hand, have seen Muslims' opposition to reform by means of a UCC as anti-national, a threat to national security, and as a sign of barbarism. In their view, their opposition to reform not only testifies their backwardness, but also their refusal to participate in the national mainstream (ibid., 79). The strident critique by right-wing political parties of the backwardness of Muslim Personal Law on the one hand, and the Muslim clergy's opposition to change the lot of Muslim women by means of a UCC on the other, has turned legal reform and gender equality into an issue of national and Muslim identity. So in a post-partition environment, where Muslims have become increasingly dissatisfied with the nationalist endeavours of the Hindu majority and their increasing economic and political marginalisation, the Indian state – eager to appear secular – adopted the principle of non-interference so as to 'appease' the Muslim leadership who have called for substantive equality for religious minorities (Subramanian 2014). So, the manner in which the Constitution was adapted and adopted in the Indian context resulted in what political philosopher Marion Young (1990, 258) termed 'differentiated citizenship'. In such a scenario, individuals are seen as incorporated into the political community not only as individuals, but also as members of specific groups (Bhargava 2007 and 2004; Subramanian 2014, 266).

Such state policy had far-reaching consequences for (Muslim) women's position under the law – especially in the area of the family. The Indian state assumed that for women religious rights are stressed over gender rights. In fact, in many ways, Muslim women's citizenship was reduced to the rights of the community (Narain 1998, 51). The women's organisations and the national women's movement have long been protesting against the discriminatory nature of personal laws of all religions. Against the backdrop of the political struggles of minority communities to establish their community rights under Articles 25 and 29 of the Indian Constitution, they have lobbied the state for establishing a UCC after independence. They saw codification as better than the arbitrary implementation of diverse customary laws in the area of the family (Chhachhi 2005, 229). In fact, to reform the Hindu law in favour of women was a pressing concern of women's groups (and of President Nehru) at the beginning of independence in 1947. The Hindu Code Bill that was suggested by Nehru in 1947 was highly welcomed by feminists and reformists. The Bill would have raised the age of consent and marriage, given women the rights to divorce and to claim for alimony and inheritance, and treat dowry as *stridhan* (Kumar 1998, 97). Although the majority of the Congressmen supported the Bill, the ardent political struggles around secularism and religion, as outlined above, was enough to pressure Nehru into stalling it until 1955–56, when sections of it were passed as four separate Acts: The Hindu Marriage Act, the Hindu Succession Act, the Hindu Minority and Guardianship Act, and the Hindu Adoption and Maintenance Act. A UCC founded on Brahmanical Hindu law would have curtailed the rights of *dalit* and tribal women, who enjoy greater freedom within their substantive jurisdiction. In face of the strong opposition of minority groups, such as Parsis, Christians, and especially Muslims, to state interference in the area of personal laws, the Indian state did not codify the laws of minorities. Instead, it enacted the secular Special Marriage Act 1954 that governs interreligious marriages (Agnes 1999; Sezgin 2013; Solanki 2011)

A little over a decade after independence in the 1960s, various women's groups began to realise that despite the successful lobbying of social reformers and feminist activists for legal reform in the public and private realms of women's lives, little seemed to have been altered in women's day-to-day experiences (Kapur and Cossmann 1996, 11; Sen 2004, 192; Sunder Rajan 2003, 157).[13] Moreover, the idea of such a uniform legal system also evoked critique from eminent feminists. For instance, the activist, women's rights lawyer and writer Flavia Agnes has in the early 1980s criticised endeavours for a UCC arguing that by means of a UCC the state would impose reforms upon people without creating a social consensus. And while these new codifications in the Hindu law may have brought some gains to Hindu women by granting them a right to absolute ownership of property, monogamy, and the right of divorce, as stipulated above, these rights are, according to Agnes (1999, 90), more conceptual than actual. So, instead of establishing legal uniformity in the area of family law, the UCC, or rather the debate about it, has provided an ideal political platform for the Muslim leadership, civic, and women's organisations to contest notions of religious identity and secularism.

However, the landmark judgement in the famous Shah Bano case in 1986 has once again reinvigorated the lobbying and advocacy activities of urban and middle-class women's rights activists and the secular national women's movement for the establishment of a UCC under which *all* women are granted their rights as citizens rather than as members of their respective community. In this case, the Muslim woman Shah Bano was granted maintenance from her ex-husband as according to the secular Section 125 of the Criminal Procedure Code (CrPC).[14] The judgement outraged the Muslim clergy, or more precisely the AIMPLB, who felt that the court had interfered in Muslim Personal Law by making a decision that did not accord with Islam. The ensuing political debates and controversies around the judgement centred on the question of whether or not the court has the authority and jurisdiction to determine rights in the area of family in regard to the Muslim community, thus completely sidelining the question of women's rights and citizenship. The insistence of conservative forces to exclude Muslim women from the purview of Section 125 of the CrPC caused the Indian government under Prime Minister Rajiv Gandhi to pass the Muslim Women (Protection of Rights on Divorce) Act in 1986 (MWA). This Bill prevents Muslim women from claiming maintenance under Section 125 CrPC in the state courts. Instead, according to the Muslim clergy, destitute Muslim women, who do not receive any support from their family, shall be supported by funds provided by the community such as *waqf*[15] or charitable organisations (Pathak and Sunder Rajan 1989, 561).

Even with such a provision, the Muslim Women Act still failed to resolve the crisis the Supreme Court judgement sparked with its judgement in the case of Shah Bano. The Muslim community found itself divided into the 'progressives' (those supporting the judgement) and the 'orthodox-conservative' (those opposing it) (Pathak and Rajan 1989, 561). Progressive and secular women's organisations (for example, Forum against Oppression of Women, All India Democratic Women's Organisations) have denounced the deprivation of Muslim women of Section 125 of the CrPC and the enactment of the MWA as a backlash against the legal position of Muslim women. Those feminists who ardently critiqued state and non-state violence against women criticised the continued placement of women's rights within religious laws and sought to institute a series of changes to the law.[16] As a result, a consensus that uniform laws would put an end to suppressive mechanisms against women emerged among feminist groups (Suneetha 2011, 57). The orthodox and ideologically conservative Muslim leadership has deployed the Shah Bano case to frame the issue of Muslim Personal Law in a rhetoric that stresses the need to protect Islamic tradition, culture, and identity from state interference.

Legal Longings: Muslim Women's Rights Activism

This call for a return to tradition and religion, or to use Subramanian's (2014) term 'cultural accommodation', directly addresses women's rights and lives. For one thing, the symbolic representation of Muslim women became crucial in the process of creating a protected legal space of MPL. The image of the pious and incorruptible Muslim woman as a symbol of the authentic Islam was once again generalised as a symbol of the Muslim community and of the Muslim family (Sarkar 2004, 238–9). In order to 'protect' the legal space of Islamic family laws, the AIMPLB was able to monopolise the interpretation of what it means to respect Muslim women and protect their honour.[17] The Shah Bano case has, in this regard, substantially hardened the borders between the state and the Muslim leadership and established ground for nurturing a political discourse on women's rights and Islam that emphasises the conflicting nature of state laws and religious identity (Hasan and Menon 2005, 1). Right-wing Hindu parties such as the BJP, Hindutva, and the RSS, on the other hand, deployed the debates around Shah Bano as a means to further legitimise the need of a 'secular' agenda so as to 'protect' minority women from cultural and patriarchal oppression on the hands of their community leaders and family members. Such rhetoric served as a legitimising ground for right-wing Hindus to support a UCC in order to establish a majoritarian society geared at integrating, and hence rendering invisible, minorities such as the Muslims. In so doing, the Hindu Right used the UCC and its policy of cultural accommodation as a vehicle to establish and normalise the supremacy of Hinduness (Kapur and Cossman 1997, 116). Ultimately, in the context of such political contestations between the Muslim leadership, right-wing Hindus, and the state, the image of the Muslim woman has been muted as either a symbol of Islamic authenticity and piety or as an object of secular reform.

However, it is important to note that the government's policy of appeasement toward its Muslim minority does not mean that the state is redundant as a means of achieving gender reform within Muslim Personal Law. For example, a case of precedent publicly known as the *Danial Latifi v. Union of India* (2001) was a great success for Muslim women's rights. In this case, the Supreme Court held that the Muslim Women (Protection of Rights on Divorce) Act 1986, which was enacted in the aftermath of the above-discussed Shah Bano case, did not conform to Articles 14 and 15 of the Constitution. These Articles prevent discrimination on the basis of sex. The critical issue in the Danial Latifi case was whether it was necessary to create a new Act where there was already a secular legal provision in place under Section 125 of the CrPC. In this instance the Supreme Court approached a middle path. It held that Article 3 of the Muslim Women (Protection of Rights on Divorce) Act of 1986, which states that 'a reasonable and fair provision of maintenance has to be made and paid her within the *iddat* period by her former husband', has to be reinterpreted in a way which calls upon the husband to make a lump-sum payment to his ex-wife. This payment not only includes the maintenance during *iddat* and the payment of the dower (*mehar*), but also a generous amount of money, which economically secures the woman's future.[18] Recent Supreme Court judgments in the Iqbal Bano case (2007), the Shabana Bano case (2009), and the Shamina Farooqui case (2015) further strengthens the Supreme Court's course geared toward establishing sex equality under the law. In all cases, the Supreme Court upheld the rights of divorced Muslim women for maintenance under Section 125 of the CrPC by referring to Articles 14 and 15 of the Indian Constitution.[19]

Nevertheless and despite the Supreme Court's shift toward realising Muslim women's constitutional rights in the above-mentioned cases, it is the issue of, rather than the concern about Muslim women's rights that is central to the debates on freedom of religion vs secularism between the orthodox leadership, especially between the AIMPLB and the current Hindu-right government. The *fatwa*-controversy from 2014 nicely illustrates such claim. This nationwide controversy was ultimately triggered by the famous *fatwa* released by the Muslim clerics in 2005 regarding the 28-year old Muslim woman named Imrana who was allegedly raped by her father-in-law in a small village in western Uttar Pradesh. In this case, the *Jati Panchayat* decided that by having had sex with her father-in-law, Imrana had in fact become the mother of her husband. Her husband was henceforth *haram* or illegal. Imrana ignored the decision made by the *Jati Panchayat* and continued to live with her husband.[20] In the aftermath of this case, which sparked national outrage amongst feminists, activists, and academics, a journalist approached the orthodox Sunni-seminary *Darul Uloom Deoband* in Lucknow to ask for their hypothetical opinion in case a woman who gets raped by her father-in-law. A cleric affiliated with the *Darul Uloom Deoband* opined that a victim's marriage in this case would no longer be valid. In fact, her husband would be *haram* (forbidden) to her.[21] This *fatwa*, which was based on the *quranic* stance which commands men to 'marry not the woman whom your father married', led the Delhi-based private attorney Vishwa Lochan Madan to approach the Supreme Court by way of public interest petition.[22] There he alleged that the conservative Muslim clerics (read: the AIMPLB) who have set up *darul qazas* all over India and who are giving judgements in forms of *fatwas* are running a parallel system of law.[23] The petition charges the AIMPLB with interfering with the country's legal system and requests the court to take effective steps to dissolve all *darul qazas* (Hussain 2009; Redding 2010).[24] After the Respondents of India's Supreme Court did not rule *darul qazas* and *fatwas* illegal in 2005, the matter came up for hearing in the Supreme Court in 2014. There the Supreme Court echoed the Respondents of India's Supreme Court decision confirming the constitutionality of *darul qazas* and *fatwas* while arguing that *fatwas* however should not violate the rights of individuals guaranteed under the law. In so doing, the Supreme Court ruled that it was up to the individual to decide whether or not to follow the often highly misogynist *fatwas* issued by the clergy as well as the decisions made by the various *darul qazas*. The AIMPLB opposed the Supreme Court's decision arguing that *fatwas* should have legal standing as the Shariat Application Act, 1937 makes provisions for personal laws to deal with cases regarding divorce, maintenance, and inheritance.[25] Despite the dissatisfaction of the Muslim leadership, the fact that the Supreme Court's decision did not ban *fatwas*, for many illustrates once again the government's commitment to a liberal approach to religion rather than gender equality.[26]

This decision, however, needs to be further understood against the background of growing communalism between the Hindus and Muslims in India which has been on the rise since the 1980s. Hindu–Muslim communalism again affects political struggles for gender legal reform. For example, in December

1992, fundamentalist right-wing Hindus destroyed the Babri *masjid* (mosque) in Ayodhya, claiming that the mosque was the original birthplace, known as Ram Janambhoomi, of the mythical Hindu warrior King Rama. At the time of the ten-year anniversary of the demolition of the mosque, the right-wing *Vishwa Hindu Parishad* VHP (World Hindu Council) affirmed their intention to build a temple on the site of the Babri Masjid. As a result, the tension among Hindus and Muslims culminated in the Godhra attack on February 27, 2002, when a Muslim mob attacked a train in Godhra which was believed to carry Hindu pilgrims from Ayodhya. At that time 58 people were killed. This in turn prompted a series of retaliatory attacks against Muslims and general riots, which broke out simultaneously in cities and towns throughout North and Central Gujarat. Not even 24 hours after the Godhra attack, on February 28, Gujarat began burning, and hundreds of Muslims and Hindus were massacred in Ahmedabad. It is assumed that about 2,000 people, mostly Muslims, were killed. Some have even described the deaths of Muslims as a genocide in which the state was complicit.[27]

The demolition of the Babri *masjid* in Ayodhya (1992) and its aftermath as well as the Gujarat riots (2002) not only demonstrate the rise of an aggressive Hindu fundamentalism, but also render blatantly visible the religion-based social exclusion and physical insecurity of Muslims in India. Here it is important to note that Former Chief Minister of Gujarat and India's current Prime Minister Narendra Modi was, to summarise the academic view, according to Martha Nussbaum (2009), Nivedita Menon (2002b), and Ratna Kapur (2006), substantially involved in the 2002 Gujarat riots. In fact, Modi's relationship with Muslims is to this day characterised by a Hindu supremacist mentality and politics, which substantially reinvigorates political aspirations of the Muslim leadership, and especially the AIMPLB, to 'protect' and strengthen Muslim identity through the law.[28] In fact, the reinvigorated public debate about the economic, social, political, and educational marginalisation of Muslims in the aftermath of Gujarat, sparked the United Progressive Alliance (UPA), which succeeded the BJP-led government in 2004, to set up the Sachar Committee to analyse and capture the conditions of Muslims in India and give policy recommendations. While the United Progressive Alliance, as in contrast to the BJP, fully endorsed the findings of the Sachar Committee Report, it has however failed to spark a rigorous debate amongst politicians, academics, and the civil society regarding Muslim issues.[29] At the same time, the government commissioned a report on religious and linguistic minorities in India, which was chaired by the former Chief Justice Ranganath Misra. This report, once again, illustrates the social and economic backwardness of minorities and makes recommendations for improving welfare, introducing quotas in political and educational institutions, and for designing legal and administrative modalities for the implementation of these recommendations. In essence, both government-issued reports illustrate the failure of the government-led appeasement policy toward minorities. Especially considering that such policy although wrapped in the garb of secularism and democratisation was, and still is, geared toward establishing a Hindu nation.

So, today, in the context of the troubled relationship between secularism and democracy in India and in light of the exacerbation of Hindu nationalism, a considerable number of women's rights activists and organisations have abandoned the idea of a UCC as a vehicle for the realisation of gender justice on the ground (Narain 1998, 71). Instead, these activists argue for reform within formal and informal religion-based family laws. For example, the Delhi-based feminist activist Kamla Bhasin, who has worked for the national women's movement for over 40 years, points to the conflict a 'secular' agenda posed in regard to the Muslim members of the women's movement. In an interview, conducted at Bhasin's apartment in a well-off enclave in South Delhi, she explained that the national women's movement focused on issues of rape, violence, education, and the secularisation of personal laws. However, by supporting an egalitarian UCC for the realisation of gender justice, the Indian women's movement found itself pursuing the same goal as the fundamentalist Hindus. 'Suddenly', Bhasin says,[30]

> We were on the same page as right-wing Hindu parties. This created a great deal of discomfort *vis-à-vis* our Muslim members. In my view, Islam cannot simply be deemed as anti-women and abolished in the name of secularism. So rather than rejecting Islam and its laws, as aspired by right-wing parties, the secular state should act as a promoter of gender equality within ethnic and religious communities.[31]

Such multicultural stance speaks to a wider trend in South Asian women's rights activism. Women's organisations and movements all over the country – be it tribal, Hindu, Parsi, or Muslim – increasingly adopt an integrated grassroots approach where women's rights are framed in terms of community values and norms as well as of citizenship rights.[32] Liberal feminists have criticised a multiculturalism approach to gender reform as they see such political policy as a means to leave women's fate in the hands of all too often corrupt and misogynist community leaders (Okin 1999). Other feminists, especially postcolonial and critical legal feminists, stress the opportunity such policy offers for various actors to tackle cultural and systemic factors that contribute to women's marginalisation from within the very context women's lives are given meaning (Merry 2003; Narain 2014; Nussbaum 1999; Volpp 2001). The latter scholarship assumes culture as a flexible and contested category and thus receptive to gender and legal reform endeavours.

While the fast and steadily growing religious and political conservatism in the 1980s ossified the categories of culture and religion, women's rights activists and feminists started to counter such perspective by advocating for a conception of culture and religion as epistemological flexible concepts. Conceptualising culture and religion as contested, hybridised, and dynamic, in fact, animated women's rights activists to advocate for reform from *within*. Muslim women-led networks and organisations started emerging in the late 1980s and early 1990s in urban centres (Kirmani 2011, 74). Despite the symbolic centrality the category of Muslim woman has in the context of the debates on secularism and democracy in India, the actual voices of Muslim women were hardly heard. The national women's movement was, and still is, the main platform from where women voice their dissatisfaction around issues related to domestic violence, employment, political participation, and the just recently reinvigorated controversy around rape. It is important to note that the national women's movement contains numerous organisations and groups which vary in forms of location, form, types, and activities. As Subramaniam (2004, 635) writes, these organisations and groups are 'urban, rural, small, large, formal, informal, localised, national, internationally affiliated and combinations of these three forms such as local informal branches of national organizations'. The goal of the Indian women's movement was to focus on women's common oppression. However, as expressed by Kamla Bhasin earlier, rising communalism in the 1980s brought to light the salience of class and religious identities (*dalits* and Muslims) – creating tensions and divisions within the movement (Subramaniam 2006, 637). While some Muslim members remained dedicated to the secular cause of the movement, others redefined themselves vis-à-vis the Hindu majoritarian women's movement in terms of their religious identity. The lack of Muslim women's rights advocates during the Shah Bano controversy in the national women's movement was the last straw for those middle- and upper-class Muslim women who have been dissatisfied with the movement's hesitation to address Muslim women's issues (Kirmani 2011a).

Consequently, a small number of Muslim women split from the secular Indian women's movement in the late 1990s to found their own women's organisations (for example, Muslim Women's Forum in Delhi, the Mumbai-based Women's

Research and Action Group (WRAG) and *Awaaz-e-Niswan*, *Huqooq-e-Niswah*, Muslim Women's Youth of India, the Muslim Women's Rights Network, or the earlier mentioned BMMA). This 'nascent Islamic feminists movement', in the words of Sylvia Vatuk (2013), or 'minority feminism', as Nida Kirmani (2011a and 2011b) terms it, has in the last decade gained considerable visibility within the public space (see Chapter 4). In fact, women's activism and organising around the earlier discussed Imrana 2005 and Gudiya 2004 cases further contributed to the growth in Indian Muslim women's activism since the 1980s. The aim of many Muslim women's rights organisations and networks in India is thus to challenge the masculine bent of current interpretations of the religious texts and history, as they, for example, materialised in the debates around the Imrana and Gudiya cases (Kirmani 2009; Vatuk 2013). In so doing, these organisations and networks publicly contest misogynistic interpretations of the religious texts as well as Muslim women's political and economic discrimination and marginalisation – issues that are by and large left unaddressed by the state as well as the Muslim leadership. Today, these women's rights organisations and networks offer women's 'protection' through a variety of strategies and approaches, ranging from demonstrations, petition drives, and signature campaigns to courting arrests, and the use of new web and communication technologies (Pathak and Rajan 1989, 580). Although growing, Muslim women's rights organisations and networks are still few in numbers.[33]

I note that unlike the Mumbai-based *Awaaz-e-Niswan* or the Women's Research Action Group (Kirmani 2011; Solanki 2016), none of the Lucknow-based Muslim women's organisation analysed in this book adopts the label of 'Islamic feminist' or describes their strategies as being a part of the domestic and global 'Islamic feminist movement'. In fact, the presidents of the Lucknow-based organisations all see themselves as activists rather than feminists. Although acknowledging the fact that a lot of their activism corresponds with Islamic as well as liberal feminists' endeavours to further women's participation in the spheres of politics and law, Shaista Amber (AIMWPLB), for example, strongly feels that a feminist label could discredit her community membership. Naish Hasan (BMMA), on the other hand, rejects the feminist label due to its association with Western feminism of sexual liberation and because she feels that the upper caste and upper-class feminists in India are out of touch with the everyday reality of especially poor rural women. Shehnaz Sidrat (*Bazme Khawateen*), in turn, is not familiar with the term feminism.[34] To this end, I am cautious to amalgamate Muslim women's organising around Muslim family law in Lucknow with India's 'nascent Islamic feminists' movement' as for example Sylvia Vatuk (2013) does.

In India, Muslim women's organising around women's rights does not happen in a vacuum but can be linked to transnational struggles led by Muslim women's rights activists, feminists, and organisations around the globe. In fact, the contested politics of gender, selfhood, secularism, and community identity in contemporary India resonates with current global struggles on nationalism, religion, and democracy. The 1980s witnessed a proliferation of transnational Muslim women's networks such as Sisters in Islam and Women Living Under Muslim Law, which seek to promote 'an understanding of Islam that recognises the principles of justice, equality, freedom, and dignity within a democratic nation state'.[35] By deconstructing gendered Islamic discourse, these Muslim women's rights activists, often termed as 'Islamic feminists' (Badran 2008; Mirza 2008), produce alternative proposals of Islamic justice that challenges the authority and power of conservative religious circles and/or the state.[36] The terms Islamic feminism and Islamic feminist arose in the 1990s to categorise those Muslim women's activists who specifically work toward gender justice within a *quranic* framework, as opposed to Muslim (secular) feminists which included respect for religion within a liberal model of religious pluralism, democracy, and citizenship (Badran 2008; Mirza 2008; Moghadam 2002).

Besides such transnational movements, there exists a growing number of grassroots movements for Islamic gender justice that feed off the language, ideas, and strategies developed by the larger organisations. For example, during the anti-regime uprisings in Tunisia, Egypt, Yemen, and Syria in 2011, also known as the Arab Spring, women from all walks of life rallied to the streets to protest against the increasing violence against women (for example, child marriage, female genital mutilation) and their lack of economic, political, and social rights. Instead of adopting a Western secular agenda of rights and justice, women's rights activists in the Middle East and North Africa increasingly strive toward infusing international legal standards of justice into religious legal discourse that underpin their struggle for a more democratic society (Al-Ali 2012).[37]

So instead of turning away from religion, these women try to bridge the apparent 'gap' between conservative religious laws and secular notions of political, economic, and social freedom. To this end, these progressive activists and policymakers are eager to re-interpret religious tenets on women's sexuality and identity and align it with secular standards of social justice. As the Egyptian women's rights activist Sherine Ibrahim says,

> The more established women's movements and organisations need to establish a dialogue with grassroots activists, young men and women, in order to find a common ground. This is to bridge the gap between secular ideals and daily

realities on the ground. That is crucial! There are some very interesting and progressive attempts to re-interpret the religious basis of justice and women's rights.[38]

Similarly, Muslim feminists in Indonesia currently advocate for their right to interpret (*ijtihad*) the *Hadith* and the *Quran* so as to dismantle gender stereotypes that severely restrict women's rights within the public and private sphere. Using gender analysis, they deconstruct women's position as derived from orthodox interpretations and bring it in accordance with the national Constitution as well as international legal standards such as the Convention on the Elimination of all Forms of Discrimination Against Women (CEDAW) (Ezeilo 2006, 7). Muslim women's lack of access to secular and religious education in Afghanistan engendered a wave of 'gender jihadists' who currently seek to break down discriminatory codes of behaviours that derive from patriarchal interpretations of the *Quran* (Jacinto 2006, 12). Like in India, the backdrop of current Muslim women's rights activism worldwide is the proliferation of hard-liner patriarchal groups, the spread of fundamentalist thought and practices, and the growth or reappearance of political Islam. Within such a harsh political context, progressive Muslim women's activists' endeavour to create a space where religious identity is balanced with democracy, human rights, and social justice.

Configurations of Muslim Women's Rights: Theoretical Framework

This preoccupation of Muslim women's organisations and networks globally, nationally, and locally with bridging the 'gap' between secular and religious ideals of gender justice, as well as that between national or international human rights standards and informal local laws or traditions, speaks to a wider intellectual trend in the area of law and society. From the late 1980s, sociologists and anthropologists were increasingly concerned with unravelling the unevenness and complexity of the categories of women's and human rights within an ever more politically, economically, and ideologically fragmented world. Focusing on counter-hegemonic legal struggles, articulated through transnational, national, and grassroots networks and organisations, in the global South (for example, India, Mozambique, and Egypt) as well as the global North (for example, the United States), their work engages with the crucial question of how international legal standards become meaningful in local social settings.[39] To this end, this scholarship examines the role of legal intermediaries such as NGOs, as well as social movements and community actors, in translating legal concepts from the global arena down and from the local arena up. Using complex analytical tools that stress the instability and porosity of legal (and social) borders – such as Santos' (1987, 2002) idea of interlegality or Kleinhans and Macdonald's (1997) account of critical legal pluralism – these scholars break with cultural relativism and universalism approaches.[40] Then, unlike modernists, who draw on a conventional account of legal transformation as a top-down process, or cultural relativists, who theorise law as a direct reflection of a specific cultural system of norms and values, this empirical-based scholarship on law and globalisation views legal change as a process of contestation, negotiation, and translation producing (new) forms of legal subjectivity. Thereby, legal discourses are produced and shaped within multi-dimensional and multi-levelled legal worlds, spanning from national and transnational justice systems' jurisdiction over community courts, NGOs, social movements, corporations, and transnational networks to the intricacies of everyday life. Law in this context is conceptualised as fluid and flexible, crossing and blurring legal, social, and moral boundaries. Critical law and society scholars discuss the predicament between secular and non-secular religious discourse as an area of intellectual inquiry. The apparent dilemma between liberal ideals of gender justice and Islam is conceptualised in terms of an intermediary space of analytical uncertainty. This opens up room for analysis geared towards revealing the unevenness of the categories of women's rights and gender justice within an ideologically contested world.

There exists a considerable body of anthropological and sociological literature that scrutinises local processes of adaptation and vernacularisation of global human rights discourse (for example, Abu-Lughod 2010; Merry 2006; Rajagopal 2005; Sousa Santos 2002; Wilson 2006). This work is specifically concerned with bridging the divide between secularism and religion, East and West, and formal and informal law. The goal of these scholars is to produce work that asks for a nuanced understanding of normative categories of justice and equality within contested local, national, and transnational settings. This is to overcome theoretical underpinnings prevalent in political, legal, and feminist scholarship that stress the incommensurability of secular legal standards with local customs and traditions.[41] In so doing, these scholars set out to discover and examine the (sometimes) hidden corners and niches where legal discourses are pluralised and fragmented, or, where law becomes alive within a 'third space' (Bhabha 1990, 211) – a space beyond essentialism and universalism.[42] These above-mentioned law and society scholars follow 'the trajectories of law' (Abu-Lughod 2010) through a multiplicity of sites within which ideas about law are shaped, contested, and transformed. This fosters a view on law as fragmented, fluid, and constantly in flux.[43]

In the area of women's rights, scholars of law and globalisation have produced important work that stresses the interpenetration of legal discourse over its analytical binaries. Their work engages with the manners in which feminist discourse is translated, disseminated, and lived on the ground (Abu-Lughod 2010; Agosin 2001; Ezeilo 2005; Relis 2011; Yuval Davis 2006). This scholarship underscores the importance of having the knowledge and understanding of social actors without essentialising local culture or religion and oversimplifying the complexity and fluidity of local practices. Here are two examples. Firstly, drawing on the vernacularisation theory in law and anthropology literature, Merry (2006) illustrates the ways transnational activists and national elites (for example, human rights lawyers, social activists, academics, and community and NGO leaders) in India translate and explain international human rights ideas into local terms to deal with particular issues such as gender violence.[44] Crucial to the process of vernacularisation, she argues, are 'knowledge-brokers', who operate in the 'middle' or in between the local and the global. These are, for instance, human rights activists, lawyers, and policymakers who 'refashion global rights agendas for local contexts and reframe local grievances in terms of global human rights principles and activities' (Merry 2006, 39). These new legal ideas and norms are then situated within local structures of the community and the family. This also includes structures of power and meaning.[45] Whereas Merry offers a useful analysis of how ideas on gender and the family are translated from the global arena down and from local arenas up, the anthropologist Abu-Lughod (2010), specialising on the Arab world, theorises the 'social life' of women's rights from a different angle. Unlike Merry (2006), Abu-Lughod (2010) did not primarily focus on individuals' and organisations' contribution to the transformation of right discourses. Instead, she scrutinises the manners in which right discourses shape the social and political worlds they penetrate. Drawing on multi sited ethnographic methods, Abu-Lughod (2010, 2) traces Muslim women's rights as they travel through various worlds and projects. These rights appear in debates, documents, and policies produced in a variety of sites, governmental bodies, religious establishments, women's rights organisations and networks as well as everyday life. Abu-Lughod (2010) illustrates how discourses, debates, documents, and talks on Muslim women's rights organise social and political worlds and produce organisations, projects, and forms of governing. At the same time, Muslim women's rights are shaped and transformed by the very sites they travel through. For Abu-Lughod (2010, 33) such a multi sited approach allows us to 'better understand the complex dynamics of gendered power, global, national, and local'.

Although different in their approach, both Merry's vertical and Abu-Lughod's horizontal analysis of the 'life of the law' illustrates women's rights as deeply intertwined with structures of power. In fact, discourses on women's rights structure and shape power relations within different and often overlapping social and political fields. Therefore, an analysis of the life of women's rights on the ground yields important insight into the ways in which (trans)local contestations on hegemonic images and ideas on gender and the family affect the deeply-seated power relations within sociopolitical and legal fields. Analytically spoken, to theorise law as an 'object of humanistic inquiry', as Annelise Riles (2005) puts it, 'a traveling concept' (Abu-Lughod 2010) or as 'a subject of transformation and translation' as Merry (2006) does, renders insight into often hidden dimensions of power struggles. Drawing on grassroots women's rights activism in Muslim Lucknow, I will illustrate in the subsequent chapters how struggles for legal and political authority render visible the permeability of ideological and legal boundaries. In this context, the categories of law and gender are not conceptualised as monolithic and unchangeable, but as subject to transformation and reinterpretation. Such an approach opens up room for the analysis of alternative conceptualisations of freedom, autonomy, and agency that are not (necessarily) commensurate with liberal parameters (for example, the privatisation and individualisation of religion).

Feminist scholars concerned with gender in Islam have over the last decade increasingly contributed to a more differentiated understanding of Islam, gender, and political agency as contested and transformed in the context of social movements, nation-building, and processes of modernisation. In line with Merry's and Abu-Lughod's work discussed above, these post-structural feminists speak out critically on exegetical approaches that study the question of women's rights and women's agency through an undifferentiated notion of Islam or Islamic culture, a view wherein women's identity is relegated to the private sphere and reduced to a symbol of authentic Islam. Such an image of the Muslim woman as a signifier of Islamic identity stands in sharp contrast with the Western liberal ideal of autonomy, freedom, individualism, and consequently, agency.[46] Drawing our attention to such popular islamophobic and orientalist underpinnings of secular conceptual frameworks, political scientists Alev Cinar (2005) and Nilüfer Göle (2000, 1996) show how, in Turkey, political projects around concepts of nationalism and secularism do not engender teleological processes of liberalisation in terms of self-fulfilment, individuality, and self-empowerment, or individualisation and rationalisation. Rather, their work effectively illustrates that processes of modernisation and secularisation create space for 'subjective constructions of meanings, cultural identities, and social conflict' (Göle 1996, 6–7). In a similar vein, Saba Mahmood's (2005) excellent ethnography on a women's piety movement in Cairo shatters analytical certainties of freedom, autonomy, and agency as exclusively restricted to the Western tradition of liberalism. Mahmood exemplifies such claims by arguing that women's piety, although rooted within patriarchal structures, produces a form of political agency. From such a perspective, Muslim women's blatant adoption of an orthodox lifestyle, orchestrated through the public display of their chaste body and pious mind, does not stifle women's agency. Instead, it opens up opportunities for political participation.

Both trajectories reveal that the formation of subjectivities, religious identities, and political agency are situational and can only be understood through a critical approach to political projects of modernisation and nation-building. In this vein, Deniz Kandiyoti (1991a, 4) insists that the issue of women's rights and Islam has to be studied through the different political projects of nation building, which utilises a distinct use of the female image to create a visual identity for different nationalisms, state ideologies, and oppositional social movements. In so doing, Kandiyoti and her co-authors in the collection *Women, Islam and the State* (1991) voice a certain cynicism about state endeavours for women's emancipation and point to the fact that although liberal women's rights were a central plank of modernisation and secularisation processes, such claims were political rather than factual. Then, while these newly independent states in the Middle East and South Asia sought to promote an image of the 'modern' woman by harnessing women into the state's economic development, male prerogatives within the family still remain unquestioned. In such instances the communal control over women was occasionally even intensified. Drawing on Kandiyoti's notion of women's rights as a hotly contested terrain, Lila Abu-Lughod and her co-authors in the collection *Remaking Women* (1998) have analysed and theorised Muslim women's engagement within the scenario of modernisation and state building. In this edited volume, Abu-Lughod (1998, 13) points to the alternative ways Muslim women's activists negotiate modernity and projects of modernisation. These methods open up new experiences and possibilities of agency and do not necessarily correspond with Western/liberal notions and ideals of female subjectivity.[47]

Such a shift away from evolutionary reasoning and methodological positivism requires multidimensional and context-bound interpretations of

Muslim women's grassroots struggles for justice and equality. Maintaining some distance from the universalistic master narrative of modernisation and secularism, this scholarship opens up a space for the examination of alternative conceptualisations of freedom, autonomy, and justice. To this end, post-structural and critical feminist studies on Islam and gender resonate with critical legal and globalised approaches to human and women's rights. Both disciplines establish a conceptual framework that destabilises the seemingly universal categories of women's rights and freedom and agency, vying for a critical analysis of seemingly universalising categories in a context where women produce their own understanding of justice and equality. In so doing, this scholarship sets the groundwork for a context-sensitive analysis that does not measure women's grassroots experiences against parameters of the modern liberal West, or the experiences of middle-class heterosexual white women. Like postcolonial scholars (Code 2000; Mohanty 1988; Narayan 2000; Shohat 2001), post-structural feminists and law and globalisation scholars push for a critical mode of inquiry. This is a mode where analytical certainties that produce differences – or the gap – are questioned and contextualised from an inter-relational, counter-hegemonic perspective. The analytical spaces that emerge from such scholarship are similar to Homi Bhabha's (1990) idea of the 'third space', a space producing transformation and configurations rather than differences.

Beyond the State–Society Divide: Academic Debates in South Asia

In South Asia, context-sensitive empirically based analysis of the highly heterogeneous and contested legal landscape constituting postcolonial India's religious family-law system is thus far under represented. Surprisingly, in the country with the world's second-largest Muslim population, the controversy of Muslim women's rights is long on polemics and ideological positions but often short on facts. The manners in which Muslim women's rights activists as well as other legal actors, ranging from state officials over women-centric NGOs to the religious clergy currently negotiating women's rights both inside and out of the formal legal system, are analysed is insufficient. Both political science and women's studies have shied away from including the category of non-state legal forums in their debates on the plurality of personal and family laws. Consequently, the question of women's rights and Islam in India has largely been discussed and debated within the framework of the political and academic debates on the issue of religion-based personal laws *within* state structure. There is also an urban and statist bias inherent in these debates.

Further, there is a tendency within the vast body of scholarship on gender and Islam to reproduce the trope of the Muslim woman as a symbol of either a religious 'tradition' or a secular 'modernity'. The growth of political re-Islamisation and the release of several reports related to the position of Muslims as a minority,[48] which clearly state the overall social, economic, political, and educational marginalisation of Muslim women (and men), motivated a series of studies that criticised the Indian state for not fulfilling its promise to 'protect' Muslims and, especially, enhance the legal situation of Muslim women. This literature revolves around the issues of religious identity, gender, and the state in postcolonial India and can generally be divided into two categories: those criticising the communitarian approach of religious authority and those lamenting the state's controversial politics of ssecularism . The first group discusses the ways gender serves as a bulwark to protect religious authenticity and tradition by pointing to the steady erosion of the rights of Muslim women due to patriarchal interpretations of the *Shariat* and the *Hadith* (Engineer 1999; Khory 2005; Jeffrey 2000; Lateef 1998, 1990; Minault 1998a and 1998b; Mukhopadhyay 1998; Rouse 1996). The second group discusses the role of the state that has abdicated responsibility toward Muslim women as citizens by acknowledging the authority of the religious leaders over familial legal matters in the area of the family (Agnes 1999; Chhachhi 2005; Hasan 2000, 1999 and 1998; Hasan and Menon 2005 and 2004; Narain 2008 and 1998; Patak and Rajan 1989; Rajan 2003). Additionally, much of the work on Muslim women in India is on *purdah* (gender segregation) and women's participation in politics or education. These studies depict women's entrance into the public sphere in these areas as radical and new (for example, Forbes 1982; Minault 1982a; Papanek 1982).

So, scholarship on Muslim women in India tends to posit the issue of women's rights in Islam within a binary paradigm of the Muslim community versus the state and religious laws versus the Constitution. However, such a reductionist view, wherein Muslim women are analysed only in relation to a religious identity or to the modern state, fails to take into account the sensibilities and dynamics that are at work within the Muslim community itself and thus within non-state legal and societal institutions. This is especially true in a context where Muslim women's NGOs, social activists, and the Indian Muslim Women's Movement currently prefer to work towards gender justice within formal Muslim Personal Law and informal Islamic laws rather than within a secular UCC.

The representation of religion and religious law, either through the lens of liberalism or a religious tradition, has been criticised by the sociolegal scholar Werner Menski. Menski (2001, 7) argues that religious laws – and, in this case Hindu law – can no longer be theorised as outside of, or as deviant from, contemporary legal practice in modern India. Considering the current revival of Hindu law as an important phenomenon for the construction of a justice-focused legal system as distinct from Western concepts of law, Menski (2001, 11) advocates for an approach that conceptualises non-state law as an inherent feature of India's legal system. Without denying the state legal system as an important instance of adjudication in postcolonial India, Menski (2001, 28) argues for 'a remarkable shift of emphasis, away from law and the state's claim to rule the roost, towards society and greater recognition of the potentially beneficial role of social norms and obligation'.

Menski's call for scholarship that discusses religious laws beyond the binary state vs society dichotomy resonates with Shalini Randeria's (2002) work on caste councils and their relation to civil society in Gujarat, West India. There, the sociologist and legal anthropologist maps the changing contours of state–society relationships in a context where non-state institutions function in varying degrees of autonomy from and/or entanglement with state courts and state law. The result is a legal landscape of fractured sovereignties (Randeria 2002, 308), discursive overlap, and institutional interrelations of what Santos (1987, 2002) has termed 'interlegality'.

So far, very few legal anthropological studies on women's rights in Islam situate their analyses on an understanding of 'interlegality'. Rather, they tend to provincialise women's struggles for justice by locating them either within *Shariat* courts (Hussain 2006), rural village councils (Moore 2002), or Muslim women's organisations (Vatuk 2005). However, there are signs of a nascent scholarship that focuses on the ways religion and women's rights are negotiated within *both* state and non-state legal forums. For instance, Sylvia Vatuk (2005) has examined women's rights under Muslim Personal Law in regard to divorce, inheritance, and maintenance in formal and informal courts. Although Vatuk convincingly portrays the pluralistic institutional landscape as a complex sociolegal field, she does not explain the interrelationship and/or the entanglement of state and non-state legal institutions and discourse. Nor does she provide an understanding of the ways social and religious identities are contested through law on the ground.[49] In this respect, Gopika Solanki's *Adjudication in Religious Family Laws* (2011) is a welcome micro-level study that unravels some of the institutional and discursive complexity that shapes

Muslim and Hindu women litigants' struggles for religious identity and justice on the ground. Based on rich empirical material gathered from within Mumbai's formal and informal institutions of law, this study offers compelling new insights into the ways in which state/society interactions create spaces for legal actors from each side to 'rework cultural meanings of the family, gender relations in the family, and religious membership' (Solanki 2011, 30). Similarly, Katherine Lemon's dissertation (2010) explores the manners in which Muslim women negotiate justice at the margins of the state – within women's organisations, *darul qazas,* and mosques in Delhi. Her study opens up new thinking in terms of how the law is constituted through religious and gendered norms in contemporary India.

Such studies that throw light on Muslim women's experiences with the law and religion within various settings are of great importance. How do women (and men) experience the law? What is their motivation to engage in adjudication, or not? To what extent structure ideas of justice and equality Muslim women's everyday lives? How do views on justice intersect with poverty, family background, education, security, and employment? As Zoya Hasan and Ritu Menon (2004) argue, a pure focus on religion is not sufficient to explain and capture Muslim women's struggles, discrimination, and opportunities – categories often illuminated from a perspective of Muslim Personal Law. Hasan's and Menon's unique analysis of Muslim women's socio-economic positionality shows that poverty, education, and employment determine the extent to which and how everyday Muslim women engage with law and religious ideology. An analytical lens that captures everyday scenarios as they intertwine with ideas of justice, gender, and Islam is thus necessary.

So, while empirical micro-level legal studies on Islam and gender in contemporary India are still in their fledging stages, there exists, however, a growing body of feminist work that highlight Indian Muslim women's everyday experiences in terms of religious identity, community membership, and agency within the context of theirs messy social realities (Khan 2007; Kirmani 2013; Phadke et al. 2009). Using innovative methodologies and research techniques, involving audio documentaries, photography, social media etc., these studies render insight into Muslim women's lives as they unfold within the intimate sphere of the family, in the context of urban ghettoisation, poverty, local politics, and, on a larger scale, neoliberal politics. For example, Nida Kirmani's *Questioning the 'Muslim Woman': Identity and Insecurity in an Urban Indian Locality* (2013) highlights Muslim women's everyday negotiations around law and community membership in an urban setting. And while Khan (2007) looks at the political, social, and ideological forces that complicate Muslim women's access to Mumbai's public space, Phadke, Ranade, and Khan's study (2009) probes the counterintuitive idea of the possibilities and opportunities public loitering would hold for Mumbai's women (Muslim and Hindu). This work, without a doubt, enables insight into the intricacies of Muslim women's everyday lives in urban India. However, it does not contribute to the scholarship on Muslim women's rights activism.

Following the methodological suggestions of Kirmani (2013), Solanki (2011), Phadke et al. (2009), and Khan (2007), and sharing an affinity with culturally pluralist, post-structuralist, and deconstructionist approaches to law and gender, this study pays special attention to micro-level understandings of justice and equality within 'the discursive tradition of Islam' (Asad [1986] 2009).[50] *Muslim Women's Quest for Justice* thus fills a gap in present literature on Muslim women in India in that it provides a careful empirical scrutiny of the institutional and discursive complexity that shapes Muslim women's struggles for justice. This multi sited urban ethnography on Muslim women's activism in Lucknow intends to offer a critical analysis of the workings of law, Islam, and gender on the ground. Following Muslim women's rights discourses as they 'travel' (Abu-Lughod 2010) through formal state and *Shariat* courts, the offices of women's organisations and people's talk and minds, this book explores the intertwined workings of legal discourse and institutions. I show how in this context any neat demarcation between the state and non-state or between the religious and secular spheres is constantly blurred. This study thus demonstrates the entanglements between state and non-state law and also explores the diverse uses and outcomes of the latter for attaining women's rights and gender justice. To this end, the empirical material discussed in this book highlights the *opportunities* Islamic discourse provides for Muslim women's activists to destabilise patriarchal and hegemonic positions on justice as well as structures of power within Lucknow's complex legal landscape. This book contributes to the dialogue about the unevenness and complexity of the categories of women's rights and gender justice within politically and ideologically contested settings.

Organisation of the Book

Following this Introduction, this book opens in Chapter 2 with a sensitive analysis of the entrenched institutional setting in the city of Lucknow. Identifying the multiple sites from where ideas on law, gender, and religion emerge, this chapter explores the complex institutional dynamics that are at work amongst men-dominated state institutions and religious legal bodies, such as the *darul qaza*s, and the various Muslim women's rights organisations in the city of Lucknow. It sets the ground for a better understanding of the specific social and political settings within which legal discourses in the city of Lucknow are produced and shaped.

Chapter 3 looks pointedly at the manner in which the presidents and founding members of the aforementioned women's organisations carve out women's spaces within the male-dominated political and legal landscape. This chapter lays bare the jockeying for prestige and legitimacy among women activists as they use the local and national media in their struggle to build coalitions against conservative religious authorities and to mobilise support against powerful, entrenched institutional interests. Chapter 3 illustrates that Muslim women's increasing visibility within the public space contributes to the emergence of finely crafted legal spaces of semi-autonomy from which deeply engrained power structures and hegemonic discourses on Islam can be effectively weakened.

Chapter 4 portrays dilemmas of these activists as they navigate the highly politicised and polarised terrain of Muslim family law reform. This is a terrain where claims in the name of Islam serve to bolster patriarchy and are often countered by demands in the name of universal citizenship rights that only thinly disguise majoritarian Hindu right-wing agendas. This chapter also contains an analysis of how women's rights activists make use of the recently carved out spaces of legal semi-autonomy to advocate a variety of different models of gender-just *nikahnama,* or the Islamic marriage contract. In contemporary India, this contract constitutes an important terrain on which the parameters of the family and female subjectivity under Islamic law are currently contested amongst different sections of the orthodox religious leadership and women's rights organisations. This chapter reveals how alternative discourses on equality and justice, both secular and religious, find their way into these contracts, where they are mingled and vernacularised, thus questioning the dichotomy of Islam and women's rights.

Chapter 5 considers the specific ways Muslim women's rights organisations negotiate legal reality on the ground. This chapter foregrounds the working and functioning of the state-administered Family Court, the *Darul Qaza,* and two mediation centres headed by the presidents of the All India Muslim Women's Personal Law Board (AIMWPLB) and *Bazme Khawateen*. It delineates the modes in, and extent to, which the latter two challenge and reshape legal reality on the ground. Given the multifaceted ways justice is expected and framed by activists and litigants within these exclusively female spaces, this chapter highlights the effects that the unstable nature of the categories of women's rights and Islam has at the grassroots level. It provides a critical account of the meaning of liberal (individualised) categories of women's rights and justice in a context where women's legal subjectivity is bound up to the social networks of their kin and community, rather than liberal ideas of individual freedom, autonomy, and choice.

The concluding chapter pulls together the many threads of the book's arguments on the 'trajectories of Muslim women's rights' (Abu-Lughod 2010) and the contested nature of women's autonomy and freedom (Cinar 2005; Göle 1996; Mahmood 2005), and their articulation in everyday life. In closing, Chapter 6 teases out the policy implications of this study and its findings.

Endnotes

1. According to the Census 2011, 14.2 per cent of India's overall population are Muslims. These are roughly 172 million people. The great majority belongs to the Sunni branch of Islam with a substantial minority belonging to the Shia and an even smaller minority to the Ahmadiyya and Quranist branches. See the Census 2011, available at: http://www.census2011.co.in/religion.php (accessed April 11, 2016).
2. Deniz Kandiyoti (1991a, 4) conceptualisation of women's rights as a 'hotly contested terrain' reflects the ambivalences surrounding ongoing processes of economic change, nation-building, and secularisation in the Muslim world.
3. Already in 1976, the Indian anthropologist Imtiaz Ahmad criticised the fact that sociologists and anthropologists have left unquestioned the homogeneous understanding of Islam and the belief that all Muslims adhere to the same religious principles as laid down in the *Quran* and the *Shariat* (1976, xvii). This tendency of framing Islam, and hence the Muslim community, in postcolonial India as a bounded entity has, despite this early critique, continued to dominate academic writings in the area of law and gender. In this book, however, I understand Muslim women's right struggles as a contributing factor to the increasing fragmentation of the religious authority, and the pluralisation of both doctrine and practice.
4. In colonial as well as contemporary India, the religious leadership involved in interpreting religious sources was, and still is, divided by class, language, geographic location, religious school and practice, and political affiliations.
5. Benda-Beckmann (2001, 185) and Mukhopadhyay (1998, 15) speak in this context of a reinvention or a rediscovery of customary law that is a distorted interpretation of the local legal situation.
6. The Judicial Plan of 1772 formulated by the Governor-General Warren Hastings, envisaged a religion-based civil and criminal court system. In the suits pertaining to inheritance, succession, caste, and marriage Hindu law was applied to Hindus and Muslim laws to Muslims (Fyzee 1964, 47–8).

7. In 1921, these religious courts were brought under the auspices of the newly formed umbrella organisation *Amarat-I-Shariat*. This organisation offered an extensive judicial training programme (*tarbiyati-I-Quadat*) to prospective *qazis*. Only two years later, six other *darul qazas* were established in Bihar. However, I will note that in practice, disputes in the realm of personal and family laws were still negotiated within the so-called 'traditional' or 'customary' forums rather than the British courts or the *darul qazas* run by members of the influential Deoband Sunni school.
8. The Muslim League, a political party composed of rich landowners, was formed to represent Muslim's interests in colonial India (Narain 1998, 47).
9. The *ulema* are the religious clerics. They are authorised to interpret the *Quran, Sunnah,* and *Hadith* from a legal and theological perspective (Narain 1998, 47).
10. This Act, however, grants Muslim women the right to petition for judicial divorce on certain grounds by adopting a more liberal perspective of the *Maliki*-school as compared to the *Hanafi*-school. The *Hanafi*-school of jurisprudence, followed by the majority of Muslims in the subcontinent, is the strictest school that gives the wife almost no grounds for a divorce (Minault 1998, 154). This new law on divorce has been codified on the basis of a selection of legal rules that have been approved by the legal scholars in Medina. This Act makes provisions for divorce in cases where the husband has disappeared, has been imprisoned for a long time, or has failed to provide maintenance for his wife. In *Hanafi*-school the wife has to wait ninety years if her husband disappears without trace (Agnes 1999, 37; Pearl and Menski 1998, 301). Further, this Act facilitates divorce for Muslim wives who either could not obtain a divorce from their husbands, because they were unwilling to set them free, or, because classical *Hanafi* law offered them no grounds on which a divorce could be justified. In this situation, the only way a Muslim wife could divorce her husband was by resorting to apostasy (the abandonment or renunciation of a religious or political belief) (ibid., 302). For the first time, this Act gives Muslim women the right to seek divorce from their husband in the state courts (Hasan 1999, 123). However, the right of the husband to unilaterally divorce his wife by uttering the word *talaq* (divorce) three times in one sitting or over a time period of three months, has been left untouched by that Act. The Bill, based on the principles of the *Maliki* law, is the result of careful deliberations amongst Sunni scholars and the support of the colonial government.
11. In: 'Why Codification of Muslim Personal Law,' *Countercurrents.org*, May 2, 2009. See: http://www.countercurrents.org/engineer020509.htm (accessed November 1, 2010).
12. Talal Asad (2003) argues that while secularism as a political doctrine is often seen as a response to Euro-American problems of nation-building, secularism has been understood and applied differently – for example – in the Middle East. Drawing on Benedict Anderson's term of the 'imagined community', Asad theorises secularism as an imaginary geared toward creating unity in diversity. In this respect, secularism not only denotes the separation of the church and the state but also includes the creation of a civil society, political participation, building a fair market system, and the creation of citizenship that encompasses different identities built on class, gender, and religion (ibid, 5).

13. In this respect, the Indian feminist Rajeswari Sunder Rajan (2003, 165) laments that the Indian state has so far failed to deploy its role on behalf of women to initiate social reforms within the legal body.
14. Under section 125 of the CrPC, the wife can approach the magistrate to order the husband to make financial payments or face criminal charges. Section 125 of the CrPC is a territorial law that is hence applied to all citizens regardless of their faith and community belonging.
15. *Waqf* is a charitable Islamic trust and means endowment of property, moveable or immovable, tangible or intangible dedicated to God by a Muslim, for the welfare of needy and poor people. A visit to the *waqf* board in Lucknow, however, revealed that these boards are highly indebted and there is no evidence that needy or poor people can resort to this institution for financial support.
16. For a detailed discussion of women's legal activism in postcolonial India see Radha Kumar (1993) and Gail Omvedt (2004).
17. Scholarship on the AIMPLB tends to reduce this informal body to its role as an ardent defender of MPL vis-à-vis the modern Indian state. However, as Justin Jones (2010, 183–4) points out, it is important to keep in mind that the AIMPLB does not restrict its activities to political activism. Instead, the AIMPLB offers guidance and advice to its followers on a range of issues of personal and family comportment within an Islamic framework. For instance, the AIMPLB regularly holds meetings and seminars in major cities where women and men are invited to talks and discussions on issues such as divorce, abortion, and adoption. Jones (2010, 183) states that the AIMPLB has been increasingly involved in such activities so as to establish personal ties to Muslims that do not have access to the elite circles of Muslim society.
18. Contrary to the Shah Bano case, this judgement did not evoke the political mobilisation of conservative Muslims. This is partly because the judgment was more moderate and partly because there was a lack of concerted mobilisation within orthodox circles (Subramanian 2008, 647–9).
19. For more information on these recent cases see: Flavia Agnes, December 15, 2009. 'Shah Bano to Shabana Bano': http://archive.indianexpress.com/news/shah-bano-to-shabana-bano/554314/ (accessed March 24, 2016) and Tahir Mahmood, April 27, 2015. 'For all the Shah Banos. Constitution and Not Communitie's Code, Should Decide Religion-based Disputes': http://indianexpress.com/article/opinion/columns/for-all-the-shah-banos/ (accessed March 24, 2016).
20. The Imrana case was a significant topic of discussion among legal practitioners working at the state courts and sociolegal activists, which includes Muslims as well as non-Muslims. In these discussions, the case was read as an example of how a *fatwa*, which is a mere opinion and not binding, can undermine the rights given to women under Indian law. For instance Tulika Srivastava, a human rights lawyer and founder of the legal organisation AALI (Association for Advocacy and Legal Initiatives) in Lucknow, contends in a personal conversation that the Imrana case is a criminal case and has nothing to do with personal law. She argues that the whole debate is misplaced given that rape is a criminal offence. Whatever *fatwa* has been issued is in

her opinion completely irrelevant to the case. Various Muslim activists and lawyers such as Syeda Hameed (see: http://www.boloji.com/index.cfm?md=Content&sd=Articles&ArticleID=5849, accessed May 17, 2016) and Tahir Mahmood (see: http://www.thehindu.com/2005/06/29/stories/2005062903831300.htm, accessed May 17, 2016) have also publicly contested the *fatwa*. Arguing from an Islamic point of view, they contend that the *fatwa* was misplaced and relies on a contestable interpretation of the *Quran*. The proponents of such a view stress the fact that the *Quran* provides options for women in such a situation and that this *fatwa* is the result of patriarchal misinterpretation. This legal activism resulted in the imprisonment of the father-in-law in 2006, where he serves a sentence of ten years (Lemons 2010, 99). The *fatwa* in the Imrana case was, on the other hand, supported by some of the women in the AIMPLB. For example, AIMPLB-members Fauzia Naseem and Begum Naseem Iqtedar Ali agreed with the *fatwa*, which stipulates Imrana as *haram* (forbidden) to her husband after having had intercourse with her father-in-law. But they lament that in a country like India, the Islamic law cannot be fully applied, otherwise the rapist would have been stoned to death. (Interview with Fauzia Naseem in Lucknow, February 24, 2010 and Begum Naseem Iqtedar Ali Khan in Lucknow, October 23, 2009).

21. For a good discussion of the *fatwa* controversy and the 2014 Supreme Court of India *fatwa* decision see Saif Mahmood's article in *The Hindu*: http://www.thehindu.com/todays-paper/tp-opinion/misunderstanding-a-good-judgment/article6226896.ece (accessed June 4, 2015).
22. Although *fatwas* are not legally binding, legal opinions issued by one of the most important seminary worldwide influence public opinion-making to an important extent.
23. A similar case concerns the young Muslim woman Gudiya, who was carrying the child of her current husband when her presumed-dead first husband returned after five years from the Kargil war. In this particular case, the elders of the village council forbade Gudiya to stay with her husband of three years, whose baby she was expecting at that time. Instead, in the name of Islam, the religious authorities ordered Gudiya to return to her soldier husband to whom she was originally married for only two weeks before he was called to service. The attempts of her second husband to reinstate the marriage were futile, and Gudiya died a year later of blood poisoning, at the age of twenty-six (Kirmani 2009, 74). See also: http://www.hindu.com/2006/01/03/stories/2006010316481200.htm (accessed June 11, 2012).
24. For a more elaborate discussion on the *Vishwa Lochan Madan v. Union of India* suit, see Jeffrey A. Redding, *Institutional v. Liberal Contexts for Contemporary Muslim Non-State Dispute Resolution Mechanisms*, 2006. The paper can be downloaded here: http://papers.ssrn.com/sol3/papers.cfm?abstract_id=1648945 (accessed August 3, 2012). See also: In *The Hindu* (July 19, 2014): http://www.thehindu.com/todays-paper/tp-opinion/misunderstanding-a-good-judgment/article6226896.ece (accessed June 4, 2015).
25. See: 'AIMPLB Refutes Govt, says Fatwas have Legal Standing' by Faizan Ahmad, August 25, 2005, The *Times of India*: http://timesofindia.indiatimes.com/india/

AIMPLB-refutes-govt-says-fatwas-have-legal-sanctity/articleshow/1210052.cms (accessed March 31, 2016).

26. The outcome of and debates around the *fatwa* controversy were highlighted by the media in India, England, and the US See for example: http://jurist.org/paperchase/2014/07/india-high-court-forbids-enforcement-of-fatwas.php, http://www.bbc.com/news/world-asia-india-28205895 or, http://timesofindia.indiatimes.com/india/Fatwas-have-no-legal-standing-Supreme-Court/articleshow/37975016.cms (all accessed June 3, 2015).
27. See also: http://news.bbc.co.uk/2/hi/south_asia/4543177.stm (accessed March 5, 2012).
28. See for example: 'A Lynching Over Beef-eating is Part of a Rising Tide of Hindu Nationalism in Modi's India'. Rama Lakshmi, The Washington Post, October 5, 2015: https://www.washingtonpost.com/news/worldviews/wp/2015/08/17/how-life-in-india-has-changed-under-modi-and-why-some-muslims-arent-happy-about-it/ (accessed March 31, 2016).
29. See Economic Professor Rakesh Basant's article 'Perspectives on Muslims in India: Sachar Committee Report and its Aftermath,' published by the Center for the Advanced Study of India, University of Pennsylvania. See more at: https://casi.sas.upenn.edu/iit/basant#sthash.q29wBcBT.dpu (accessed March 31, 2016)
30. Personal interview in Delhi with Kamla Bhasin on February 29, 2010.
31. Tulika Srivastava, a Lucknow-based lawyer, activist, and Executive Director of the South Asia Women's Fund, also embraces the cause of grassroots justice from a religious/community perspective. Similar to Bhasin, Srivastava points to the failure of the conservative state to secure justice for its female citizens within an ethnically, economically, and religiously diverse society. 'In a highly pluralised society such as India', she told me, 'the idea of a uniform set of laws that fits everybody is unrealistic. How can you extract law from its community context? In India, the individual is bound to its family and community. To my mind, women are better off struggling for justice from within – making sure their Constitutional rights are not infringed upon by conservative interpretations of their laws'.
32. Shalini Randeria (2007, 103–6) advises against hastily conceptualising religious laws and institutions as alien or opposed to processes of legal and gender reform in modern India. Instead, she theorises caste and community councils as a sign of India's uneven or entangled modernities. Randeria (2002) develops the concept of entangled modernities as a response to modernisation theories more generally, and to the macrosociological paradigm of *multiple modernities* as theorised by Shmuel Eisenstadt (2000) in particular. Whereas Eisenstadt theorised the variety of responses nation-states offer to Western ideas of modernity and hence considers Western ideas and norms of modernity as the frame of reference for other articulations of modernity, Randeria, together with sociologists such as Beck, Bonss, and Lau (2001), calls for a theory of 'reflexive modernisation' or 'modernisation of modernity' that entails a more critical enquiry that re-structures and re-conceptualises widely-accepted concepts of Western modernity. In so doing, Randeria suggests a relational perspective of the

entangled modernities, where non-Western configurations of modernity are explored as a result of transnational interaction and intermixture – as a part of a 'shared history'. The term *entangled modernities* points to the fact that non-Western modernities can neither be explained by 'histories of analogy' nor viewed as failed attempts to mimic the West, but have to be endorsed as a part of a shared transnational history (Randeria 2004, 155–7; Randeria 2002, 287). Such an outlook of *entangled modernities* defies Western modernity as the benchmark for non-Western societies and challenges the widespread phenomena of methodological nationalism and Eurocentrism in the field of social sciences.

33. Despite this recent proliferation of Muslim women's organisations, I note that Muslim women's rights activism in India is by no means a new phenomenon. Already in colonial India, some reform-oriented Muslim women discussed issues of education and *purdah* in elite 'clubs' (Minault 1998; Lateef 1990). These 'clubs' were spearheaded by elite and well educated Muslim women such as for example the well-known Muslim women's activist Rokeya Sakhawat Hossain, who founded the Bengal branch of the *Anjuman-i-Khawateen-i-Islam* in 1916. Under her aegis, prominent Muslim women set up vocational trainings for poor Muslim women, helped widows in distress, supported women from lower socio-economic background to find a suitable groom and get married, and encourage economically privileged women to go to the slums and train women (and men) for different kinds of income-generating activities (Hossain 2005, x). Like *Anjuman-i-Khawateen-i-Islam,* Muslim women's organisations in contemporary India are still by and large spearheaded by upper-class Muslim women and theirs activities are geared towards social welfare. However, the organisations and activists at the centre of this study differ from colonial organisations such as the *Anjuman-i-Khawateen-i-Islam* in that they openly challenge the masculine bent of current interpretations of the religious texts and history.
34. Personal interviews and email conversations with Shaista Amber, Shehnaz Sidrat, and Naish Hasan
35. See Sisters In Islam's website: http://www.sistersinislam.org.my (accessed January 28, 2015).
36. In the context of the Middle East and Northern Africa there exists a large body of scholarship on Islamic feminism. See for example Margot Badran (1995) for Egypt, Anouar Majid (2002) for Morocco and Iran Valentine M. Moghadam (2002), Ziba Mir-Hosseini (1999) or Afsaneh Najmabadi (1993) for Iran.
37. In the context of the Middle East and Northern Africa there exists a large body of scholarship on the women's movement in the context of Islam. See for example Margot Badran (1995) for Egypt, Anouar Majid (2002) for Morocco, and Valentine M. Moghadam (2002), Ziba Mir-Hosseini (1999), or Afsaneh Najmabadi (1993) for Iran.
38. Sherine Ibrahime is the Deputy regional director for CARE International in the Middle East. On January 30, 2014 she presented the CARE report on women's rights in the Middle East and North Africa at the Woodrow Wilson International Center for Scholars in Washington, D.C. (see: https://www.youtube.com/watch?v=XF0toA-ePFY, accessed September 8, 2014).

39. Santos (2002, 472) theorises counter-hegemonic struggles as 'subaltern cosmopolitanism'. This term stands for the projects and struggles of those who are socially, politically, and geographically outside of the hegemonic power structure. Santos' idea of subaltern cosmopolitanism highlights the ways in which the oppressed articulate their own conceptions and concerns about equality and difference.
40. The concept of interlegality defies legal centralistic approaches that assume the state's monopoly of the production of law. Interlegality also speaks against classic legal pluralism, which, although acknowledging various socio-legal systems, conceptualises state and non-state law as parallel systems of ethics and morality (Santos 1987, 280–1). Unlike these static approaches, interlegality stresses the porosity and fluidity of legal boundaries that results in the entanglement of legal codes and morals among the different legal systems (ibid.). It promotes a view of law as fragmented and of normative orders as overlapping rather than distinct (Santos 1987, 298).
41. In feminist scholarship on social justice and gender equality the universalism-relativism paradigm is still alive and well. Social activists and theorists such as, for example, Susan Moller Okin (1990, 1994) and Charlotte Bunch (1990) have argued that despite the fact that there are cultural differences among women it is possible to generalise aspects of inequality over the broad spectrum of cultural differences. Hence, the Western construct of (women's) human rights clearly applies in all geographical and cultural contexts. As a response, scholars and feminists who work with women in the global South have challenged such holistic top-down approaches to gender equality, where justice is defined as according to a set of Western parameters that neglect the social reality of the social actors to whom these rights should apply.
42. Bhabha (1990, 211) theorises the 'third space' as a space where the essentialism of a prior given original is denied. Within the 'third space', meanings and discourses are put together without giving them the authority of being prior to the others. This gives rise to something different, new, and unrecognisable (1990, 211). Within such a 'third space' other positions and new structures of authorities and political initiatives are enabled to emerge.
43. For example, Wilson (2006, 78) advocates a multi sited approach to law in order to open up ways to think of the social life of law apart from existence within the formal world of law. Wilson (ibid., 81) explains the need for such an approach with the lack of attention paid to the actual epistemologies of rights as they are translated into practice and as they affect subjectivities and social realities.
44. Merry (2006, 44–8) uses the terms 'replication' and 'hybridisation', both of which she categorises as a form of vernacularisation, to explain how ideas of human rights get disseminated and translated. Her terminology is helpful to explain how the translations of global human rights from the global to the local and the other way around are often paradoxical, unexpected, and partial. Replication is a process where international rights models are replicated domestically. Thus, the idea and the language of the law remain the same but the cultural understanding and shaping the way it works is different. However, whereas the process of replication does not change the form or ostensible ideology of the law, the process of hybridisation does.

Merry describes hybridisation as the more active form of vernacularisation. In the process of hybridisation, symbols, ideas, and ideologies of international women's rights merge with those of other localities to produce new hybrids. In the context of global women's human rights, Merry explains vernacularisation as a process that entails the extraction of the human rights language and its adaptation in the local context. Crucial to such a process are 'knowledge-brokers', who operate in the 'middle' or, in between the local and the global. These are for example rights activists, lawyers, and policymakers who 'refashion global rights agendas for local contexts and reframe local grievances in terms of global human rights principles and activities' (Merry 2006, 39).

45. Santos (2002, 472) describes legal vernacularisation as phenomena that mix heterogeneous legalities by disintegrating and fragmenting the latter. This gives rise to new constellations of legal and political meanings. He argues that vernacularisation is an inherent feature in trans-local struggles for legitimacy, acceptance, equality, and difference. These are struggles about the demarcation of boundaries of what does and what does not constitute a specific social and legal space, defining constellations of power and forms of authority and legitimacy.

46. Interestingly, both, the proponents (Nadja Hijab (1998); Ahmed Leila (1992), as well as the detractors Fatima Mernissi ([1987] 1998), Yvonne Yazbeck Haddad (1998) of modernity and modernisation as the 'solution' for Muslim women's liberation of patriarchal and religious shackles, locate Islam in the realm of tradition that stands in opposition to modernity as engendered by nationbuilding, secularisation, and modernisation. As a consequence, gender and law as analytical categories have largely been discussed within the dichotomies of 'tradition' and 'modernity'. Thereby Muslim women appear either as objects of reform or religious ideology in political debates and discourse.

47. For further reading on Muslim women and the modern nation state see for example: John L. Esposito (1998) on the Muslim world in general, Aihwa Ong (1990) on Malaysia, Yvonne Yazbeck Haddad (1998) on the Arab world, and Maitrayee Mukhopadhyay (1998), Amrita Chhachhi (1991), and Gail Minault (1998a and 1998b, 1982a) on India.

48. These are the earlier-mentioned non-governmental Seema Kazi's Minority Report (1999) and the government-initiated Sachar Committee Report (2005) and the report of the Ranganath Misra Commission (2007).

49. In this regard, Livia Holden's book *Hindu Divorce: A Legal Anthropology* (2008) on Hindu divorce and remarriage practices in the urban court system, notary offices, and customary settings in rural India is a welcome exception. Holden examines the way semi-official legal actors – such as the village notary – negotiate divorce and remarriage agreements in favour of women by interpreting both customary and official law. She shows how local discourses on customary divorce and remarriage are 'juggled' against normative conceptions of the 'sacred Hindu marriage' so as to reach a compromise. Unfortunately, Holden's study does not detail the dynamics through which these seemingly oppositional discourses are merged in local discourses on law and gender. Amrita Basu's article entitled 'Playing off Courts: The Negotiation of Divorce and

Violence in Plural Legal Settings in Kolkatta' (2006) is yet another welcome study. In this article, Basu focuses on the ways 'courts are played off' by Hindu women and their families in negotiating divorce and violence in a variety of legal settings, ranging from state institutions such as the Family Court and the police to local informal judiciary bodies in Calcutta.

50. Talal Asad ([1986] 2009) in his essay *The Idea of an Anthropology of Islam* encourages anthropologists to study Islam as a discursive tradition rather than as a fixed system of belief and practice. He argues that '[a]n Islamic discursive tradition is simply a tradition of Muslim discourse that addresses itself to conceptions of the *Islamic* past and future with reference to a particular Islamic practice in the present' (2009, 20). He rejects a universal notion of Islam and maintains that tradition as such is contestable and changeable (2009, 24).

Chapter 2

A Multidimensional Approach to Muslim Women's Activism

Mapping the Legal Landscape in the City of Lucknow

The legal landscape in the city of Lucknow is complex, featuring a variety of non-state legal bodies which are currently involved in the discursive struggles over the institutional power to uphold, regulate, or adjust 'correct' Islamic practices regarding marriage and the family. Within the last decade, the city of Lucknow has experienced an extraordinary proliferation of Muslim women's organisations which aim at publicly overturning chauvinistic ideals of women's subjectivity in Islam within a contested sociopolitical landscape. The current rise of political Islam in the city of Lucknow, nourished by ideological tensions between Sunni and Shia groups (Freitag 1989, 249), galvanised both Sunni and Shia women to openly destabilise relations of power and question established ideas of gender equality in Islam. However, whereas Shia women tend to debate issues of Islamic law and practice within the intimate comfort zone of their traditional spiritual meetings called *majlis*, which usually take place on religious sites such as mosque courtyards, Sunni women have more recently carried their struggle for justice into the politically and ideologically contested public sphere. As mentioned above, the presidents and founding members of the All India Muslim Women's Personal Law Board (AIMWPLB), Indian Muslim Women's Movement or the *Bharatiya Muslim Mahila Andolan* (BMMA), and *Bazme Khawateen*, which are at the centre of this study, are amongst the most vocal Muslim women's activists in the city. These newly emerging Muslim women's rights activisms in the city of Lucknow is part of and constitutive to a highly linguistically, ideologically, economically, and politically scattered Muslim community.

The activists and members of the different Muslim women's rights organisations featured in this study speak different languages, prefer different Islamic clothing styles, live in different neighbourhoods, interact with different institutions, and, not surprisingly, cultivate unique relationships with the state and with the Muslim leadership. As Shaista Amber (AIMWPLB), a well-known Lucknow Muslim women's rights activist, puts it: 'I hardly collaborate with other women's rights activists in the city despite the fact that our goals are so similar. To my mind, our different styles of interpreting the Islamic texts and of talking about what Islamic justice means, sets us apart'. Similarly, Naish Hasan (BMMA), another eminent Muslim women's rights activist from Lucknow, contends, 'my activism differs from those of other organisations in the city in that I work with the state and not some dubious *mullahs* who think of themselves as political and legal representatives of Muslims in India'. Listening to these voices, it becomes obvious that there is no such thing as *the* Muslim women's rights movement. Rather, as many conversations with members, presidents, and founders of the AIMWPLB, the BMMA, and *Bazme Khawateen* show, these organisations and activists consider themselves as separate players within a highly competitive political and discursive field in Lucknow.

Considering the institutional diversity as well as the wide range of precepts on Islam and gender, I consider Lucknow a particularly good place to map the diversity of Islamic voices in the subcontinent and to capture current grassroots-level reform efforts, especially those geared toward destabilising the well-accepted discourse on gender and Islam produced by the Indian state, the AIMPLB, and other patriarchal societal institutions such as the All India Shia Personal Law Board (see below). In short, Lucknow's institutional complexity allows substantively for a nuanced understanding of the categories of gender and justice within contested local and national settings and methodologically for micro-level study of institutional interaction, discursive complexity, and everyday understandings of justice and equality. In this chapter, I will unravel some of the institutional complexity that characterises the sociolegal landscape in the city. I argue that formal and informal legal institutions in the city are part of a larger power system where issues of religious and legal authority and understandings of justice and equality are constantly contested between sections of the Muslim clergy, the state, social activists such as those featured in this study, and everyday people.

Fragmented Muslim Communities

The above-described fractured relationship amongst Muslim women's activists is by no means a pure coincidence, but indicative of the complexity of the political and legal terrain within which they operate. Muslims in India were never a homogenous block but disaggregated in terms of caste, race, and class, and of the urban–rural divide (Gayer and Jaffrelot 2012). Historically, the city of Lucknow has always been a site where different sections of the Muslim community have contested interpretations of Islamic practice, ideology, and experience. The city of Lucknow is home to a sizeable Muslim minority. Muslims constitutes about 20 per cent of Lucknow's overall population of 2.8 million people.[1] Generally, Muslims in Lucknow are either a member of the Shia-minority or Sunni-majority sect. The latter is divided into different schools (for example, *Maliki*, *Hanafi*, and Shaafi), which draw on different interpretations of the religious texts. This results in differences in religious practices and jurisprudence. In the city of Lucknow, '[s]ocio-economic divisions are [further] compounded by doctrinal and sectarian schisms', writes the political scientist Mushirul Hasan (1998, 8).

Muslims tend to reside in the old part of the city in areas called Chowk, Riverbank Colony, Wazirganj, Wazirbagh, and Saadatganj. These areas still bear heavy imprint of *nawabi* architecture and lifestyle. It is easy to get lost in the narrow and labyrinthine alleys (*galliyan*) in old Lucknow and one can still imagine the former beauty of the, nowadays, mostly crumbling old mansions (*haveli*) that seam the little lanes in the old city. Such houses enclose a courtyard and feature a men's area (*mardana)* that is segregated from the women's area (*zenana*). Many families retain such spatial segregation which also translates into the structuring of the public space (see Chapter 3). These Muslim-dominated neighbourhoods are located just south of the river Gomti which divides 'new' and 'old' Lucknow – as the Lucknowites call it. Most important religious institutions (for example, *Bara Imambara, Chota Imambara, Chattar Manzil, Firangi Mahal*, and others) are thus located in the old city south of the river Gomti. The only two institutions across the river are the Sunni seminaries *Nadwatul Uloom* and the *Barelvia Warzi*. In certain pockets in old Lucknow, Sunnis and Shias co-reside with Hindus.

'New Lucknow', which sprawls on the former outskirts of 'old Lucknow', is mostly the result of the urban planning growth periods in the 1940s and 1980s. The influx of poor urban migrants into the old part of the city combined with the growth of the educational sector resulted in the creation of new neighbourhoods in the north, east, and west of old Lucknow (for example, Mahanagar, Gomti Nagar, or Aliganj). These areas, often segregated in terms of religion and class, are home to Lucknow's expanding (upper) middle class who prefer these lofty neighbourhoods with its 'modern' one-family homes and big gardens to the dark and crowded lanes of the old city. From a perspective of class, Muslims living south of the river, in old Lucknow, tend to be poorer than those living north of the Gomti (Susewind and Taylor 2015). Despite this tendency, however, it is important to keep in mind that there is money in old Lucknow too.

The localities of the three Muslim women's activists at the centre of this reflect – to a certain extent – their socio-economic positionality. For instance, Shaista Amber resides in a newly constructed house outside Lucknow near the city's airport. The large compound with its lush garden is located within a Hindu-dominated upper-middle class neighbourhood. Naish Hasan's Lucknow apartment is also located in a predominantly Hindu-dominated area. The multi-storey complex situated north of the river Gomti near Lucknow University is home to middle and upper-middle class families, who can afford to live in Lucknow's new (and rapidly growing) residential developments. Shehnaz Sidrat lives in her husband's family simple two-storey house in the old part of the city. The *haveli* built during colonial time is located near the prestigious former British Residency of Lucknow – a famous historical landmark. The Residency, now mostly in ruins, was staging ground of the Mutiny and thus an important relict of Lucknow's rich history and relevance in the Indian Rebellion of 1857. Today, the neighbourhood features a mix of elegant old houses built during or after British occupation and India's typical red and yellow concrete residential complexes. Sidrat's classical Islamic house is divided in to women's (*zenana*) and men's (*mardana*) area. The latter has been removed from its original purpose and serves nowadays as *Bazme Khawateen's* office.

Like Amber, Hasan, and Sidrat, the majority of Muslims in Lucknow identify as Sunni. However it is important to keep in mind that Lucknow is home to the largest Shia population in India.[2] Lucknow's Shia population is dense in the East-West of Lucknow's old city – in Hussainabad and Kashmiri Mohalla. These areas, also known as 'Shia ghetto' (Verniers 2012, 105), are home to some of Shia Lucknow's most important religious institutions (for example, *Shia Jaama Masjid, Asafi Masjid, Bara Imambara, Chota Imambara*, and *Imambara Ghufran Maab*). While Shia Islam in Lucknow is often represented as a part of a transnational religious tradition rooted in Najaf and Karbala, Iraq and Qom, and Iran. I note that Lucknow has developed its distinct interpretation and practice of Shi'ism. For example, religious rituals such as mourning meetings (*majlis)* and elegies (*marsiya*), which are often performed in Lucknow's *Imambaras*, are unique to Lucknow Shi'ism (Susewind and Taylor 2015). Interestingly, there seems to be a correlation between political affiliation and religious identity. While Lucknow's Sunni population generally aligns with the popular Samajwadi Party,[3] Shias do not align with any specific party.[4]

However, while Muslims in Lucknow are hardly concerned with their friends' and family's affiliation with a specific school or sect in their everyday lives, and sectarian distinctions are usually a side note, these distinctions become relevant in conflicts surrounding Islamic authenticity amongst different sections of the multilingual and ideologically fragmented Muslim community – and, especially amongst the clergy.[5] During my research, I saw the fact that the relationship amongst Muslims in the city is conflict-laced seeping through formal and informal conversations with Muslims from various socio-economic backgrounds, as well as in local newspaper articles. However, it was on a nice early winter day in November in Lucknow's old city that these tensions actually materialised at the occasion of *Muharram*. *Muharram* marks the first month of the Islamic calendar and the period of mourning for Imam Husain, grandson of the Prophet of Islam, who died during the Battle of Karbala in the seventeenth century (Hasan 1997, 114). Every year, the event of the religious procession – when black-clad Shia women and men walk through the lanes of old Lucknow beating their chests and carrying *tazia* (replicas) in commemoration of Imam Husain – fuels hatred amongst other Muslims in the city. A young Shia woman and student at Lucknow University who lives in Avadh Point, a Shia-dominated neighbourhood, told me about how young men arduously throw stones at those who they deem to be of a different Islamic sect or school and of how everyday Muslims engage in fights on the streets during the procession. These fights end with a few bruises at best and with death at worst. According to this young woman, the city employs thousands of security personnel to intervene in case of violence; often a curfew is imposed throughout *Muharram*.[6] The sectarian violence that erupts at this time every year is a tangible manifestation of Lucknow's Muslim communities' conflicted positions on the authenticity of Islamic ideology and what people are authorised to practice – or protect.

These contestations, however, are not new phenomena but date back to colonial times. Mushirul Hasan (1997) describes how before the arrival of the British in the nineteenth century the sectarian lines of demarcation amongst Muslims were blurred and fluid. Sandria Freitag (1989, 250) writes that '[I]n Lucknow, community identity impinged on an age-old conflict in Islam, shaping and recurring ideological tensions between the two [Sunni and Shia] groups'. Back in the nineteenth century, Muslims married across ideological and sectarian lines and commonly engaged in trade and commerce with each other (Hasan 1997, 128). However, the decline of the Shia aristocracy after the British annexed the city in 1857, which helped bring about the impoverishment of the Shia upper-class, combined with the relative prosperity of some Sunni groups, deepened the sectarian gap as economic classes shifted. The British further compounded this Sunni–Shia division by giving legal definition to these two categories (ibid.). Then, near the end of the nineteenth century, Lucknow's Sunni population split into two ideological schools, the Deobandi and Barelwi (Hasan 1998, 8), causing a further rift in what had previously been a relatively monolithic subset of the city's Muslim population. Under British rule, the different Sunni sections and Shias established their own seminaries of Islamic teaching and learning (for example, *Darul Uloom, Firangi Mahal*), dedicated to 'protect' Islamic lifestyle and ideology from the encroachment of British thought and/or sectarian onslaught (Graff, Gupta and Hasan, 1997, 8–9), but each according to their own set of beliefs. Such ardent efforts to 'protect' Islamic ideology within the ideologically fragmented Muslim community, directly affects issues of Muslim family law. Similar to (post)colonial contestations around family laws on a national level (see Introduction), ideas around marriage and the family become central markers of religious identity at the local and even personal level. Thus today the different Islamic schools and sects in the city engage in highly political contestations about issues concerning the 'true nature' of Islamic laws, especially in regard to family and conjugality. This can be explained with the fact that the clerics have genuine concern with the structure and preservation of families as they see it in their own schools. During colonial times such contestations by and large took place between the British colonisers and different sections of the Muslim community. In postcolonial India, however, these struggles, although involving the state, are by and large carried out amongst different political players *amongst* Muslims. Within such a context, meanings around the ideal family and marriage get institutionally pluralised and fragmented along lines of religious ideology and practice.

Muslim women's organisations are a part of this. They currently contribute to the fragmentation of Islamic law and practice within Lucknow's 'shared legal space' (Solanki 2007, 47). Engaging in institutional negotiation and communication regarding the content of law, women's rights activists and organisations in the city are an integral part of the working of Lucknow's complex legal landscape. Given the conflicting nature of institutional interrelationships that prompt orthodox hegemonic discourses on religion and gender justice to shatter and disperse, I ask: How can we adequately understand and theorise Muslim women's activism and its implication for the 'active social life of Muslim women's rights' (Abu-Lughod 2010) within such a complex political and discursive field, where boundaries of knowledge, meanings, and practices on religion and justice are constantly shifting? To this end, this chapter aims to trace and partially untangle the seemingly *messy* institutional reality in the city of Lucknow by analysing the relationships that exist amongst these institutions. This is to understand the institutional imbrications within Lucknow's legal landscape, a landscape characterised by its heterogeneity of institutions rooted in different historical, political, and social developments. Moreover, it is to uncover the institutional interrelationships in the city of Lucknow as forged and cultivated through personal networks, historical connections, institutional ties, political debates, and public contestations on the production of legal and religious knowledge. Such an approach not only allows for institutional comparison, but also for an interrelational perspective on law and gender.

Lucknow's Multi Sited Legal Landscape: Some Thoughts on Methodology

An inter-relational perspective is clearly underrepresented in the existing anthropological and feminist scholarship focusing on Muslim women's organisations. Only a few studies theorise Muslim women's rights organisations and activists in terms of their entanglement with state and community institutional bodies (Kirmani 2011a, 2011b, and 2009; Solanki 2011). Otherwise, feminist, political, and anthropological scholarship tends to analyse Muslim women's activism either in isolation from the larger institutional context, or in juxtaposition with the secular or theocratic state (Ahmed 1992; Badran 1991 and 1994; Hijab 1998; Kandiyoti 1991). What marks these studies is that they tend to be caught up in explaining why advocates of Muslim women's rights often reject the state and religious bodies rather than engaging with them. The task of explaining institutional ambiguities and ambivalences as a structural element of Muslim women's activism remains neglected. Too often, the complexity of the political and legal field is overlooked. Equally often, the relationship between gender justice and religion is reduced to one of conflict between rights activists and the state, as well as the Muslim leadership, or the AIMPLB to be more precise. This posits Muslim women's rights activism in oppositional terms. The fact that activists' agendas penetrate and overlap with state and community bodies, blurring the line of demarcation between the state and the religious community as established through political debates and discourse, remains in the penumbra of scholarly analysis.

In contrast to such scholarship, I am compelled to conceptualise Muslim women's rights activism in Lucknow as a part of the inner logic of the sociolegal field. Taking the voices of female activists, lawyers, and litigants seriously, I agree with Risha Syedi, a young female advocate working at Lucknow's Criminal Court, who once told me,

> I am not very good at dealing with men – both the clergy and the state officials. However, because women in India struggle for justice not only through the state legal system, but increasingly using the *Darul Qaza* or the local mosque as a more efficient and cheaper way to solve their problems, I have to know how such institutions work.... I have to learn everything about them so as to become more attuned to the ways in which women use different laws and institutions for achieving justice.

I took Syedi's contemplations as an important premise for my research. Instead of discarding state and non-state institutions as separate from Muslim women's rights activism, I consider awareness of the plurality of institutions and laws as a necessary condition for a context-sensitive analysis of women's rights activism in postcolonial India.

Predicating my study on such institutional plurality, I adopt a multidimensional approach to law and politics, as discussed in the Introduction (AbuLughod 2010; Merry 2006; Rajagopal 2005; Santos 2002 and 1987; Wilson 2006). This allows me to trace the trajectories of ideas, images, and beliefs about law and gender as they travel through grassroots organisations, political institutions, quasi-judicial bodies, and individuals' lives – shaping women's struggles for rights on the ground. An ethnography designed by a multidimensional approach to law does not look primarily to the existing similarities and differences between the various legal institutions. Instead, it appraises the inter-relationships among legal institutions and discourse. Such a conceptual framework calls for qualitative research methods with which to effectively document the trajectories of Muslim women's rights discourse and activism. These methods should also identify the ever-shifting boundaries of knowledge, meanings, and practices that shape these pluralistic legal realities. Hence, a sound anthropology moves beyond a *single sited* to a multi sited approach.

The method of *multi sited ethnography*, as theorised by George E. Marcus, sets the mode for situating and designing ethnographic research in the contemporary world. By a *contemporary* world, Marcus means that the 'global collapses into and is made an integral part of parallel, related local situations rather than something monolithic or external to them' (Marcus 1995, 102). The goal of such an approach is to allow for a focus upon the interconnectedness of phenomena that occur within different social spaces. Such an ethnographic practice turns against a rigid comparison of the local and the global and conceptualises the field in terms of interrelations and processes. A multi sited ethnography is, therefore, indispensable to the goal of tracing the complex and changing social and political dynamics of communication that exist among and within the various sites.

During nine months of fieldwork in Lucknow, I had the opportunity to access a wide spectrum of sites where Muslim notions of women's rights and justice are currently shaped and contested. Besides the aforementioned women's grassroots organisations – the AIMWPLB, the BMMA, and the Women's Club *(Bazme Khawateen)* – I visited orthodox, male-dominated institutions such as the All India Muslim Personal Law Board (AIMPLB) and the All India Shia Personal Law Board (AISPLB). My research journey took me from the bustling state-run Family Court situated in a former American library in the heart of Lucknow to the Islamic seminary *Darul Uloom Nadwatul,* whose impressive mix of colonial and Islamic architecture dates back to the late nineteenth century and which hosts a *Shariat* court, a mosque, a library, and a *Madrasa*. I ventured to the former palace of a French trader, which today hosts the religious higher education school *Firangi Mahal*, and to the tucked-away Shia quarters in old Lucknow, with their shiny copper domes and winding alleys. I visited a women's mosque situated in an empty patch of agricultural land on the outskirts of Lucknow, as well as the city's colonial-style university, the Sunni colleges, the public congregation halls located in the heart of the city such as the Uttar Pradesh Press Club, the first and only women's park in Lucknow (*Zenana* Park), and the homes of women's rights activists, *maulanas*, and individuals working at the grassroots level.[7]

To uncover inter- and intra-institutional dynamics of power that shape Lucknow's sociolegal landscape, I applied a mix of several qualitative research methods. Between October 2009 and March 2012, I conducted over 70 open and semi-structured interviews with representatives of the state courts and of the different religious organisations, as well as with litigants and Muslim women and men from various economic and ideological backgrounds. On the institutional level, I conducted expert and semi-structured interviews with judges from the *Shariat* court, advocates from the Family Court, and founding members of the AISPLB, the AIMWPLB, *Bazme Khawateen*, and the BMMA. The latter three organisations are at the centre of this study. These interviews provide insight into the lives of teachers, doctors, seamstresses, shopkeepers, academics, feminists, housewives, and politicians. Thus, they reveal a broad spectrum of possibility with respect to the interpretation of religious authenticity and practice concerning women's rights and obligations under Islam. Moreover, these biographical accounts highlight Muslim people's day-to-day understandings and lived experiences regarding sexuality, morality, honour, *purdah*, mobility, and marriage. In other words, these life stories provide insight into the relationship between religion and gender and its manifestation in daily life. These interviews were conducted in English, Hindi, or Urdu. Despite my considerable language skills in Hindi, I decided to work with a translator, who assisted me for the interviews where the interlocutor did not speak any English.[8] Through non-participant observation and semi-structured interviews with litigants, I further gathered ethnographic snapshots of 26 disputes that were negotiated and mediated either in the Family Court, in the *Darul Qaza* or *Shariat* court, or within the all-female forums *Bazme Khawateen* and the AIMWPLB. All of these cases highlight the ways in which female sexuality and gendered morality become important sites for the negotiation of 'justice'. I have further gathered secondary material (for example, court rulings, media statements, letters, pamphlets, etc.). This data set has been systematised and codified according to the approach of *grounded theory* (Glaser and Strauss 1967). The qualitative data gathered in these diverse sites brought out the complexities of legal subjectivities, politics, and institutionalised power relations.

These diverse research sites prompted me to evaluate the specific conditions of the fieldwork – as well as my positionality therein as a New York City-based female researcher with a European background. For this purpose I adopted a critical approach to qualitative research that embraces reflexivity. I am aware that no research can be untainted from the researchers' experiences, knowledge, and prejudice. However, recognising the power relations that influence the dialogue and intersubjectivity between the researcher and its interlocutors helps to understand – at least to some extent – how my own positionality in the field in terms of class, race, gender, age, marital status, and educational background affect data collection and analysis. It further helps to reflect on how my privileges and prejudices influence the questions I ask and the assumptions I make. I consider such approach as indispensable in a context where most of my interlocutors and I speak different languages, draw on different experiences, and aspire different goals in our life. Moreover, we are equipped with different prejudices, interests, and values. In my own use of the reflexive and critical research methodology, I tried to interrogate discursive certainties that derive from my own experiences as a European researcher, mother, wife, and white middle-class woman by applying feminist postcolonial theory of Western hegemony, imperialism, racism, and classism (Doezema 2001; Grewal and

Kaplan 1994; Mohanty 2002; Shohat 2001; Spivak 2000). This means to reflect on systemic power configurations globally and locally. Consequently, my methodological efforts were geared towards understanding the forms of knowledge, meanings, and attitudes that constitute the very social situation within which my interviews took place and within which I interacted with a variety of actors from different socio-economic, racial, educational, ideological, and political backgrounds. Such approach is further necessary to carefully reflect on preconceived notions of 'the Muslim woman', 'Islam', 'equality', and 'justice' in the process of data gathering and analysis.

My own social identity as a wife and mother has proved to be an enormous advantage in establishing rapport with the Muslim women who are the subject of this research. In many conversations, my marriage and motherhood have given me the social status needed in the local context to inquire about marital discord, legal strategies for its resolution, and transformations in family, kinship, and gender relations. My identity as a married woman and mother of a young child has further facilitated my access to Muslim women's rights organisations. The presidents of the AIMWPLB, *Bazme Khawateen*, and the BMMA very generously included me in their activities as an onlooker and/or a researcher to whom they could pass on their ideas about rights, gender, lifestyle, and Islam. My access to men-dominated institutions such as the high-profile *Darul Uloom Nadwatul* or *Firangi Mahal*, and the Family Court, however, was only possible due to pre-established contacts in the field.[9] At the *Darul Uloom Nadwatul* and the *Firangi Mahal* I was screened and interrogated regarding my professional background, religious affiliation, and of course, purpose of my visit. Nevertheless, and against my initial prejudice against the Muslim clergy, the *qazi* at *Darul Uloom Nadwatul* welcomed me with due respect. In fact, he was pleased to see me after I assured him that I was not a journalist. The *qazi* supported my research project in many ways. He not only gave me permission to look at some of the court files (I was not allowed to make copies), but he also allowed me to observe a mediation session in the *Darul Qaza* (see Chapter 5). During the course of my research I interviewed the *qazi* twice. Whereas the first interview was more formal and took place in his office, the second interview took place at his home. There he introduced me to his wife and five children. I also visited the Family Court in the company of two young advocates who worked at the adjacent Criminal Court. They both kindly put me in contact with a friend of theirs, a Shia advocate, who has been working in the Family Court for almost two decades. He was open to share his experiences with litigants and defendants as well as his perspective on the state courts and his perception of Muslim Personal Law.

In order to understand more deeply the institutional and discursive fields of power sketched above that shape Muslim women's activism in the city of Lucknow and beyond, I consider it necessary to first get an idea of the broader hegemonic power relations. So, before discussing the historical and political trajectories of those three Muslim women's organisations that are at the centre of this study, I will open my analysis with an introduction of the two most powerful arenas for the of adjudication and production of Muslim family laws in the city of Lucknow: the state-administered Family Court and the informal *Shariat*-court system set up by the politically powerful All India Muslim Personal Law Board (AIMPLB).

Legal Hegemonies: The Family Court and the System of *Darul Qazas*

The Family Court

In Lucknow, the great majority of cases related to marriage, divorce, custody, and maintenance are processed in the state-administered Family Court.[10] The Family Court is a District Court that was established in India under the Family Courts Act of 1984.[11] The Family Court in Lucknow is under the administrative control of the High Court in Allahabad, Uttar Pradesh. It is located on the premises of a former *baradari*,[12] which was later converted into an American library under colonial rule. The Family Court is an extremely busy place. Mopeds and bicycles are parked everywhere. Litigants stand in corners or sit with advocates at small plastic tables in the shade, discussing their cases. *Chaiwallahs* are busy delivering traditional Indian sweet black tea with milk to the advocates and their clients. Whereas the two chambers are accommodated in the former American library, the advocate's offices are located in the courtyard in open air. These rudimentary offices are covered with a corrugated metal roof and separated from each other by metal mesh. The equipment is simple: a plastic table, a few plastic chairs, a single light bulb, and one or two old metal lockers to store files. In 2011, only a few advocates possessed a computer. The case files are still predominantly written by hand or with a typewriter. The number of female advocates is very small, according to my observations only five out of around 120 advocates.

In general, Muslims (and Hindus) perceive the Family Court as corrupt, indifferent towards the grievances of especially the lower-income echelon, and above all untrustworthy, sluggish, and inefficient.[13] The frequent absences of the judge and of the advocates considerably delay the process of dispute settlement, resulting in a large backlog of pending cases. There are an estimated 20 million cases pending in Indian courts (Shackelford, 2009, 7). Two-and-a-half million are pending at the High Courts and about 40,000 at the Supreme Court. This can be compared with the 69 pending cases at the Supreme Court in the United States in 2006 (ibid., 8). The court rulings I have collected in the Lucknow Family Court evince that the time that elapses between the filing of the petition and the judgment ranges from two up to thirteen years. The latter number is by no means an exception. On the contrary, these legal documents show that most cases take an average of five to seven years before a decision is made.[14] This long process can be explained by the frequent absence of judges in the court, the resistance of husbands to come to the Family Court, and the lack of financial means on the part of the litigants, which hinders them to proceed with the case. Hence, it can take several years or even decades until a decision is made, if at all (see Chapter 5). In conversation, one Muslim advocate working for the Family Court in Lucknow likened the institution to 'a spider web' – especially for the poor. There, they are easily caught and end up wasting both money and time. Wealthier people, however, are able to obtain a directive from the High Court, which considerably speeds the process of dispute settlement in the Family Court.[15] In a similar vein, the social activist and former secretary of the AIMWPLB, Parveen Abidi, says: 'If a woman is not financially sound enough to buy a good judgment then she has a problem. Today, money is everything. Judges are not judges and they do not give the right statement. They are all corrupt'. Despite its widely perceived apathy, inefficiency, and costliness, the Family Court is by far the most commonly used legal institution in Lucknow.[16]

The AIMPLB and its system of *darul qazas*

As mentioned in the Introduction, the postcolonial Indian state never had and most probably will never have a legal monopoly in the area of family laws. Rather, as Shalini Randeria (2002, 308) suggests, the Indian state's sovereignty is 'fractured' and 'partial', leaving room for societal institutions and associations to claim authority in the area of adjudication and lawmaking. Because of the vast plurality of religious communities, each with their self-regulatory legal bodies, the postcolonial state seeks to regulate the scope of these societal institutions' legal autonomy under Article 26 of the Indian Constitution. This Article stipulates freedom for religious groups to maintain and establish institutions for religious and charitable purposes, and to manage their own affairs in matters of religion.

The Deoband scholars affiliated with the AIMPLB have taken advantage of this constitutional legislation. From 1973 onwards, following the foundation of the AIMPLB, this increasingly influential body set up six *darul qazas* in the northern state of Bihar. One of the most pressing concerns of the AIMPLB is to establish and strengthen the *Shariat*-court (*Darul Qaza*) system throughout India.[17] *Darul qazas* (lit. house of adjudication) are intended as an alternative dispute resolution mechanism for Indian Muslims to resolve family issues in accordance with the *Shariat* and the *Quran*. *Darul qazas* do not issue *fatwas* or administer criminal law. Especially in the northern part of India, where Islam is more prevalent, *darul qazas* have become an integral component of legal plurality, particularly concerning family matters. Today, *Shariat*-courts hold considerable power within the legal landscape. As a result, claims to judicial power are constantly re-negotiated by the state and by the orthodox-conservative sections of the Muslim communities within the legal landscape in postcolonial India. Whereas the state de facto recognises the legal authority of the *Shariat*-courts, the orthodox clergy views the state court's partial power over adjudication and interpretation of Muslim laws as an ideological encroachment upon the private sphere of Muslims (as mentioned in the Introduction).

Pointing to the inefficiency and corruptness of the state legal system, the AIMPLB has legitimised its intention to establish *Shariat*-courts all over the country. Lucknow's own *Darul Qaza* judge, Ateeq Ahmed Qasmi, views *Shariat*-courts (*Darul Qaza*) as a viable solution for delivering fair, affordable, and speedy justice to Muslims. In the *darul qazas,* cases are solved amicably, taking into account the concerns of each party and delivering swift verdicts in accordance with the *Shariat* and the *Quran*. In the opinion of the *qazi*, the *Darul Qaza* benefits both state and secular factions, relieving the burden of the state courts while providing Islamic justice.[18] Although the *Shariat*-court system is located outside of the official legal system, the latter acknowledges these courts as an alternative for dispute resolution that is cheap, amicable, and in close relationship with the community.

However, underlying the efforts of the AIMPLB is the agenda of the Muslim leadership to resist all state intervention into Muslim Personal Law. As previously discussed in the Introduction, the verdict in the disputed Shah Bano case – coupled with the increasing political polarisation of Hindus and Muslims – helped prompting the Muslim leadership to 'protect' their religious laws from the ideological incursion of the state. The vibrancy of this political stance against the state is made visible in an excerpt from an interview with one AIMPLB member, *maulana* Khalid Rashid,

> We must keep in mind that the decisions in the state courts should not interfere in our personal laws. I am afraid to say that this is often not the case. We [AIMPLB] have written to the various government authorities at the central level, even to the Prime Minister and the law minister, to the chief justice of the Supreme Court ... but ... you know, the Constitution gives us our fundamental right to follow our practices. For example, if a person has given *talaq* thrice in one or two sittings and even on the premises of court, as far as the Islamic *Shariat* is concerned, it is considered a divorce. So, in cases where the High Courts and the Supreme Court pronounced judgements against our personal laws, there should be an amendment.

Many Muslims view the primacy of the *Darul Qaza* over the state courts in the same way, making it arguably the most influential legal body for Lucknow's Muslim community. The *Darul Qaza* is an influential legal body among the Muslim community in Lucknow. In 1995, the Deobandi section of the AIMPLB set up two *darul qazas* on the premises of the Islamic teaching and learning seminaries *Darul Uloom Nadwatul* and the *Firangi Mahal*.[19] These *darul qazas* mediate cases that fall into the purview of family laws such as divorce, inheritance, property, and custody.

Functioning and working of *darul qazas*

Darul qazas are highly bureaucratised and formalised institutions. The *qazi*, or judge, is the spiritual, moral, and legal authority. In providing judgements he consults Islamic texts such as the *Quran*, *Shariat*, *Sunnah*, and *Hadith*. He is, therefore, also highly knowledgeable about Islamic texts, having gained his expertise through a lengthy educational training in a religious seminary (*Madrasa*), most commonly within India. There are only a few *qazis* in India trained outside of the country in the Middle East (Solanki 2011). Most *qazis* are registered under the Qazi Act of 1880. Apart from their legal work, the *qazis* take over a wide range of duties, such as performing marriages and other religious rituals and advising community members in regard to religious ideology and laws.[20] State-administered Muslim Personal Law is not of relevance in the *Darul Qaza*.

Notwithstanding the orthodox Sunni clergy's disaffirmation of the state legal system, the organisational structure and day-to-day procedures of the *darul qazas* in Lucknow, as elsewhere in India, are similar to that of the state courts. The cases that are mediated in the *Darul Qaza* in Lucknow are all well-documented. The hearings are recorded in writing, the verdicts written on a stamp paper and registered. The language of the documents is Urdu and the script Arabic; between 1995 and 2010, Lucknow's *Darul Qaza* had registered a total of 917 applications pertaining to divorce, property, maintenance, and restitution of conjugal rights. The offices of the *Shariat*-court are also well organised. They each feature a large desk and telephone, chairs for visitors, and a generous register where the files are kept. In the city's second *Shariat*-court, located on the premises of the Islamic school *Firangi Mahal*, the rooms are spacious and equipped with books on law and on Islam written in English, Arabic, and Urdu. However, this apparent adoption of the bureaucratic formality of state-run courts does not interfere with the *darul qazas*' goal of distancing themselves from the state.[21] For instance, the *qazi*'s assistant in the Lucknow *Darul Qaza* expresses his scepticism toward litigants who approach the *Darul Qaza* only after unsuccessful attempts at state-court settlements. In his view, such couples approach the *Darul Qaza* on bad terms. He describes the Family Court as a place where hatred is fuelled rather than doused. Reconciliation between the disputants, in his opinion, is almost impossible under such circumstances.

The institutional boundary, drawn on the part of the clergy between itself and the state courts, is based not only upon the dichotomy of amicable versus non-amicable, but on that between the concepts of Islamic versus un-Islamic. Authorities in the *Shariat*-court view justice delivered by the state as un-Islamic, due to ignorance on the part of the state judges regarding Islamic laws. The majority of the judges in the state courts are Hindus. Consequently, real Islamic justice is only guaranteed in the *Shariat*-courts.

Here is a brief outline of the court procedure in the *Darul Qaza*: First, the *qazi* summons the disputants and their family for an informal hearing. In the event that the parties are unable to compromise, the case then proceeds to a formal hearing. These are held in the hearing room in the *Darul Qaza,* and are presided over by the *qazi*. The *qazi's* assistant takes minutes of the hearing and the *ulema* (usually a few religious scholars) witness the process of dispute settlement. Similar to the state courts, the parties can request a formal challenge to the *qazi's* verdict. A first option is for the parties to appeal to the *Darul Qaza* committee comprised of two or three senior judges. If still dissatisfied, the next option is for the parties to appeal to the central *Shariat*-court in Delhi. According to the *qazi* in Lucknow, this appeal system is rarely utilised, since both parties generally agree on the verdict, which is perceived by them as God-given. One elderly man – a religious scholar – whom I met on the campus of the *Darul Uloom Nadwatul* in Lucknow and with whom I engaged in a conversation, told me, 'The decisions in the *Darul Qaza* are taken in a fast manner because ultimately it is God who calls the believer to account. As a Muslim you first serve God the Almighty who ultimately calls you to account for your faults. So people who do not respect the verdicts delivered by the *Darul Qaza* will receive punishment at doomsday'. The religious scholar describes the *Shariat*-court system in India as a legal space of religious self-representation informed by discourses of piety and divine justice. Justice in the *Darul Qaza* is thus seen as natural law – as God-given – and hence unquestionable. Such narrative evinces *darul qazas* as a space of religious self-representation within which notions and procedures of justice that are conceptualised as part of Western modernisation and/or political secularisation are rejected as un-Islamic, irrelevant, or even obstructive.

The verdicts of the *Darul Qaza*, however, are no more than recommendations and advice, hence not enforceable by state authorities. However, as mentioned above, the judge might take into consideration the decisions made in the *darul qazas*. Otherwise, the *darul qaza's* pronouncements are only binding *inter partes;* dissatisfied parties cannot approach the state courts to enforce or appeal the verdicts. This has been further established in 2014 where the Supreme Court ruled that although *fatwas* and the *darul qazas* are not unconstitutional, they must refrain from violating individuals' civil rights.[22] This ruling came as a response to a petition launched in 2005 by the Delhi-based private attorney Vishwa Lochan Madan, who was deeply concerned with the very controversial *fatwas,* or, legal opinions, issued by the *Darul Uloom* (see Introduction). These are *fatwas* that prohibit women from holding a private or government job, from becoming judges, and that forbid girls to ride a bicycle, or *fatwas* that accept the validity of three pronouncements of divorce (triple *talaq)* given by the husband to his wife on Skype and that re-enforce *ḥalala*. Such *fatwas* have outraged civil rights organisations and women's organisations all over the country.

The Emergence of Muslim Women's Organisations and New Personal Law Boards

In line with such criticism, Lucknow-based Muslim women's activists have each openly challenged the religious and legal hegemony of the AIMPLB with its *Shariat*-court system. As mentioned above, the *Darul Qaza* system has been repeatedly criticised outside of and within the Muslim community as a 'parallel system of law'. Women's rights activists in particular have strongly voiced their distrust of the *Darul Qaza* system and of the AIMPLB, stating that such men-run institutions are deeply biased against women. For instance, Muslim women's rights activist and founding member of the Indian Muslim Women's Movement (BMMA), Naish Hasan, told me about the story of a young Muslim woman who has been repeatedly raped by her father. She gave birth to four children fathered by her own father. This young woman has approached the *Darul Qaza* in the hope the *qazi* would call her father to account for his actions. However, as Hasan regrets, the *qazi* did not bother to properly investigate the case. Instead, he found fault with the woman, whom he accused of not having complied with the Islamic concept of female modesty (*purdah*). Shaista Amber, president of the AIMWPLB, offers a similar image of the *Darul Qaza*. In her opinion, the fact that the *Darul Qaza* issues divorce decrees without even listening to the women's version of the marital conflict illustrates the misogynist approach of this men-dominated societal body. Shia clerics, on the other hand, have criticised the AIMPLB and its *Darul Qaza* system as sectarian and as ignorant toward Shia culture. They feel that Shia scholars and the Shia perspective on law has been severely underrepresented in the AIMPLB and the Sunni-dominated *Darul Qaza*.

Bazme Khawateen (Women's Club)

One of the very few Muslim women's rights activists, I got to know during the time of my research, who is more lenient toward the often misogynist AIMPLB, is Shehnaz Sidrat, the president of *Bazme Khawateen*. Despite criticising the *Darul Qaza* for being a men-dominated system that allows for men to easily divorce their spouses through the practice of triple *talaq*, frequently leaving the often-illiterate women with no shelter and financial support, she leaves unquestioned the political representative role of the religious authorities. Aligning herself with the orthodox religious leadership along ideological axes of identification, Sidrat hopes for the AIMPLB to recognise her organisation as part of this umbrella organisation. 'I would like *Bazme Khawateen* to become the women's wing of the AIMPLB. Although they have failed to regulate triple *talaq* or to effectively adjudicate family matters in the *Darul Qaza*, they are still 'the only body' representing our community. We have a lot of things in common, such as the struggle against the practice of dowry and female foeticide'.[23] As a result of such aspirations, Shehnaz Sidrat recently moved the head office of *Bazme Khawateen* from the family residence to the *Firangi Mahal* – a famous religious centre for Sunni Muslims in Lucknow.[24]

Bazme Khawateen is a family establishment that works with the Muslim community in Lucknow, and with women living in remote rural areas in Uttar Pradesh.[25] The majority of *Bazme Khawateen* members are from the lower socioeconomic strata, and only a minority belong to the middle and upper-middle class. *Bazme Khawateen* was established in 1934, while India was under British rule, on the location of the first women's park in old Lucknow (*Zenana* Park). The period of the organisation's inception marked the advent of the growing institutionalisation of Muslim women's activism, which had begun in the early part of the century. The founder of *Bazme Khawateen*, Begum Sultana Hayat, belonged to those elite Muslim women who were actively engaged in setting up reform-oriented Muslim women's organisations and Muslim women's clubs.[26] The main concern of these organisations and clubs was to push for education of Muslim women and to discuss *purdah* (Lateef 1990; Minault 1998b). Moreover, these organisations and clubs offered a setting for Muslim women to address issues of Islam and gender while outside of their homes. These publicly active Muslim women were not concerned with challenging or overthrowing the authority of the religious leadership. Rather, their intention was to add a gendered perspective to current debates on Islamic reforms, and to strengthen the Muslim identity vis-à-vis the colonial state. The emergence of these different associations and clubs led to a new exchange of ideas and to the greater participation of upper-class Muslim women in addressing the social and educational issues of colonial India.[27]

Begum Shehnaz Sidrat carries on the legacy of her mother-in-law and primarily focuses upon educational issues. Every month, Begum Sidrat organises a meeting in the *Zenana* Park in old Lucknow, where 80 to 150 members from all parts in the city gather at a time to enjoy some snacks and afternoon tea while learning about *quranic* issues related to women's rights, health, education, and spirituality. The several thousand members of *Bazme Khawateen*, the great majority hailing from Uttar Pradesh, include housewives, students, and working women with various economic and social backgrounds. The monthly gatherings in the park, which are exclusively female, also feature a stage for the performance of marriages, the reciting of poems and songs, and the offering of *namaz* (prayers). Since women in the city of Lucknow as elsewhere in India are strongly discouraged from offering *namaz* in the mosque, this provides the rare opportunity for Muslim women to pray in a public space (see Chapter 3). According to Sidrat, the Hindi newspaper *Nai Duniya* (New World) reported *Bazme Khawateen* to be the biggest women's club in the world.

In addition to meetings in the park, Sidrat regularly invites members of *Bazme Khawateen* to her office for workshops and special events. Up to 50 women gather in her rather small and scarcely furnished office – divided by a thick curtain from her living room. Apart from a great desk, where a large amount of loose papers, folders, and newspaper clips are piled up, there are a few chairs lined on each side and at the centre of the room. *Bazme Khawateen* provides legal and literacy trainings, offers legal counselling, and mediates family-dispute cases according to *Shariat* law. More recently, *Bazme Khawateen* began running a 'match-making bureau'. Having built up a vast network of members amongst mostly Sunni Muslims in Lucknow, Shehnaz Sidrat receives letters and phone calls almost daily from parents who are looking for a suitable wedding match for their sons and daughters. The letters include vital statistics: age, height, hair, eye, and skin colour, as well as personality traits and education. They also stipulate the clients' specific expectations for the prospective groom/bride (for example, education, character, skin colour, domestic responsibilities, profession, etc.).

Operating in the shadow of orthodox religious establishments, *Bazme Khawateen* offers a public 'comfort zone' for Muslim women who often find themselves alone and without a voice either within their family or in the male-dominated state and non-state systems of adjudication (see Chapter 5). In the office of *Bazme Khawateen*, Muslim women are offered room to share and discuss their life stories, receive lessons on proper readings of the Islamic scripture, and pray in public. Although it is occasionally criticised by other Muslim women's activists as 'puppets in the hands of the Muslim authorities', *Bazme Khawateen* faces no major institutional opposition. *Bazme Khawateen* is not interlinked with other local, national, or transnational (Muslim) women's organisations. The organisation is entirely funded by its president, Shehnaz Sidrat.

The All India Muslim Personal Law Board and the AISPLB

However, while until 2004 the AIMPLB has been largely unrivalled as the representative forum of Indian Muslims, members of the Barelvi sect of Sunni Muslims linked with spiritual Sufism, the Shia clergy, and the newly emerging Muslim women's organisations are much less favourably disposed toward this dominant Sunni body with its Deobandi-Wahabi orientation. For instance, in 2004, *maulana* Tauqeer Reza Khan, grandson of Barelvi sect founder *maulana* Ali Shah Mufti Ahmad Raza Khan, initiated a partial split from the AIMPLB. This spurred a wide rift among the influential Sunni clergy on different issues regarding the *Shariat*. In an interview featured in the *Times of India*, *maulana* Tauqeer Reza Khan explains the reason to form the parallel All India Muslim Personal Law Board (Jadeed) with the AIMPLB's failure to adequately protect the spirit of Muslim *Shariat* law. Moreover, the Barelvi member of the AIMPLB felt that its Deobandi members discriminated against them.[28]

Just a few months after the establishment of the AIMPLB (Jadeed), prominent Shia leaders of the Shia Ulema-e-Hind echoed such concern. As mentioned above, Shia–Sunni relationships in the city of Lucknow were and are fragile. The 1986 anti-Shia edict, a *fatwa* of apostatisation against Shias issued by the Deobandi seminaries in Lucknow and Pakistan, further exacerbated the sectarian rift between Sunnis and Shias in the city. This *fatwa,* which declared Shias as non-Muslims (*kafir)* and therefore liable to extermination for succumbing to apostasy, fuelled sectarian violence in Pakistan, so the political analyst Khaled Ahmed in *The Indian Express*.[29] Over the last decade or so, more than 12,000 Shias have been systematically killed by militant Sunnis in Pakistan.[30]

So, a major factor that caused the populist Shia cleric from Lucknow, *maulana* Athar, to establish his own personal law board in 2005 was the fact that the AIMPLB is dominated by the Deobandis. In his view, the AIMPLB thus works primarily for the interest of its Deobandi members. In a personal conversation in February 2011, Athar explained that although the AIMPLB also represents sects other than the Deobandi, 'it does not take into account the problems and demands of the others. Other religious groups, such as for example Barelwis and Shias, are not well represented. After my efforts to increase the representation of the Shias within the Board failed, I found myself compelled to establish our own Muslim Personal Law Board'. Justin Jones in his article on the fragmentation of the AIMPLB, however, reminds us to be cautious not to frame the AISPLB as a unified Shia operation to oppose the AIMPLB – as Athar tends to present it. Rather, Jones (2010, 197) argues, another, and perhaps equally strong motivation that led to the formation of the AISPLB, was the Shia Board member's ambition to assert themselves against the long-established Lucknow-based *Khandan-i-Ijtihad* clerical family. The latter has, according to Jones (2010, 197), held authority over Shia institutions in the city over the last 200 years and has strong ties to the AIMPLB.

Although somewhat reluctant, Athar set up the *All India Shia Personal Law Board* (AISPLB) in January 2005. The AISPLB operates from the home of its president, *maulana* Athar, and is thus located in the winding alleys in one of old Lucknow's Shia quarters. According to Athar, the AISPLB offers a platform for Shias to openly identify and discuss social, political, and economical 'backwardness'. He felt that the issues of their community had been constantly sidelined – by the government as well as by the Sunni-dominated Muslim leadership – ever since independence. The Shia clergy believe that their community lags behind other Muslim communities in terms of education, employment, and political representation. They are, for instance, often excluded from the process of creating government policy for the aid of the Muslim community. Given the Shias' considerable population – 50 million – in India, the Board demands Shia representation in parliament and state assemblies, with the reservation of seats for Shias.

The AISPLB further stakes claim to Muslims' religious rights as set forth in the Constitution. They call for separate management of Shia *waqf* (properties),[31] autonomy over their educational system (for example, to set up their own schools and formulate their own curricula), subsidies for Shia pilgrims going to places of worship, and the protection of Shia personal law. In order to protect their family laws, the AISPLB seeks to establish a committee consisting of eminent elderly authorities (*ulema*) to advise in legal matters. The intention of the AISPLB is, first, to render visible the political, economical, and social concerns of the Shias, and, second, to unite the scattered Shia community in India in their struggle for political and social recognition.

The Board holds regular meetings in different cities across India and organises seminars and workshops to discuss pressing issues (for example, terrorism, and religious rituals and practices). In order to disseminate their agenda and to recruit new members they have established their own website.[32] They further intend to share their localised experiences and analysis across borders, establishing a transnational network with other Shia communities outside of India. Hence they are planning the launch of a Shia television station and newspaper in order to reach other Shia populations. Although the mission of the AISPLB is almost exclusively political, the Board recently engaged in public debates concerning the legal scope and limitations of Muslim women's rights within marriage, releasing their own model-*nikahnama* (see Chapter 4). In the context of its aspirations, the AISPLB has also, according to media accounts, decided to launch a toll-free telephone helpline for women suffering domestic violence so as to strictly ostracise men who misuse women.[33] Such a foray into the legal arena of gender reform must be understood in terms of this group's efforts to bring Shia-specific interpretations of the religious texts to the fore. Their endeavour is to contrast with the well-established, and among legal practitioners, widely recognised Sunni, or more precisely *Hanafi*, interpretations of Muslim law.

The AISPLB, however, has not succeeded in corralling support from all sections of India's internally fractured Shia community. An earlier member of the Board has stated in the media that the members of the Board are few and that its founders are unfortunately more concerned with promoting their self-interests than the interests of the community.[34] Moreover, Shia women lament their lack of representation on the Board. The AISPLB in fact has no female members. Shia women argue that the Board was formed on the premise of establishing ties with the state in order to demand representation. Women, however, were absent from the Board, boding poorly for their inclusion in this agenda. So, the lack of full support of the AISPLB on the part of India's Shia population illustrates how 'inner-Shia and Shia-Sunni conflicts could be deeply intertwined', as Jones (2010, 198) rightly put it.

The All India Muslim Women's Personal Law Board

Lucknow's men-dominated institutional landscape has thus prompted a few Shia and Sunni women to launch, as a female counter-voice, the All India Muslim Women's Personal Law Board (AIMWPLB). As a Board composed of Shias and Sunnis they hope to bridge the gap between the otherwise strongly divided members of the different Islamic schools in Lucknow. The founding members of the AIMWPLB opine that the politics surrounding religious identity, where the differences between Shias and Sunnis are expressed through ideological differentiations, had become obstructive to the realisation of Muslim women's rights. Shaista Amber, the Board's president, has said, 'All *maulanas* do is to discuss what is Islamic and [what is] not. Nobody thinks about all these women who suffer from violence and poverty every single day. They have nowhere to go! That's why we have established the AIMWPLB'.[35]

In March 2005, just a few months after the establishment of the AISPLB, a few middle-class Sunni and Shia women from Lucknow set up the AIMWPLB. The founding members of the AIMWPLB all initially met at a wedding, where they conceived of the idea due to the common belief that the dignity and freedom of Muslim women were being subverted by chauvinistic and selective interpretations of the *Quran* and the *Shariat*. However, internal fractions that focused around the Board's current president Shaista Amber reportedly arose shortly after the AIMWPLB's launch. Several women on the committee accused Amber, who is a member of the Communist Party, of misusing the AIMWPLB as a platform from which to pursue her political agenda. They also accused her of using the name and cause of the Board in order to promote her own celebrity status. As a consequence, the Women's Board split two years after its inception, leaving Amber to lead the AIMWPLB single-handedly.[36]

She contends that the board was established as a response to the Muslim clergy's patriarchal and essentialist interpretation of Islamic texts and law regarding marriage and divorce. The sphere of the AIMWPLB's activities varies, from spiritual gatherings and religious education to legal advocacy and mediation of family disputes. The AIMWPLB operates out of a mosque located on the outskirts of Lucknow. Entirely financed by Amber, these headquarters facilitate the meetings and programs of the women's Board. There, Amber conducts religious debates and lectures and organises meetings called the *khuli adaalat* in which women are called upon to discuss their grievances with Islamic scholars (*maulana*). This mosque is further intended as a place of worship, allowing women and men to pray together. The events of the AIMWPLB such as the commemoration of the terrorist attacks in Mumbai in 2006, a workshop on human rights, and talks held on International Women's Day are well-frequented by newspaper journalists and reporters. The AIMWPLB is therefore well-documented and discussed in local and national newspaper articles.

Whereas the media praises Amber's step to challenge the authority of the clergy with the establishment of a women's personal law board as an 'effort to prove their mettle' (*Milligazette*) and as 'a victory for Indian feminism' (*The Telegraph*),[37] the well-known *Imam* Khalid Rashid from the *Firangi Mahal* considers such new boards, including the AISPLB, irrelevant for the larger Muslim community in India and of no national importance. At one of my visits at the *Firangi Mahal*, Rashid explained to me,

> The AISPLB and the AIMWPLB are local organisations that are of no national relevance. Whereas the AIMPLB includes all those people who are considered Muslim in the eyes of the Indian Constitution, these Boards consist of a few self-appointed leaders that have no hold within the Muslim community. Since the AIMPLB is host to all prominent scholars belonging the various sects and schools in India, the other boards simply do not matter for the community.

Along similar lines, Shehnaz Sidrat, president of *Bazme Khawateen*, told me in an interview that for her the AIMWPLB served merely as a platform for Amber to promote her celebrity status and to make money.[38]

Despite this criticism, which nicely reveals the schisms that run through the Muslim community in Lucknow, the AIMWPLB is increasing in popularity and membership. This popularity is mainly catalysed through the media and word of mouth. In 2009, at the beginning of my research, I found it very difficult to talk to women associated with the AIMWPLB. However, when I visited Amber again in February/March 2011, her organisation seemed to have substantially grown. For the first time, I had the chance to meet some of the AIMWPLB's members. These women came from different socioeconomic and educational backgrounds. However, the majority of the women I met were poor and live in the slums (*bastis*) of Lucknow or in nearby villages. The women who came from as far as Delhi, Punjab, Madhya Pradesh, and Bihar were usually economically better off. These women had heard about the AIMWPLB through the newspapers or television and had made contact with Amber via telephone or email. Also, since my first field visit a proper committee – counting fifty members – had been set up, and a considerable number of new members had been won. Most of the committee members came from outside of Lucknow, and I was hence only able to interview a few. In early 2011, Amber estimated the number of AIMWPLB members to be several thousand. However, these numbers cannot be verified as the AIMWPLB does not ask for registration and therefore does not have its members on file. In order to recruit new members and to gain publicity, the Board regularly organises seminars and campaigns. It also utilises the Internet to reach a greater audience. The AIMWPLB works autonomously and has no affiliation with any other NGO. The board receives funding from charity and donations. Although AIMWPLB is registered under the Foreign Contribution Registration Act, Shaista Amber has until now not applied for international funding due, as she says, to lack of knowledge about the procedure.

In courses and workshops Amber reads and discusses the *Quran* together with her mostly poor members in regard to women's rights and gender relations. She teaches them about their rights as mothers, wives, and daughters and as citizens. These are rights, Amber complains, that are often jeopardised by people's ignorance of women's *quranic* rights at the grassroots level on the one hand and at the national level, where competing political and religious ideologies abound, on the other hand. To illustrate the latter, Amber refers to the two famous and controversially debated cases – the Imrana and the Gudiya cases, which I discussed already in more detail in the Introduction. In a nutshell: The first case is about a young woman called Imrana who was raped by her father-in-law. The village then decided that this incestuous rape made her the mother of her husband who was subsequently *haram* (forbidden) to her. The *Darul Uloom Deoband* issued a *fatwa* stating that Imrana is no longer rightfully married to her husband. The second case concerns another young woman, Gudiya, who was pregnant with the baby from her second marriage when her first husband, believed to be dead, returned from the Kargil war after five years. In this case, the AIMPLB released a *fatwa* declaring her marriage to her second husband of two years void.

In our conversation, Amber was seemingly outraged by the manner in which the AIMPLB bluntly prioritises religious identity politics over women's rights. With an angry voice, she told me,

> The *fatwas* released in the Imrana and Gudiya case illustrate the AIMPLB's ignorance toward women's issues. They just don't care! Rather than releasing *fatwas* that disturb women's lives, the AIMPLB should ensure the well-being of Muslim women in India. Thousands of women suffer from such nasty (*kharab*) politics that totally undermine women's virtue and the fact they too are human beings.

Amber went on explaining her incentive to form the AIMWPLB, saying, 'These *fatwas* are not according to Islam. It is therefore my duty to reinstate women's rights in Islam in political debates and in people's mind. I continue to fight for our rights until Muslim women in India can live peacefully!' In this vein, the AIMWPLB publicly speaks out against ultra-conservative rhetoric regarding gender and Islam. As a part of their strategy, the AIMWPLB lobbies the state to secure the rights of Muslim women as citizens under the Constitution and as Muslims under Islamic laws, within state adjudicated Muslim Personal Law. They furthermore endeavour to enhance women's political representation. Another tactic of the AIMWPLB is to call on the state to restrict the legal power of the *darul qazas* and the Islamic seminaries whose misogynist verdicts and *fatwas* have, according to Amber, made the lives of many Muslim women miserable.

This all-female legal institution is a distinctive feature within the legal landscape in Lucknow, offering an important discursive space of resistance within which the legal and religious authority of the AIMPLB is challenged. Moreover, the AIMWPLB widens the religious space by establishing an informal dialogue with the state. As I will illustrate in the subsequent chapters, the AIMWPLB represents an arena within which a progressive understanding of Islam – one that transcends stereotype and essentialist constructions – is publicised. In so doing, the Board adopts a two-pronged approach. First, it lobbies the state to acknowledge Muslim women's rights in accordance with the Constitution and to reform women's rights within MPL. Second, it creates a public forum within which patriarchal notions of women's rights in Islam are reshaped through a dialogue with 'women-friendly' religious authorities (for example, *maulana, mufti,* etc.) as well as with individuals at the grassroots level. Therefore, the AIMWPLB marks out a space that furthers a dialogue with the state, the clergy, and individuals.

Bharatiya Muslim Mahila Andolan (BMMA)

Naish Hasan, a Lucknow native and one of the founding members of the Indian Muslim Women's Movement, or *Bharatiya Muslim Mahila Andolan*, criticises the AIMWPLB for their approach of discussing Muslim women's rights by and large in relation to the Islamic texts and ideology. In her opinion, this approach detracts from the goal of understanding the wider political, economic, and social circumstances within which gender asymmetry is rooted. Hasan views the state of gender inequality among Indian Muslims as one result of the overall social, educational, and economic marginalisation of the Muslim community. Drawing upon the Sachhar Committee Report from 2006,[39] Hasan contends that the Muslim community in India suffers from severe economic, social, and educational 'backwardness'. She and her fellow activists believe that this condition derives from, amongst other things, the exclusion of Muslims from governmental policy on the one hand, and the rampant violence that has seized the community on the other.[40] For Hasan, communalism and fundamentalism has further compounded the Muslim community's alienation and physical, political, and economical insecurity within postcolonial India. Moreover, the negative impact of capitalism upon Muslims, accompanied by escalating terrorism and resulting hostile perceptions of Muslims by non-Muslims, has contributed to Muslims' vulnerability. This has also had a substantially negative impact upon Muslim women's lives. The current reactionary conservative movement within Muslim communities, which endeavours to strengthen patriarchal values, has, combined with extreme poverty and marginalisation, pushed Muslim women to the fringes of Indian society. In Hasan's opinion, popular misconceptions about the basic features of Islamic jurisprudence, coupled with unavailable democratic opportunities, enhance the social marginalisation of women. Therefore, the current state of Muslim women can only be substantially ameliorated by seriously downsizing the power of the conservatives on the one hand while creating access to democratic possibilities for Muslims on the other.

Despite the political, social, and legal hardships of Muslim women in postcolonial India, the secular women's movement in India, which fashioned its criticism of institutional modernisation and postcolonial politics into tools of protest, did not pay special consideration to Muslim women. Unlike their Hindu and *dalit* peers, Muslim women have by and large remained off the political and social reformist agenda. For Hasan, the modern Indian women's movement, established in the 1970s at a time when Indians were still in the throes of the particular kind of Indian modernity as well as colonialism, prompted middle- and upper-class women to take up the struggle against their political exclusion, domestic violence, rape, and dowry deaths. These women's activists, who Hasan describes as 'good leaders that plotted a secular path toward a future predicated upon questions about their relationship with the state', however, were all Hindus. 'Muslims', Hasan laments, 'have not been approached in this process. Their specific needs and problems have, therefore, been neglected'. Moreover, Hasan regrets that the national Indian women's movement as well as other secular NGOs have failed to address religion in positive terms in the context of their commitment to the project of secularism. As Hasan contends, secular organisations have been wary to openly broach Muslim women's issues in a context of political and religious polarisation, currently taking place locally and globally.

The BMMA follows an existentialist-secular path predicated upon questions about who they are, what their relationship with the conservative leadership and the state is, and how Muslim women's future will look like. Hasan's strong disaffirmation of the clergy's identity politics – where ideological ideas about the 'truth of Islam' are marshalled as tools to disregard 'issues of school [education], water, sanitation, the Ration Card or identity card and other government schemes for Muslims' – worked its way through our many conversations. Questioning the religious authority of well-known *maulanas* affiliated with the Deobandi-run AIMPLB, the Shia-organised AISPLB, as well as that of Shaista Amber, Hasan challenges their legitimacy as political leaders. 'Who appointed them as leaders?' she distrustfully asks. 'I don't consider them as leaders of our community. I did not vote for them nor did anyone else!'

Refuting the political authority of orthodox *maulanas* as well as their strategy to discuss Muslim issues within a purely doctrinal framework, Hasan distances herself from the AIMPLB, the AISPLB, and the AIMWPLB. Her decision to work with and for the downtrodden Muslim community in postcolonial India derives, according to her, not primarily from her identity as a Muslim but from her grit to improve the everyday situation of those who are amongst the poorest in postcolonial India. 'The community really needs to be improved,' Hasan affirms,

> And this can't be done by setting up separate personal law boards. Rather, our struggles toward justice need to be based on our Constitutions and state-administered religious personal laws. We need some changes within state-administered personal laws. There should be a law that sets out to improve the position of Muslims in general and of Muslim women in particular. Let's fight for this kind of legal change at the state level rather than setting up alternative courts!

Like the Muslim leadership and women's rights activists such as Amber and Sidrat, Hasan formulates religion positively, as a category through which political and social justice can be asserted. However, in order to truly ameliorate the situation of disenfranchised Muslims, and especially Muslim women, Hasan feels that it is important to reconcile issues of religion and gender with matters of secularism and democracy. Hence her outlook indicates an important shift toward a conceptualisation of the categories of religion and secularism as congruent rather than disparate, and therefore equally conducive to social change.

With this aim in mind, Naish Hasan, together with Muslim academics and activists, formed the Mumbai-based Indian Muslim Women's Movement or the BMMA in January 2007. The BMMA is an autonomous organisation that is organised as a network of local groups affiliated on the state level. The BMMA works hand in hand with grassroots organisations and is well interlinked with a variety of local, national, and transnational organisations, movements, and networks that are all involved in advocating for social equality, peace, communal harmony, and justice. For instance, BMMA is a part of Musawah, a global movement for gender justice in Islam. The BMMA further allies with (trans) national organisations for joint research projects such as the Mumbai-based Observer Research Foundation or UN Women.[41] Hasan labels the BMMA a secular organisation since it endeavours to initiate and implement gender reforms in the area of Muslim family law primarily through the state legal system.

As according to their website 70 per cent of their members must be Muslims and 30 per cent of its members can be 'men and women from any caste, community or religion'.[42] According to a 2015 blog entry, the BMMA counts 60,000 members dispersed across fifteen states.[43] Every state is assigned a state leader who organises the BMMA's activities on the state level. The structural core of the BMMA is the National Council, comprised of its founding members and state leaders. The National Council makes all decisions regarding the BMMA's agenda, activities, and strategies. This body meets every three months to exchange experiences, share each other's work, and make decisions on important matters. The BMMA has offices in the states where the organisation is currently active. Until 2013, the office of the BMMA in Lucknow was located in the home of its founding members Naish Hasan and Zakia Jowher. The BMMA very recently shifted its Lucknow office to Mumbai due to internal restructurations.

As Hasan told me, the secular BMMA was set up as a national arena for Muslim women to voice their rights within a Constitutional framework. The English-language press such as the Lucknow-based *The National Herald* describes the BMMA as 'a lone voice fighting for the voiceless'; the *Sunday Times of India* described it by saying 'India's Muslim feminists join global "jihad" for gender justice'.[44] The BMMA is intended as an alternative and progressive voice for change and democracy, one that derives from within the Muslim community. Locating women's oppression and inequality within a wider set of circumstances, the BMMA works for the amelioration of Muslim's political, educational, social, and legal 'backwardness' while fighting for 'justice'.[45] In order to achieve these goals, they work to develop leadership skills among Muslim women of especially the lower economic strata, while lobbying the state for reforms of MPL and political inclusion. As Naish Hasan tells me, the BMMA is primarily funded by individual donations and membership fees.[46] Furthermore, the BMMA gets support from the community and civil society in kind such as sponsoring of meeting venues and lunches and donations such as sewing machines etc. as well as *zakat* money. In addition, Action Aid supports the BMMA state leaders' professional development opportunities with small fellowships.[47]

One of the most important strategies of the BMMA is to establish leadership qualities among grassroots activists, who then advocate for change on the district level. These newly recruited grassroots leaders act as pressure groups, presenting their plights with local authorities and demanding action. As a second strategy, the BMMA plans to build a network of academics, policymakers, and politicians to lobby the state. Together with civil society actors and academics, the BMMA conducts research on women's daily realities and experiences. The findings are discussed at regularly organised roundtables where the issues of Muslim women's rights are addressed. These roundtables are attended by academics, activists, journalists, and civic groups, as well as individuals who are concerned with the plight of Muslim women. Based upon their studies' empirical findings, the BMMA develops action plans, manifestos, and strategies for legal reforms.

Another goal of the BMMA is to gain public visibility. For this purpose they organise street rallies in larger Indian cities and hold awareness camps in the Muslim-*bastis* (slums) and public parks. Workshops on political, social, and economic rights are held in universities, police academies, or colleges in order to reach students, policymakers, and activists.[48] The BMMA further organises public meetings, press conferences, and campaigns (for example, covering domestic violence, inflation, the political marginalisation of Muslim women, female foeticide, excessive electricity bills, and the right to food and housing) in order to bring women's issues to the fore. Held in major cities across India, the activities are consistently covered by the press (see Chapter 3). The BMMA also makes use of social media, such as feminist blogs, Internet forums, social networks, and podcasts in order to disseminate their agenda of legal, social, and political change.[49] In April 2013, Hasan travelled to the United States as a Visiting Fellow at the University of Wisconsin, Milwaukee. There the Institute of World Affairs interviewed Hasan regarding her activism and her ideas of Muslim women's rights. This interview aired on Milwaukee public television.[50]

The BMMA's structure, principles, and strategic method mark it out as a very different organisation from the ones heretofore discussed. The very 'language' by which it describes its own structures, strategies, and activities is reminiscent of transnational human (women's) rights networks. Its goals are framed upon the tenets and principles of universal human and women's rights and are legitimised by the values of the Constitution. The BMMA is a local movement, but its range of influence nonetheless spans villages/communities and districts across the nation to the globalised world – typically the reserved audience of transnational organisations such as the UN. Participating in public debates and engaging with state institutions, the BMMA has contributed to the widening of the democratic space.

Drawing on the secularism argument, the BMMA acknowledges the supremacy of the Indian Constitution in the legal and political life of Indians and aligns its activism accordingly. In this manner, Naish Hasan, founding member of the BMMA, rejects any kind of parallel society that is geared toward institutional separation from the state back in 2010. Back then, the BMMA, in contrary to *Bazme Khawateen* and the AIMWPLB, did not offer legal mediation on its own accord. Any effort to establish a parallel religious leadership in order to govern its members was considered a threat to the constitutional system, jeopardising women's rights as citizens. This attitude, however, has changed since my last field visit. Giving in to community pressure demanding non-male arenas for the adjudication of Muslim laws, the BMMA set up legal aid cells called Women's *Shariat*-courts in Mumbai, Pune, Ahmedabad, and Dindigul in Tamil Nadu in 2013. These Women's *Shariat*-courts are, as stated on the BMMA's website, intended to safeguard the interests of women and children in the area of the family and ensure their citizenship rights. These women's courts are further designed to provide speedy justice as according to the *Quran*. In the near future, the BMMA plans to set up a national bench comprised of eminent activists and scholars 'who will give opinion on complex matters of Muslim Personal Law'. All BMMA counsellors and advisers sitting on the Women's *Shariat*-court benches receive paralegal training, so the report.[51] The BMMA's main goal, however, is to codify Muslim Personal Laws *within* state law, which, if successful, would render such alternative dispute mechanisms redundant. For this purpose, the BMMA paired with the Delhi-based Centre for Study of Society and Secularism (CSSS). The CSSS, which was funded by the reformist Islamic scholar and activists Asghar Ali Engineer, is a democratic organisation established as a response to communal riots and violence that gained momentum in the 1980s (see Introduction). Together with the BMMA, the CSS is currently involved in the codification of Muslim marriage laws (see Chapter 4). Naish Hasan, who never approved of 'parallel systems of law', as she called it, separated from the BMMA in 2013. This is due to her disapproval of the 'BMMA's new agenda'.[52]

In conclusion, the structure and functioning of the BMMA – its very activism – is based upon a unique approach to secularism, one that allows Muslim women to go beyond polarising debates of Islam versus secular constitutional values. Such an approach echoes the position of state-oriented and independent Muslim feminists, as for example in Iran, Malaysia, Turkey, and Egypt (Badran 2008; Foley 2004; Moghadam 2002; Kandiyoti 1991a), who endeavour to enlarge the democratic space with the reform of laws concerning Muslim women's freedom in social, political, religious, and individual domains.

The Multidimensional Complexity of the Legal Field

The amorphous legal landscape portrayed in this chapter is imbued with internal conflicts, rejection as well as collaboration, and overlap. In this context, single coherent legal spaces do not exist. Instead, each adjudicative site, formal or informal, provides a platform for interaction between the state and/or societal actors. The result is a highly interactive institutional landscape, characterised by complex and changing social and political dynamics of communication – existing among and within the various sites.

This chapter shows that within the last decade, the often too readily accepted antagonism between the Muslim community and the state has been destabilised. In fact, my analysis of Lucknow's institutional landscape reveals a turbulent shift in religious authority in contemporary India brought about by the emergence of alternative personal law boards and Muslim women's organisations. This institutional 'churning process' (Jones 2010, 200) amongst the religious leadership, schools, and activists brings to light the instability of the inter-institutional relationships. In fact, the overall impression is one of significant institutional fluidity/overlap between the state, the ideologically diverse Muslim leadership, and women's activists. The above discussed Muslim women's activists have, together with other legal and political players such as the Shia leadership and the Barelvi Sunnis, contributed to the fragmentation of the religious leadership affiliated with the AIMPLB – evoking a fragmented view on issues of MPL and Muslim life on an institutional, political, and personal level. Such fragmentation shows the instability of institutional borders and local and national power relations. For example, the longstanding Muslim women's organisation *Bazme Khawateen* aspires to work toward women's citizenship rights by lobbying the powerful AIMPLB to include a gender perspective in their programming and policymaking activities. The AIMWPLB and the BMMA, on the other hand, openly oppose the AIMPLB and call upon the state to extend Indian citizens' political, social, and economic rights to Muslim women. In so doing, both organisations seek to widen the democratic space and to engage in a dialogue with the, often reluctant, Indian state. For instance, the AIMWPLB lobbies the state to back up their women-friendly proposals for Muslim laws and to curtail the legal authority of the orthodox Muslim clergy – especially the Deoband section of the AIMPLB. The secular BMMA, which works toward the political inclusion of Muslims and Muslim women in particular, not only looks to the state to back up their agenda but considers this body the ultimate dispenser of justice, seeking active collaboration between the two. Consequently, the BMMA aims at reconciling religion with principles of democracy and secularism on all levels. The BMMA rejects all kind of self-appointed legal and religious authorities and lobbies against attempts to establish a separate legal system for Muslims. In short, Muslim women's activists positioning is neither uniform nor simple, but fragmented along lines of politics and religious ideology.

We may conclude that Lucknow's legal landscape is especially suitable to shatter the twin fiction of the 'homogenous Muslim community' as brought forward by the state as well as by the AIMPLB, and, of course, of a singular legal ideology – the *Shariat* – that is static and unchangeable. In this regard, my analysis illustrates that we may need to look beyond state-community antagonism to capture the vibrancy and flexibility of India's institutional landscape and the law. Then such 'interpenetrative legal sphere', to speak with Solanki (2011, xxii), is characterised by various strands of institutional interrelationships – tied up in polymorphous formulations of Muslim family law – mutually constitutive and penetrative institutional boundaries and fluid and changeable power relations. It is precisely this flexibility, it seems, that allows for the above discussed civic actors to participate in debates on gender, law, and Muslim lifestyle while at the same time questioning the existing balance of authority (Eickelman and Piscatori 1996; Jones 2010). Within each of the ensuing chapters, I explore such idea by focusing on the manner in which these Muslim women's rights activists shape and design their activism so as to destabilise hegemonic patterns of power, authority, and legal consciousness. I start with an analysis of how Muslim women's rights activists navigate the highly patriarchal public space by making their bodies seen and voices heard.

Endnotes

1. Hard data on Lucknow's Muslim is difficult to come by since the Census of India does not record data regarding class, religious school, literacy, gender, and sex ratio amongst Muslims. However, several governmental and non-governmental reports on Muslim's socio-economic status in India, namely the Seema Kazi's Minority Report, the Sachar Committee Report, and the report of the Ranganath Misra Commission, evince Muslims as the most disadvantaged religious group in terms of education, employment, and economic security. My discussion of Muslim's socio-economic positioning in Lucknow is based on Raphael Susewind's interactive map designed in 2013. Based on data derived from electoral rolls, the Census of India, Election Commission of India, MapmyIndia, and other online sources, Susewind created a detailed map taking into consideration the geographical, economic, and sectarian aspect of Muslim life in the city. Raphael Susewind's interactive map on Muslim India can be accessed on his blog: http://www.raphael-susewind.de/blog/2012/mapping-lucknow-muslim-life (accessed June 1, 2015).
2. India has the highest number of Shias after Iran.
3. The Samjawadi Party is primarily located in Uttar Pradesh and has a secular democratic outlook. The Samajawadi Party does not believe in communal forces. It claims to work for the upliftment of the weaker section of the society. For more information see their website: http://www.samajwadiparty.in/ideology.html (accessed June 26, 2015)

4. See Susewind: http://www.raphael-susewind.de/blog/2012/mapping-lucknow-muslim-life (accessed June 1, 2015).
5. In a personal interview, Naish Hasan (BMMA) reminded me that in daily reality Muslims rarely know the religious school their family belongs to. In contrast, they do have knowledge about their affiliation with a specific sect and caste (*jati*). Similar to the Hindu community, Indian Muslims are hierarchically segregated into different castes based on the existence of numerous endogamous and generally occupationally specific groups that have their own caste appellations (for exampls, Ansari, Khan, Pathan, *nai* (barber), *dhobi* (washer man), and sweeper). In this regard, Hasan views the different Islamic schools as a political division made by the clergy, as in contrast to the caste system, which is a lived reality.
6. A *New York Times* article reports about the sectarian strife during *Muharram* in the city of Lucknow: http://india.blogs.nytimes.com/2013/11/20/the-two-lucknows-during-muslim-holy-month/?_php=true&_type=blogs&_r=0 (accessed July 10, 2014).
7. I will note that unlike in other cities in Uttar Pradesh, such as Bijnor, Saharanpur, Meetpur, Muzaffernagar, or Badpat, there exist no caste or sect *panchayats* in Lucknow. This is also in contrast to bigger Indian cities such as Mumbai. There, the legal landscape includes Muslim sect *panchayats* such as the one administered by the Khojas as well as as Hindu caste *panchayats* among the Sai Suthars or the Meghawal (see Solanki 2011). Strangely, there exists no literature on why such *panchayats* are absent in the context of Lucknow. However, as suggested by the anthropologist and professor at Lucknow University, Nadeem Hasnain, in an email conversation, such phenomenon could be explained with the emergence of the 'Arjak Sangh Movement' in the 1960s. The 'Arjak Sangh Movement' is a humanist rationalist movement in Uttar Pradesh that especially focuses on establishing social equality for *dalits*. The increased incorporation of *dalits* in Lucknow's governmental structures, which includes better accessibility to the courts, he argues, counts for the disappearance of the already very weak informal *panchayati*-like institutions in the city.
8. All interviews have been transcribed and translated into English for the purpose of analysis.
9. This includes the AIMPLB executive member Begum Naseema Ali Ikhtedar Khan and the Muslim female advocate Risha Syedi, daughter of a well-respected Sunni family in the city. As she accompanied me, Risha Syedi became a great asset to my research in the *Darul Qaza*. Well-versed in Islamic law and language and knowledgeable about the codes of conduct among the clergy, she substantially facilitated my interactions with them in the *Darul Uloom Nadwatul* and the *Firangi Mahal*.
10. The Family Court provides several guidelines under Muslim Personal Law for Muslim women in cases pertaining to divorce, maintenance, property, inheritance, and custody. In the Family Court a married or divorced Muslim woman can file for a monthly allowance from her (ex-) husband under Section 125 CrPC. However, this section only applies to women who are either still married or who have been rejected or divorced by their husband. A woman who leaves her husband on her own without any 'sufficient' reason, who lives in adultery, or who agrees on the divorce is not eligible to

claim her financial rights under this Section. However, under The Muslim Women (Protection of Rights on Divorce) Act from 1986 (MWA) – administered in the Metropolitan Magistrate Courts, the second-lowest level of India's Criminal Courts – *any* divorced Muslim woman, if she is dissatisfied with the financial arrangements made by her ex-husband, can claim her *mehar*, property, and a one-time payment (*mattaa*), the moment the *iddat* period is over. But in reality the MWA is hardly used. This might be in part due to the general ignorance of the advantages this Act provides for divorced Muslim women as well as the uncertainty many Muslim women have about the validity of the divorce, which is often pronounced by their husband in their absence. The Family Court also provides Muslim women with the guidelines to seek a divorce on certain grounds. Under the Dissolution of Muslim Marriage Act of 1939, a woman can file for a divorce given that her husband has abandoned her, failed to maintain her, is insane or impotent, treats her with cruelty, or that the marriage was performed when the bride was under the age of fifteen. Under this Act, her right to *mehar* and *iddat*-money remains–theoretically–intact. In practice however, Muslim women once again hardly make financial claims under this Act. As the advocate Hamza Abidi explains, this is because women litigants' first and foremost endeavour is 'to exit matrimony without creating further stir'. In other words: without using the law to its full extent. Cases pertaining to domestic violence and dowry are dealt with in the Criminal Court.

11. Under this Act, every city or town that exceeds the population of one million is assigned a Family Court. The Family Court has the same jurisdiction as the High Courts and the District Courts, including some criminal jurisdiction over maintenance orders (Section 125 Criminal Procedure Code). However, only a very few cases are directed to the High Court for adjudication. The national Supreme Court sets the definitive precedent for all states, while the High Court sets the definitive precedent for the relevant state. Whereas High Court benches may depart from the precedents of other benches in other states, a precedent of the Supreme Court can only be overruled by a higher bench, composed of more judges. The judges in the state courts are commonly trained in Western law, particularly common law tradition rather than religious law (Subramanian 2008, 636). For the Family Courts Act of 1984, see: http://mha.nic.in/pdfs/TheFamilyCourtsAct,1984.pdf (accessed June 12, 2012).
12. A *baradari* literally means a building with *'baarah'* (twelve) *'dar'* (door). *Baradari* refers to a garden pavilion, which were highly popular in Mughal India. During that time, the concept of the garden pavilion was imported from Persia. The typical Persian garden pavilion, as it was translated into Indian settings, was a four-sided open pavilion with three arches on each side. Three arches on four sides equals a total of twelve arches, or twelve doors. Soon enough, the word *baradari* came to be applied to all garden pavilions, even when they had more or less than the regular twelve arches.
13. A bit more information about the Family Court's operations might be in order. According to a statistic provided to me by the Lucknow-based NGO AALI (Association for Advocacy and Legal Initiatives), the Family Court in Lucknow settled

9,347 disputes between 2006 and 2010. Every day, the cases that are adjudicated in the Family Court are publicly announced in handwriting on a sheet of paper at the entrance of the court. This sheet states the number of cases, the nature of cases, and the names of the plaintiffs. It is rolled up together with the sheets from previous days and weeks and kept in a little wooden box at the entrance of the Family Court, where the actual sheet hangs on the outside of the box. There are two such boxes, one for the first and one for the second chamber. At every visit to Lucknow's Family Court, I have checked the number and nature of cases that were scheduled that day for a hearing. Each chamber dealt with about 55 to 75 cases every day. The great majority of the cases were filings for divorce or restitution of conjugal rights under the Hindu Marriage Act 1955 and for maintenance under Section 125 CrPC, showing that the majority of the petitioners are Hindus. For example, on February 22, 2011 sixty-one cases were listed on the sheet for the second chamber. On that day, all the cases were either filed under Section 125 of the CrPC (41) or under the Hindu Marriage Act (1955) (18). Out of these sixty-one cases, only ten were filed by Muslims; out of these ten cases 3 were petitioned by men under Section 13B of the Hindu Marriage Act (divorce by mutual consent) and 7 by women under Section 125 of the CrPC (maintenance).

14. On the backlog and delays in the Indian courts see for example the 77th report of the Indian Law Commission: http://lawcommissionofindia.nic.in/51-100/Report77.pdf (accessed April 30, 2013).
15. Interview with Hamza Abidi in the Family Court in Lucknow on February 13, 2011.
16. Within the last two decades, the Indian state has endeavoured to render adjudication more efficient. It has established what is referred to as 'fast-track courts' or People's Courts (*Lok Adalat*) that provide quicker, less formal, and less costly resolutions (Redding 2010, 18–19). Cases relating to family matters, partition, property, theft, injuries, and physical aggression that are pending in the courts can be directed to the *Lok Adalat*. *Lok Adalat* is a non-adversarial system focusing on compromise: cases are transferred only if both persons agree to it. If just one party requests transfer, the *Lok Adalat* will still handle the case given the court sees a good chance of amicable settlement after hearing both parties. The *Lok Adalats* are presided over by retired and/or sitting judges, advocates, social workers, and other people of repute. Similar to non-state caste and community assemblies, *Lok Adalats* use arbitration, mediation, and conciliation. The normal rules of civil procedure and evidence are suspended and informality and oral discussion prevails. There are neither court fees nor procedural requirements (for example, the parties do not have to follow regular processes required by the Civil Procedure Code or the Evidence Act), and in another departure from regular courts the disputants are able to interact with the judge directly. Once a compromise has been reached with the consent of both parties and an award made, it is enforced as a decree of the civil court and is binding on both parties, with no opportunity for appeal. In situations in which a compromise cannot be reached the case goes back to the regular courts. By creating a system of *Lok Adalats,* the state intended to provide less expensive and more participatory justice to its citizens (Shackelford

2009, 7–10). Tamara Relis (2011, 538) points out that especially people from the lower socioeconomic strata use these quasi-judicial courts as a means to obtain a compromise agreement outside of the formal legal system. Such an extra-judicial agreement is often more desirable than a formal one, as it leaves the reputations of the participating families intact. In resolving conflicts in a less formal manner, within the communities from whence they originated, these People's Courts in fact reflect the ongoing process of legal decentralisation that is currently underway in India. *Lok adalats* are increasingly important in dispute settlement and today comprise an integral part of the Indian justice system, due in large part to the enormous backlog in the formal state courts. These *informal sessions* take place in Lucknow every Sunday on the premises of the Family Court, taking up cases brought to the *lok adalat*'s attention by Hindus and Muslims.

17. *Darul qazas* have been around in India since colonial times (see Introduction). Between 1917 and 1921 Islamic scholars set up six *darul qazas* in Bihar.From the establishment of the AIMPLB in 1972 onwards, twenty-two *Shariat*-courts were established throughout the country under the aegis of the AIMPLB (Mahmood 2001, 3–4). Moreover, the AIMPLB established a committee on *Darul Qaza* that oversees the different *darul qazas* and furthers the establishment of religious arbitration councils in the country.
18. Interview with Ateeq Ahmed Qasmi, *qazi* in the *Darul Qaza* in Lucknow on January 13, 2010.
19. The Muslim intelligentsia established the *Darul Uloom Nadwatul* in the nineteenth century in order to maintain the social, cultural, and economic values of Islam. See http://www.nadwatululama.org/english/aboutus.php (accessed June 7, 2012). The *Firangi Mahall* is an autonomous body of Islamic scholars, teachers, and religious leaders that is closely connected to the well-established and Sunni-dominated All India Muslim Personal Law Board where it has representative status (Robinson 2001, 1).
20. Interview with Ateeq Ahmed Qasmi on January 12, 2011.
21. As Barbara D. Metcalf (2004, 10) points out in her study on the Deoband–school, of which the *Darul Uloom Nadwatul* is a part, the bureaucratisation and standardisation in these Islamic institutions were originally copied from the British. In the late 19th century, the Deoband–school adopted models of British bureaucratic organisation to replace more familiar and personal ones. As Metcalf writes, they used print in a way that furthered urgency to 'standardise' and 'codify' meanings of Islam.
22. Indian media: Supreme Court says 'no place for fatwa', http://www.bbc.com/news/world-asia-india-28205895 (accessed December 14, 2017).
23. Personal interview with Begum Shehnaz Sidrat in Lucknow on January 27, 2010.
24. Although the members of the AIMPLB respect her organisation and consider its work valuable for the betterment of Muslims in India, no efforts have been made on their part to actually integrate the *Bazme Khawateen* into the overall structure of the AIMPLB. In response to an internal call for greater women's perspective, the AIMPLB did increase its number of women in the forty-one-member executive committee in 2010, from one member to five. Despite the increase, the AIMPLB has not become

more women-friendly; women are still underrepresented, and the AIMPLB considers the creation of a women's wing unnecessary. (Personal interview with the AIMPLB executive member Begum Ali Naseema Iqtedar Khan in Lucknow, February 28, 2011)

25. Though accessible through their website (http://aitg.co.in/bazmekhawateen.aspx), the club gathers new members primarily through word of mouth and via its public events.
26. Begum Sultana Hayat's husband is an offspring of the well-known Ansari family, whose *ulema* has established the Islamic seat of learning – the *Firangi Mahal*. In India, the family name Ansari indicates an ancestral link to the Syed Hazrat Abu Ayub Ansari of Medina, who accommodated the Prophet Muhammed when he moved from Mecca to Medina. The descendants of the Ansari migrated at different times to the subcontinent, as scholars, government functionaries, soldiers or officers. In Lucknow, the Ansari identify themselves with the noble *ashraf*-caste. Due to this familial association, *Bazme Khawateen* maintains a close relationship with the Sunni clergy, especially to the scholars affiliated with the *Firangi Mahal*. (Personal interview with Begum Shehnaz Sidrat in Lucknow on January 27, 2010.)
27. For example, between 1907 and 1921 a series of conferences, called the All India Muslim Ladies Conference, were held. These conferences were organised and attended by urban upper-class Muslim women. At these meetings, resolutions on education and *purdah* were passed routinely and speeches against polygamy were held. These conferences reflect the concern of these Muslim women about education, polygamy, and economic independence (Lateef 1990, 82). This early Muslim women's activism, which proliferated in the beginning of the twentieth century, experienced a drastic decline in 1927 when most of the Muslim women leaders joined the secular All India Women's Conference (Lateef 1990, 83). The All India Women's Conference was concerned with educating women and the eradication of social problems concerning women (Omvedt 2004, 189). Overall, the activism of the Muslim women's clubs and associations in colonial India were not geared toward the creation of a separate female space.
28. Interview with *Maulana* Tauqeer Reza Khan featured in the *Times of India*, December 14, 2004 (http://timesofindia.indiatimes.com/city/lucknow/Barelvis-announce-parallel-personal-law-board/articleshow/961589.cms, accessed May 18, 2015).
29. Khaled Ahmed's piece 'The Lucknow Connection' (May 12, 2014) can be read here: http://indianexpress.com/article/opinion/columns/the-lucknow-connection/99/ (accessed June 5, 2015).
30. In Pakistan, Shia killings by militant Sunni forces, especially by the Deobandi, have according to a 2014 Human Rights Watch report massively increased since 2008. The Pakistani government, however, has so far failed to effectively protect its Shia minority from sectarian violence. For the full report see: http://www.hrw.org/news/2014/06/29/pakistan-rampant-killings-shia-extremists (accessed June 5, 2015).
31. *Waqf* is a charitable Islamic trust and means endowment of property, moveable or immovable, tangible or intangible, dedicated to God by a Muslim for the welfare of needy and poor people.

32. Information is extracted from an interview with *Maulana* Athar on February 24, 2011 in Lucknow and from their website. See: http://aisplb.org (accessed December 20, 2011).
33. See: http://indiatoday.intoday.in/story/shia-board-to-ostracise-those-who-beat-or-desert-their-wives/1/132344.html (accessed July 28, 2012).
34. See an interview with Hasan Ali Rajani in twocircles: http://twocircles.net/2009oct25/shia_personal_law_board_demands_reservation_legislatures_shias.html (accessed July 28, 2012).
35. Interview with Shaista Amber on December 15, 2009.
36. The former general secretary of the Board, the Shia social activist Parveen Abidi, disclosed to me the details about the AIMWPLB's internal struggles. On the contrary, Amber did not even allude to these in all our conversations. After the split of the AIMWPLB, Abidi quietly launched – together with thirty-four Muslim women from different sects and schools – a small social organisation that teaches women about *Shariat*-law and their Constitutional rights. In contrast to Amber, Abidi and her organisation do not court the media, abstaining entirely from public debates over the interpretation of Muslim law. At this point it is important to note that the city of Lucknow features a wide range of small Muslim women's organisations, dealing with issues of education, health, religion, and law, which are run on a small scale and are hardly featured in the media. A lot of better-off housewives have started their own charity projects through which they hope to distract themselves from their rather boring lives as housewives and help the community – if only in a small way.
37. See: http://www.milligazette.com/Archives/2005/16-28feb05-Print-Edition/162802200512.htm (accessed April 15, 2012) and http://www.telegraphindia.com/1050209/asp/opinion/story_4348469.asp (accessed April 15, 2012).
38. In other words, Sidrat accuses Amber of making a profit from donations made to the AIMWPLB.
39. The Rajinder Sachhar Committee was appointed in 2005 by the Indian Prime Minister, Manmohan Singh, to prepare a report on the economic, educational, and social condition of the Muslim community in India. The complete report is available at: http://www.scribd.com/doc/91192744/Exposing-Sacchar-Committee-Report (accessed August 26, 2012).
40. In 2002, Hasan worked for AALI (Association for Advocacy and Legal Initiatives), a human-rights based organisation in Lucknow. The AALI was among other organisations and advocates of human rights instrumental in bringing to light the countless cases of sexual assault against Muslim women during the Gujarat riots in 2002 (Naqvi 2006).
41. Email conversation with BMMA co-founder Zakia Soman on August 9, 2015.
42. http://bmmaindia.org/Membership.aspx (accessed July 24, 2015)
43. http://bmmaindia.blogspot.ch/search?updated-min=2015-01-01T00:00:00-08:00&updated-max=2016-01-01T00:00:00-08:00&max-results=7 (accessed July 24, 2015)

44. Both newspaper clips are published in the Annual reports of the BMMA. However, I could not find them online.
45. For their goals, demands, and activities see the BMMA-blog: http://bhartiyamuslimmahilaandolan.blogspot.com (accessed June 9, 2012).
46. The membership fee is Rs. 5 (ca. US $ 0.08) for a year or Rs. 1,000 (US $ 16) for a lifetime. The goal of the BMMA is to keep the membership fee low so as to enable women and men from a low socio-economic background to participate. (See their website: http://bmmaindia.org/Membership.aspx (accessed July 24, 2015)
47. Email conversation with BMMA co-founder Zakia Soman on August 9, 2015.
48. Interview with Naish Hasan in Lucknow on January 22, 2010.
49. BMMA-blog: http://bmmaindia.blogspot.com (accessed September 12, 2012).
50. The interview is available on YouTube: http://www.youtube.com/watch?v=DHGGX8CDk4U&feature=share (accessed May 1, 2013).
51. See their website for the BMMA's report on its Women's *Shariat*-Courts: http://bmmaindia.blogspot.com/p/reports.html (accessed June 18, 2015)
52. Personal email conversation with Naish Hasan on July 24, 2015.

Chapter 3

Destabilising Gendered Proprieties

Muslim Women's Visibility within the Public Space[1]

'One thousand four hundred years ago, at the time of the prophet Muhammed, Muslim women participated in wars, worked as nurses and doctors, owned and operated businesses and were actively involved in public religious life. I am fighting to get our quranic rights back and to make Muslim women visible in public again!'

These are words of Naish Hasan (BMMA), pronounced in a personal conversation in winter 2010. Hasan's claim to work towards women's reintegration into the public space, using Islamic history and ideology as an explanatory framework, is a central plank in the agenda of Muslim women activists in the city of Lucknow. In this respect, this short narrative succinctly captures contemporary Muslim women's rights activists' endeavour to stretch the gendered boundaries of the politically contested public legal space, as discussed in the previous chapter, via struggles over competing definitions of religious *knowledge* and *authority*.[2] They view their exclusion from public religious and political life less in terms of an ideological dictate than as the Muslim clergy's decidedness to consolidate political power structures through patriarchal and paternalistic interpretations of the Islamic texts. For example, Shaista Amber (AIMWPLB) insists that the clergy's interpretations of the *Quran* and the *Hadith*, which prevent Muslim women from becoming a *qazi* (judge), a *mufti* (law expert), an *alima* (scholar), or priest and which prevent them from praying in public mosques, need to be challenged. In a similar vein, Shehnaz Sidrat (*Bazme Khawateen*) also takes issue with patriarchal interpretations depicting women's active participation in the public space as an onslaught on their modesty and, hence, as a religious 'sin'. Recent *fatwas* released by the eminent Lucknow-based Sunni seminaries *Darul Uloom Nadwatul Ulama* reflect the patriarchal leaning in the *ulema's* interpretations of the religious texts. These *fatwas* strongly advise women against becoming a *qazi* (judge), a *mufti* (law expert), or an *alima* (scholar), and discourage them from praying in public mosques. Calling for a return to the 'true Islam', as conveyed in Hasan's quote above, Sidrat points to the opportunities Islam offers for women to engage in public life, saying: 'As long as we follow the rules of *purdah* [concept of Islamic modesty and shyness], Muslim women are free to work, become politicians and activists. No one can stop us!'[3]

By making their bodies seen and their voices heard within Lucknow's contested public space, these middle-class Muslim women blatantly disrupt generally accepted assumptions of women's respectability, egalitarianism, freedom, and equality. In this chapter, I look closely and comparatively at the manner in which the presidents and founding members of the AIMWPLB, BMMA, and *Bazme Khawateen* create space for their activism within contested local and national contexts. I argue that these public contestations over the meaning of womanhood, freedom, egalitarianism, and equity evince the fluidity of the categories of Islam and women's rights on the ground – revealing Islam as a 'discursive tradition' (Asad 2009 [1986]) rather than as a fixed system of belief and practice. Whereas scholarship on Islam, gender, and law in India tends to discuss Muslim women's rights struggles in relationship to the state and through the lens of Muslim women as the oppressed subject (Agnes 1999; Chhachhi 2005; Hasan 1998, 1999; Pathak and Sunder Rajan 1989; Sunder Rajan 2003), this chapter explores the multiple strategies of public self-representation used by these Muslim women's activists' to contest the widely accepted notions of Muslim women as relegated to the private sphere and with no political agency. Such analysis illustrates the multiple positions of Muslim women's rights activism – an aspect often neglected in liberal and modernist scholarship on Islamic gender justice struggles.

Muslim Women's Activism in Lucknow: Manufacturing Respectability within the Public Space

The visible Sunni woman who accesses the public space purposely – she organises political rallies, teaches about Islam in parks and mosques, and engages in policymaking – stretches the gendered boundaries of what is considered to be a 'good' (*shareef*) or 'bad' (*haram)* woman in ultra-conservative discourse – as for example promoted by the *fatwas* released by the AIMPLB. Within such discourse, notions of the 'good' or 'bad' woman converge with the idea of the 'private' and 'public' sphere. All too often, scholarship on Islam and gender theorises Muslim women's entrance into the public sphere as radical and new and as breaking with core ideas of Islamic ideology (Forbes 1982; Minault 1982; Papanek 1982). However, as I will show in the coming pages, to cast Muslim women's subjectivity within the binary of the public and private sphere neglects the intermediary spaces within which these Muslim women's activists currently negotiate political agency as Islamic subjects. Phadke, Ranade, and Khan (2009) make an important observation in this regard. Drawing on an intersectional analysis of gender and space in the city of Mumbai, the authors point out that women who self-assertively enter the public space tend to represent themselves as 'bearers of all moral and cultural values that define the family/community/nation' (ibid., 187). However, instead of analysing such forms of public self-representations as a form of backwardness – as modernists tend to do – they analyse the transfer of such moral discourse, or, a discourse of respectability, into the public space as an opportunity for women's participation within Mumbai's strongly men-dominated public space.

Similarly, more recent works on Islamic feminism theorise Muslim women's goal to achieve respectability in public as a means to create space for political activism, and consequently agency. For instance, the political scientist Nilüfer Göle (1996) analyses the Islamist veiling movement of university students in Turkey during the post-1983 period as an incident where a specific Muslim identity is constructed within the public space. In this context she convincingly argues that the veil emerges as a strategy for enlarging women's space for political activism in the context of modernisation and liberal aspirations of nation building in Turkey. Similarly, Saba Mahmood in her ethnography *Politics of Piety* (2005) offers a compelling exposition of the possibilities such embodiments of religious practices hold for political agency. Mahmood's work draws on the example of a grassroots women's piety movement in the mosques of Cairo to show that women's embodied religious practices are not simply a reflection of their personal beliefs, but the very means through which subjectivities are cultivated and agency acquired. Mahmood argues that this form of pious subjectivity, although seemingly incommensurate with assumptions of the liberal subject undergirding feminist scholarship, does not stifle women's agency. In fact, it constitutes an altogether different form thereof. Such a conceptual framework, as developed by critical feminist scholarship, is helpful in understanding Lucknow's Muslim women's activists' claim to assert agency through the embodiment of respectability – a claim which is often couched in a symbolic language of piety.

Eager to amalgamate their public activism with their identities as 'good' (read sexually controlled) Muslim women, these activists participate in a complex process of self-representation wherein the feminine Islamic attributes of simplicity and modesty as expressions of religious piety are infused into their public self-representations as autonomous and independent activists. In this vein, Amber, Sidrat, and Hasan show a vigorous eagerness to stretch the gendered public space by demonstrating their *quranic* knowledge and therefore challenge the clergy's religious authority through the careful orchestration of their pious bodies and minds.

Modernising the Islamic dress

Let me illustrate. Shehnaz Sidrat (*Bazme Khawateen)* is a former interior designer who later took over *Bazme Khawateeen*, or the women's club, founded by her mother-in-law in colonial India (see Chapter 2). She grew up in an upper-middle class family that has familial links to the influential *Firangi Mahal* family. I first met Sidrat in her office. Seated before her big desk, waiting for her to return with tea and cookies, I scanned the sparsely furnished and decorated room until my eye rested on a large propaganda poster. It depicted Sidrat in her late forties, wearing a knee-length and loose beige coat, a pink scarf tightly wrapped around her face and big sunglasses. Her facial expression in this highly stylised photograph was in very sharp contrast to the president's good-humoured countenance. Whereas the poster shows a rather dour woman, Sidrat's eyes usually spark with joy and her vigorous smile conveys her mischievous personality. When my host returned, she gestured humorously at the self-designed 'doctor's coat' worn in the poster. Noting my puzzled expression, Sidrat explained that although Islam allows – with the husband's permission – Muslim women to work, study, be active in politics, and engage in social work, there are certain limitations: 'If a girl goes outside, she has to be very simple, so that she won't attract dirty [for example sexual] looks or get involved in any dirty conversations'.

Sidrat has practiced *purdah* since girlhood. She hails from a small town near Lucknow, where women hardly left their homes. A favourite anecdote of hers centres on the fact that she was the only Muslim girl to study in a Hindu college. In order to do so, her father had a wooden carriage constructed for her, which featured thick curtains to shield her from the view of strangers. In addition, she designed her own *burqa* and began wearing big sunglasses. In this kind of *purdah*, as Sidrat defines it, nobody could object to her pursuit of a public college education. Since she never ceased to adhere to the strict rules of the practice, the *maulanas* could not label her a bad woman or deem her behaviour un-Islamic. And it is through this strict adherence to the principles and limitations of *purdah,* Sidrat believes, that she has garnered the respect (*izzat dete hain*) of politicians, *mullahs,* the community, and her family.

From the outset, Sidrat rejected orthodox interpretations of veiling that consist of the, in common discourse as 'traditional' conceived, *niqab,* a black, loose-fitting full-body *niqab* that engulfs head to toe – a garment often worn by Muslim women living in Lucknow's old city. In the position of the club's president she designed her own 'modern Islamic dress', as she calls it. This dress consists of a knee-length and loose beige coat, loose trousers (*salwaar),* and a colourful or black scarf tightly wrapped around her face. When in public, Sidrat often complements this outfit with a pair of big sunglasses. For Sidrat this kind of dress conforms to the Islamic tenets of 'modesty' and 'simplicity' – attributes that she considers key for women to maintaining respectability within the public space. This is to say that Muslim women manufacture their religious and gender identity in public within the complexly layered gendered hierarchies that leave unquestioned the concept of sexual difference as established and re-produced through the idea of the 'private' and the 'public'. The dress that covers her entire body allows Sidrat to forge a specific ideal of the good Muslim woman and pay respect to the clergy affiliated with Lucknow-based Islamic Sunni seminary *Firangi Mahal.* She says: 'Women do not have to hide behind a black *burqa* in public. If one follows the Islamic rule of *purdah,* as I do, women are free to go anywhere and talk to anybody and exercise both their Islamic and civil rights'.[4]

The Islamic dress as a form of political adjustment

Similarly, Shaista Amber, the president of the AIMWPLB, substantially changed her way of dressing when she became president of the AIMWPLB in 2005. It was a pleasant afternoon in late November 2009 as I sat with Shaista Amber, the wife of an Indian army officer and member of the Indian Communist Party, at a coffee table in her 'open-air office' in the backyard of her mosque. Amber is in her mid-fifties, Sunni, and upper-middle class. At our meeting, Amber wore a long and simple peach gown and her hair was partially covered with a loosely wrapped white shawl (*dupatta*), complemented by two big pearl earrings and two gold bracelets. Drinking tea and eating homemade biscuits, she explained,

> I was one of the most stylish and fashionable women. I used to wear expensive *sarees* and jewellery. I belong to the officer class and my father is from a good milieu. However, when I started to work as a social activist, I changed my dress. [...] I started to wear *hijab*. This means that I cover my body with a long gown, and my hair – the most attractive part – with a scarf. Like this, people had faith in me and started working with me.[5]

When Amber entered the public space as a politician and activist in 2005, she realised that speaking on behalf of disenfranchised Muslim women and their rights was problematic as the wife of an Army officer and a member of the more affluent Muslim middle-class. For example, the orthodox religious authorities deemed Amber's fashion and lifestyle as a sign of atheism and licentiousness. 'In an editorial of some Urdu newspaper published by the Deobandi,' Amber recalls, 'it was said that my work and lifestyle were non-Islamic and that I spoke of non–Islamic things. The Deobandi called me a *deharia,* which designates a person who doesn't believe in any religion. [...] The Deobandi spread the message that because I was from the upper-class society I didn't care about *haram* [forbidden] or *halal* [allowed]. They accused me of visiting the bedrooms of ministers and officers'.[6] Moreover, the Muslim public saw in her the rich and spoiled officer-wife, too removed from the lives and experiences of the mainly poor Muslim population in Lucknow. In an attempt to counter such accusations, Amber donned the headscarf and the simple ankle-length coat. For Amber, the bodily transformation from the upper-class and spoiled officer-wife to the 'respectable Muslim women's activist' secured her the respect and trust from the Sunni community, and allowed her to engage in politics without being labelled as a 'bad' (*kharab*) woman or a non-believer. Similar to Sidrat, Amber 'bargains with patriarchy' (Kandiyoti 1991b) – this is to conform with patriarchal ideas of women's modesty and purity – to secure the legitimacy of her presence within the public space.

There exists a convergence in methodological terms between Sidrat's and Amber's, and the conservative clergy's deployment of the discourse of 'the good Muslim woman'. Both discourses are anchored in a hierarchic framework of male supremacy. However, Sidrat and Amber instrumentalise such discourse differently. Whereas Sidrat activates the image of the 'good' Muslim woman not only to facilitate her activism, but also to express her respect towards the religious Sunni clergy in Lucknow, Amber mobilises such image to gain legitimacy as a representative of Muslim women among Muslim groups in Lucknow and beyond. The approaches used by Sidrat and Hasan are very characteristic of Islamic feminism. While none of the activists featured in this study explicitly adopt the label 'feminist' or 'Islamic feminist' for the purpose of self-identification within the public space, to decentre the power of the religious clergy through *ijtihad*, or the right to interpret the Islamic scripts, to reveal the 'true' Islam is a common strategy among Islamic feminists in Iran, Egypt, or Indonesia.[7] Critiques of Islamic feminism, such as for example Qudsia Mirza (2008) or Haideh Meghissi (1999) lament that such 'bargains with patriarchy' could be detrimental to the reformist endeavour of these women to secure women's social, economic, and political rights. Naish Hasan (BMMA) shares such concern.

Delimiting Islam: Unveiling piety

Naish Hasan (BMMA), responds with alarm to the growing number of Muslim activists who challenge public space hierarchies by 'uncritically submitting their bodies to the dictates of a bunch of self-appointed religious leaders' (read: the orthodox Sunni and Shia clergy), as she bluntly states.[8]

'Look,' she once said to me, 'whether a woman wears or does not wear the *burqa* should be a matter of choice'. Hasan continued,

> As for me, I do not like the *burqa* and all the rules and limitations the *Quran* apparently imposes on women. Many women's activists are just talking about what women should do and what they should wear instead of focusing on the most important issues, such as health, education, and employment. I am a Muslim and I believe in the *Quran*! So for this matter, I like to represent Islam as a religion that is about choice and not limitations. Personally, I do not wear such kind of costumes, which have not much to do with Islam. The b*urqa* becomes a statement for being a Muslim – I don't like that. I am a Muslim just like that – *bas!* I don't need to wear a *burqa* to be a Muslim. I do not want to convey the message that in order to be a good woman and a good Muslim you have to cover yourself up. This is not Islam. I was troubled a lot by the *mullahs* for my public appearance. However, if *purdah* means to cover and not hide the body then I can do this by simply wearing a *salwaar kurta*. There is no need for the veil! Like the many women in our Islamic history, we can go out and have our own businesses and engage in political, social and legal activities without having to hide ourselves – without losing our respect!

Without denying the importance the female body occupies in Islamic thought and practice, Hasan stresses the flexibility the religious texts offer for the interpretation of what codifies the 'respectable' Muslim woman. Although fighting a similar fight as Sidrat and Amber, Hasan focuses on the mind and not the body as a tool for destabilising ultra-orthodox notions of the public space as exclusively reserved to men. For Hasan, the terrain of struggle is the pious mind rather than the body, and her focus is inward. Therefore, Hasan questions the idea of space arguing: 'respect and dignity can be instilled through the pious mind alone.... There is no need to cover our entire bodies'. Like most Muslims in Lucknow and elsewhere in India, Hasan wears the *salwar-kurta*: a pair of loose fitting trousers combined with a long, knee-length shirt. She additionally covers her chest with a long shawl (*dupatta*). This typical Indian dress is common among Hindus, Parsis, Sikhs, and Christians.[9] Similar to many women in north India, Hasan considers this way of dressing as sufficient to cover the sexually connoted female parts of the body such as the chest, bottom, and thighs.

Islamic bodies and forms of self-representation

Muslim women's rights activists' embodiment of 'true' Islam illustrates the fact that the formation of subjectivities, religious identities, and political agency are situational, rather than rigid. However, women's visibility within the public space alone does not (yet) substantially disturb the social order of the public space – or translate in women's rights to access it (Phadke et al. 2009). Rather, there needs to be a radical shift away from the conception of the (Islamic) public space as an inherently dangerous space for women toward a feminist consciousness of the public space that establishes women's right to the public space as a 'fundamental claim for a more inclusive citizenship' (ibid., 186). In this context, the pious body and mind emerge as central elements in their struggle for full legal rights. This manner of pious self-representation, they argue persuasively, has been a suitable strategy to make everyday Muslims, as well as the clergy, listen to their voices. In this respect, these activists do not adopt the discourse of piety to oppose liberal values, as often deliberated in Western feminist theory, but, rather, to challenge the ideas of gender and Islam that are detrimental to their freedom, autonomy, and equity. Instead, the manufacturing of respectability, which often includes the practice of veiling, has become an instrument through which these women publicly dissociate themselves from some of the widely-accepted notions of women's invisibility, while safeguarding their *quranic*, political, and social rights.

At the same time, activists' aim to manufacture respectability is also tied to their endeavour to establish relationship of trust and familiarity between them and the (lower-) middle class Muslim women (and men) they cater to. The majority of lower-middle and lower class Muslims, concentrated in Lucknow's old city, practice *purdah*. This is to say that they adhere to well-accepted ideas of gender-segregation within the public space by wearing the *niqab*. In fact, the growing tendency of re-Islamisation in urban India, combined with controversial *fatwas* released by the *Darul Uloom Deboand* seminary such as the 2010 *fatwa*, which strongly encourages Muslim women to wear the full-body veil – or *niqab* – in public, led to an increase in veiling amongst middle class women in big Indian city's such as Delhi or Mumbai (Khan 2007). The same seems to apply in Lucknow. 'Here in Lucknow', Noor Khan a college teacher from Lucknow's Muslim upper class tells me, 'Muslim women have started to more rigorously practice *purdah* in public. It seems that the *niqab* and the *hijab* are experiencing a cultural revival, especially amongst Muslim women ranging from the lower-middle class to poor women, all predominantly living in old Lucknow', Khan concludes.[10]

The meaning of *purdah* is manifold, ranging from full female seclusion over the segregation of the sexes to restrictions on women's dress and mobility. Scholarship on *purdah* in the context of India (Kirmani 2013; Lateef 1973; Minault 1982a), as well as in Iran, Egypt, or Turkey (Badran 1995; Göle 2006; Hoodfar 1991), point to the complexity of practices and forms of *purdah* within contested political, cultural, and economic settings. In Lucknow, as elsewhere in India, *purdah* is understood and practiced differently – depending on family background, education, class, marital status, religious school, and locality. For some women I talked to, *purdah*, and especially the full body veil (*burqa*), signifies women's oppression and backwardness. For others, the practice of *purdah* is a safety measure, protecting women's respect in the public space. For some, in turn, *purdah* is the ultimate expression of a women's religiosity and thus illustrates her profound dedication to an Islamic lifestyle and practice. These different narratives on the practice of *purdah* reveal the discourse of *purdah* as complex and situational. This is to say that 'although there has been some commonality of themes, it [*purdah*] is an institution that has communicated different messages [...]', to borrow from the anthropologist Homa Hoodfar (1991, 321). Amber, Sidrat, and Hasan tap into this powerful and epistemologically thick discourse of *purdah* for the purpose of reconciling their – often-controversial – position as upper-class activists with the social realities – and aspirations – of their (mostly poor) constituency. I thus consider these above discussed self-representations not only coded in terms of religious ideology and gender, but also in terms of class. As I will show next, the media in India proves an excellent tool for the wide dissemination of these activists' images of Islamic justice, womanhood, and political freedom.

Muslim Women's Rights Activists: Public Visibility and the Media

Between 2005 and 2008, Sidrat, Amber, and Hasan have deployed the Hindi, Urdu, and English language press to push back the widely accepted monolithic renderings of Muslim women as a symbol of a religious tradition and as relegated to the private sphere. Using the media as an input channel, these women have – to a different extent – upset the widely accepted ideas of gender and the Islamic public space. In what follows, I focus on India's English language press as an analytical lens to analyse the manner in which these women initiate a more public debate of women's rights to equal share of religious public life.[11]

Only a decade ago, Muslim women's voices hardly surfaced in India's English language press. Similar to Western media coverage, India's English language press had heretofore employed a discursive economy in their representation of the issue of Islam and women that constructed Muslim women as stripped of their civil rights: deemed to wear the *burqa*, confined to their homes with no access to education, deprived of political participation, and victims of triple *talaq*.[12] At this point it is important to mention that the reporting by the mass media in the West has suffered from the same misinterpretations and misrepresentations of Muslim women, which substantially contributed to their stereotyping as victims and as mute. For instance, Lila Abu-Lughod (2002) has criticised the ways in which the media and the US government have deployed the popular standard knowledge about Muslim women that portrays them as oppressed, as forced to wear the *burqa*, and as relegated to the domestic sphere in their rhetoric on the war in Afghanistan (ibid., 785). Similarly, Katherine Bullock (2002, 122–33), who analysed the representations of Iraqi women in articles that were published in the *New York Times* since the official beginning of the war, argues that in the context of such press releases Islam and Muslim women have been subject to strong normative and stereotyping discourses. She asserts that the trope of the covered female body emerged as a yardstick according to which progress is measured. Along such lines, Islam is depicted as incompatible with Western notions of secularism and liberalism (ibid., 89).

Such representations of Muslim women were also criticised for being Orientalist (Said 2003 [1978]).

In the Indian context, Sabina Kidwai (2005, 392) argues that even the positive media coverage of Muslim women's issues typically affords 'no other face for Muslim women than one embodying stereotypes'. Although Indian media's emphasis upon veiling and upon triple *talaq* is still alive and well, there currently exists alongside it reportage that engage 'positively' with issues of Muslim women. Taking into account the request for a greater debate on rights of Muslim women's activists and academics, the media started creating room for making visible disagreement amongst different sections of Muslims in contemporary India, as well as amongst Muslim women's activists, in contemporary India. The result is reportage that goes beyond the political controversies and that is far more progressive and rational (ibid., 383). Such coverage increasingly features interviews with and stories about Muslim women activists and organisations (Kidwai 2005, 391; Schneider 2009, 62). This coverage offered – what is often considered from a modernist-liberal view – a 'new' identity for Muslim women: that of a heterogeneous group of individuals who critically analyse and argue for social, political, economic, and legal reform, all from varying perspectives.

Sidrat, Hasan, and Amber have taken advantage of this growing tendency of India's English language press to highlight their voices and their activities as a vital part of public life. Within a transnational media space, where Islam predominantly appears in conjunction with imagery of war, terrorism, and women's subjugation, Muslim women's activists and Islamic feminists tend to emerge as harbingers of 'women's empowerment', 'liberation', and 'freedom'. Using liberal language, the English language press portrays Muslim women's activism in terms of its progression towards the liberal goal of absolute equality – or shows the great distance it still has to go. Through the media, Muslim women's activists discuss new trends in religious thought on gender and the public space; women too could participate and perform hitherto men-assigned religious duties as knowledgeable Muslim women and Indian citizens.

Guiding prayers for women in the public women's (*Zenana*) Park

Shehnaz Sidrat (*Bazme Khawateen*) made national headlines when she invited journalists to report about the prayers that she has been leading for women in Lucknow's only women's park (*Zenana* park).[13] Located at the heart of the city of Lucknow but sheltered by high walls, the park was deemed an appropriate space because of its capacity to shield its female occupants from the gaze of men. The idea was to offer women a space outside the home in which to congregate, learn about the *Quran*, sing religious songs, recite poems, drink tea, and pray. Men were not allowed to participate in these activities. I will note that the influential clergy in Lucknow affiliated with the AIMPLB, with its conservative interpretations of *purdah*, strongly discourages women from praying in public. Glorifying an image of the Muslim woman as a good mother and housewife, the clergy sees a conflict between women's freedom to pray in public and their responsibilities as good homemakers.[14] Challenging the clergy's discursive economy that locates Muslim women entirely within the domestic sphere, Sidrat flung open the gate of the *Zenana* Park for journalists eager to report about an unusual woman-led collective prayer in 2004.

Every year, at the occasion of *Eid* (feast of breaking the fast), Sidrat organises a collective prayer in the park, entitled *Salaate Tasbeeh*. This is a special prayer – one that the devout believe may purge them of all sins. Her personal initiative to read the *Salaate Tasbeeh*, a privilege otherwise reserved for men amongst Sunnis in Lucknow, met the interest of the media. Keen to bring to the fore 'the other face of Islam', *The Times of India* described this unconventional prayer, attended by several hundred Muslim women, as 'a testimony to the free spirit of Lucknow women, who have ensured that it survived male scepticism'. Giving voice to Sidrat and some of the participants, *The Times* portrayed the event as an opportunity for Muslim women to 'bond' and to demonstrate 'female emancipation'.[15] This coverage applied a modernist discursive framework within which Muslim women's inroads into an otherwise male-dominated arena were labelled 'modern' and posited as a form of 'empowerment'.

In our interview, however, Sidrat frames her intervention within the public space beyond the binaries of women's empowerment versus Islamic patriarchy. As she tells me, Muslim women have offered *namaz* in the *Zenana* Park for over 75 years. Due to the relative seclusion of the park, the religious clergy had never opposed this. As long as the gate was shut and the women remained invisible, there was no uproar. However, when she became president of *Bazme Khawateen* in 1994, Sidrat decided to disrupt the spatial boundaries that shielded Muslim women's activism from the public eye for so long. Arguing that '*purdah* [here the term *purdah* is used in terms of the spatial segregation of the sexes] is not a hindrance for publicising Muslim women's public prayers', she started to invite the press to the weekly meetings. She explains that her motivation behind this initiative was less to solely disrupt the well-travelled imagery of the subjugated Muslim woman than to contribute to the creation of a feminist consciousness of the public space and the fact that women too can engage in religious activities outside the domestic sphere. To her mind, common understandings of the public space in Islam with their specific configurations of gendered subjectivities and senses of belonging have to be denaturalised. The publicising of Sidrat reading *namaz* is, I argue, transformative as it decentres – at least to a certain extent – the public space as a site for normalising male supremacy.

Construction of a women's mosque

As mentioned, Shaista Amber is yet another Muslim women's rights activist who currently strives to establish a feminist consciousness of public religious life. Like Sidrat, Shaista Amber has sought to create a public space for Muslim women to lead in worship, but the way she approached the problem is somewhat different. In 2008, Amber built a women's mosque on an empty plot of land near Lucknow. Drawing inspiration from STEPS, a Tamil Nadu-based women's development organisation that set up India's first exclusive women's mosque in 2004,[16] Amber works to create space for women where they have the opportunity to 'share and discuss their concerns with peers other than the family' and to 'offer *namaz* in the mosque', as she says. In the city of Lucknow, as in most parts of India, to pray in the mosque is a privilege generally reserved for men.[17] Needless to say, the construction of this women's mosque created a stir among the religious elite in Lucknow. Scholars affiliated with the *Darul Uloom Deoband* in Lucknow, for instance, argue that such 'revolutionary methods to communicate with *Allah*' compromise women's honour and reputation and create social evil.[18] As Saba Mahmood (2005, 65) argues in the context of the women's piety movement in Egypt, the reason behind restrictions on women to guiding collective prayers are twofold. First, there is the general belief that since the *Quran* makes men the guardian of women, the latter should not serve in significant positions of leadership over men. Second, there is the prevailing notion that a woman's voice can nullify the act of worship since her voice is capable of provoking sexual feelings in men.[19]

For Amber, such rhetoric does not originate from the religious texts. Rather, she argues, the clergy deploys the image of the sexualised female that poses a danger to the order of the public space as a means to, as she says, 'keep women in the dark about their rights' and to 'curtail women's freedom of movement'.[20] Evoking the iconic Islamic figure Hazrat Bibi Hafsa, one of the wives of prophet Muhammed who acted as an *Imam* and led women in offering public *namaz*,[21] Amber profoundly challenges such imagery. 'A women's mosque', Amber explains,

> Allows for women to discuss their concerns outside the family. It is an opportunity for women to mingle and share their views on religion and everyday life. Such a mosque therefore fosters women's self-esteem and community feeling. Through prayers, women can learn a lot about their rights and duties of wives and daughters and husbands and sons. To withhold women from praying in public, therefore, violates women's right to information. Also, in the future I intend to have a female *Imam* leading prayers in this mosque.

In order to finance the construction of the mosque, Amber sold her heirloom jewellery handed down to her at the time of her wedding. 'A *Maulana* with a big name', she proudly asserts, 'laid down the foundation stone of the mosque in 2006'. The mosque is a modest white-painted one-storey building featuring a sunlit prayer hall and a hostel (*dharamsala*). Its minaret – long and thin in shades of green and white – rises high in the air, dominating the otherwise undeveloped and still affordable area near the Lucknow airport. A Pakistani *Maulana* inaugurated the mosque in 2008 in the presence of 'a lot of journalists and reporters', as Amber tells me proudly.

Amber strategically involved the media to address public opinion herself. As a result, the English newspaper *The Telegraph* praised this unusual women's mosque as the 'need of the hour' and as a well-travelled concept that is 'finally knocking on the door of Lucknow, the centre of Islamic learning'.[22] With the support of the media, Amber points to the new political possibilities such a mosque could open for women in a religiously conservative city such as Lucknow. She envisions it redefining the possibilities for women's participation in public religious life. Accordingly, the media reportage stressed the relevance of such women's mosque as a marker of progress and as a timely concept representing Muslim women's possibilities in India's democratic political system. India's English language press refers to such intervention within the public space as 'highly relevant' and as a 'promise' for women's future integration into a male-dominated society.

However, 'change needs time', demurs Amber. 'Women and men in Lucknow have to realise that the prohibition for women to pray in public, which has been imposed upon them by the *mullahs*, only serves the interest of the clerics but not the community'. In fact, notwithstanding the positive media coverage, women did not frequent Amber's mosque on a regular basis until two years after it was built. At my visit in 2009 there were only one or two women offering *namaz* in the mosque behind the menfolk. However, at my second visit in 2011, the number of women who joined the men in offering *namaz* had visibly increased. Indeed, instead of just one or two there were now a handful of Muslim women from Lucknow and nearby villages who had come to pray in the mosque. One was an economics student from Lucknow University, who had just recently begun coming there. She informed me that she liked to worship Allah while in the company of men and women. She said that offering *namaz* in public gave her a sense of belonging and community. Moreover, she enjoyed discussing matters concerning women and religion with people who, like her, are truly devoted to Islam. It should be noted as well here, that both women learned about the mosque via newspapers and television.[23]

The question of whether or not Muslim women should be allowed to pray in public is widely discussed by Muslims from all over the world. In fact, a closer look at online platforms such as islamweb.net, islamqa.info, or islamicislamic.com reveals the transnational debates underway amongst Muslims worldwide. These platforms serve as discussion boards, where believers ask 'knowledgeable' Muslims for advice on various issues ranging from the *Quran*, the *Shariat*, family, politics to health and science. The construction of the mosque is therefore more than just a local phenomenon. It is a part of the 'social life', to take the phrase of Abu-Lughod (2010, 2), of international struggles and discussions on Muslim women's rights taking place across distance in geographical spatiality and religious orientation. This is to say that Amber's mosque is a visible marker of Muslim women's struggles for social inclusion and integrity as currently debated locally, nationally, and transnationally.

A female *qazi* and an unconventional wedding

The story of Naish Hasan's unorthodox wedding offers yet another example of how Muslim women's rights activists strive for a more inclusive public space. On August 30, 2008, Naish Hasan achieved (trans-) local celebrity status with her unorthodox marriage (*nikah*) to a PhD scholar from Aligarh Muslim University. The wedding was unorthodox for several reasons. First, Hasan altered her mode of dress. Deciding to break with the well-accepted custom amongst Muslims in which the bride completely hides her face behind the veil during the ceremony, Hasan instead donned an embroidered red *saree*. The end of the *saree* (*pallu*) only loosely covered her long hair, leaving her face revealed. Furthermore, Hasan abstained from wearing 'big, big jewellery', which in her opinion, reduces otherwise contracting agents to mere objects of the religious tradition.[24] Second, at Hasan's wedding the BMMA introduced its version of the 'secular' marriage contract (*nikahnama*) to the public.[25] This contract asks for registration and makes specific stipulations regarding divorce, maintenance, and property. However, the third and most important reason that this wedding received such enormous national and international media coverage was the fact that it was solemnised by a female *qazi*. Dissatisfied with the omnipresence of men at Muslim marriages, Hasan asked Syeda Hameed – a founding member of the Muslim Women's Forum, a member of the Planning Commission, and a former member of the National Commission on Women – to solemnise her marriage. Considering such a well-educated and knowledgeable woman as Hameed as well-qualified to take over the function of a *qazi*, Hasan saw no need for a man to perform the rites. After having received approval from reform-oriented *maulanas* in India, Pakistan, Uzbekistan, and Afghanistan, Hameed agreed to perform the *nikah*.

Just a few days prior to the marriage, Hasan mentioned her unusual wedding ceremony to a friend of hers – a journalist. The next day, the story was on the front page of a local newspaper. The article created a big stir among Muslims in Lucknow. Muslim women's organisations, including the AIMWPLB, supported the marriage. The clergy, as well as some scholars of the influential Sunni-dominated AIMPLB, conversely labelled the event, which would considerably push the radius of women's activities into the public space, 'useless' and 'unnecessary'.[26] For example, AIMPLB executive committee member Naseema Ali Iqtedar Khan said there is no need for a female *qazi* to perform the wedding if a man is otherwise available.[27] Likewise, Fauzia Naseema, also a member of the AIMPLB executive committee, was even more critical. She dismissed Hasan's wedding as 'nothing else than a media stunt'.[28] Meanwhile, the orthodox Lucknow Idgah Committee went as far as to deem the marriage 'invalid' and the ceremony a 'cruel joke on Islamic law'.[29] These voices reflect the lines of fragmentation that run through the Muslim community; laying bare the heterogeneity of perspectives on gender in Islam that exist on the ground.

Hasan believes this unprecedented wedding to have been the first of its kind in India if not in the entire Muslim world, and it continued to arouse wide media interest. The national press *The Hindu* described Hasan's wedding as 'unheard of', while *The Telegraph* likened its effects to 'smashing a centuries-old glass ceiling'. *India Today* dubbed the wedding as 'breaking with tradition' and the *Times of India* wrote that Naish Hasan's wedding ceremony 'breaks many shackles'.[30] Television stations all over India broadcasted footage of Hasan's wedding, which can now be downloaded from YouTube[31] and other websites. The footage neatly shows the crowd of journalists wrangling for a premium spot from which to capture the moment when 'the woman *qazi* creates history in Lucknow'.[32] The English press, without exception, viewed this unorthodox marriage as 'modern', 'progressive', 'provocative', and as a true 'challenge' to conservative conceptualisations of women's subjectivity in Islam. Within this media explosion, the protagonist, Naish Hasan, surfaces as independent, modern, self-assertive, and outspoken – qualities which challenge conservative and orthodox interpretations of the feminine ideal that stresses female modesty and subservience. In a personal conversation, Naish Hasan expressed her gratitude toward the media for publicising her unusual wedding. 'It is only through the dissemination of positive imagery of women', she asserted, and 'that the gendered boundaries proscribed by the religious authorities can be effectively probed'.

This wedding, like the mosque and the public prayers, shatters hegemonic Islamic ideology that normalises women's inability to perform religious duties, or any other functions in public life. Using the technique of *ijtihad* (interpretive science of juridical reasoning), or, what Qudsia Mirza (2008, 31) terms the 'cultural revival' strategy, these Lucknow-based Muslim women's activists have successfully demonstrated the possibilities that Islamic ideology holds for women within the public space, and they have shrewdly enlisted the media as a tool to ensure that their positions reached as broad an audience as possible. In short, such publicly visible interventions create an important environment for Muslim women to work toward a more inclusive conceptualisation of the public Islamic space. I therefore argue that current efforts by Muslim women's rights activists to resist widely-accepted ideas of Muslim women's restricted access to the public space, using religious discourse and rhetoric to do so, open up new possibilities for political agency.

Women's Spaces within the Patriarchal Legal Landscape

The comparative analysis of Muslim women activists' multiple strategies to stretch the gendered boundaries of public space, renders insight into dimensions of power that profoundly shape Muslim women's participation in the domain of politics, law, and religion in contemporary India. The three Muslim women's activists at the centre of this book challenge the authority of the orthodox clergy with their overt representations of alternative proposals of women's possibilities in Islam – through embodied dimensions of knowledge production. They provocatively challenge hegemonic ideas on gender. Instead of accepting the widely accepted definitions of *purdah*, or Islamic modesty, they reframe them. Instead of complying with the dictate of Muslim women's invisibility, either by staying at home or hiding their bodies underneath a loose *niqab*, they point to the *quranic* female icons that have earned respect with their contributions to public life. Through intellectual engagement with religious texts, these activists probe the misogynist understanding of public space. Specifically, by enlisting the media to circulate their alternative interpretations of women's rights in Islam, Sidrat, Hasan, and Amber are currently working toward the democratisation of the political and legal space – destabilising the political power wielded by various orthodox factions. In short, using the Indian mass media as an input channel, these Lucknow-based Muslim women's activists work toward carving out spaces of autonomy from which to demonstrate the possibilities that Islamic ideology holds for women within the public (and the private) space.

In its abstractions, these activists' approaches point toward an understanding of the flexibility of Islamic ideology and practice that is indicative of the unevenness of the categories of justice and gender within ideologically contested legal and political sites (Asad 2009 [1986]). Sidrat, Amber, and Hasan do not feel uncomfortable with their religious beliefs and precepts; rather, it is the power configuration that hinders their participation within the public space that sits uncomfortably with them and hinders their full participation in religious life. So instead of rejecting religion as a framework through which change can be achieved (as Western liberal feminists would do), they self-assertively appropriate religious language and practice to establish a women-friendly consciousness of gender relations in Islam.[33] Muslim women's activists efforts to consciously reshape women's subjectivity through a religious framework not only destabilises hegemonic ideas on women in Islam, but also contributes to the pluralisation of Islamic thought, practice, and law on a (trans)national and local level.

Muslim women's activists in the city of Lucknow see Islamic cultural practice as 'object of humanistic inquiry', according to the legal anthropologist Annelise Riles (2005, 1032), rather than a fixed and unchangeable ideology. In so doing, they simultaneously disrupt the category 'Muslim women'. Similar to what Nida Kirmani (2013) has argued in the Delhi-context, women's identities in Muslim Lucknow are situational and structured by class, education, family background, marital status, personal understandings of religion, politics, and regional identification. I thus consider discourses around Muslim women as a part of Bhabha's 'third space' (1990) (see Introduction) – an intermediary space of instability and transformation. So, in order to successfully challenge the widely accepted configurations of gender and power relations, these activists have to convincingly demonstrate that Islamic culture and practice are not static, but can be adjusted so as to secure women's respectability, egalitarianism, freedom, and equality.

While this chapter traced the manners in which Muslim women's rights activists in the city of Lucknow shape and contest institutional relations, equations of power and precepts of Islam and gender relating to the public sphere, the following chapter looks at how Muslim women's rights activists contest the parameters of women's subjectivity within the private sphere. Following the trajectories of institutional struggles around the meaning of women's rights within marriage and the family I will show that ideas around gender justice are in flux. I will demonstrate how institutional power struggles interpenetrate the private sphere, offering insight into alternative conceptualisations of freedom, autonomy, and agency within marriage and the family that are, as convincingly argued by feminist scholars working on gender and law (Abu-Lughod 2010; Mahmood 2005; Merry 2006), not (necessarily) commensurate with liberal ideals of gender equality. The latter stipulates equal rights for women and men and all spheres of life. Instead, such alternative, and sometimes innovative, conceptualisations of justice within the private sphere reveal the instability of legal and moral boundaries.

Endnotes

1. Parts of this chapter have been published in the *South Asia Multidisciplinary Academic Journal*. I would like to thank the anonymous reviewers for their comments on an earlier draft.
2. Santos (2002, 360) defines power as social relations of interests and knowledge. What makes social relations an exercise of power, however, is, according to Santos (ibid., 356–62), drawing on Foucault, the unequal distribution of knowledge that exists among individuals and/or organisations. According to Foucault (2010, 174–5), power and knowledge directly imply one another as there are no power relations without the correlative field of knowledge. Nor is there any knowledge that does not presuppose as well as constitute power relations. In this regard, Foucault theorises power not only in a negative way as a coercive instrument, but points to the positive aspect of power. This is in terms of its capacity to enable the production of new domains of knowledge. According to Foucault, the seemingly powerless individual is an inherent part of these power relations and thus able to move/resist the latter through the production of knowledge. Foucault hence locates power not solely on an institutional level, but power according to him is everywhere and an important aspect of everyday life.
3. The prominent Islamic feminist Amina Wadud (2009, 101) termed this form of interpreting the relationship between the sexes in Islam as 'a two pronged approach to

patriarchy'. That means that there exists an idea and practice of gross male hegemony in the private and public sphere. Therefore, patriarchy is not solely about men but about constantly privileging one kind of knowledge over another. This knowledge, following Wadud (ibid.), stems from the idea and notions about how the public space operates and, moreover, privileges the importance of the public space over the private. Notions of the public and the private space are inextricably linked with the idea of how the relationship between the sexes is structured, that is, strictly according to the matrices of the private and the public. Feminist Fatima Mernissi (1987, 136) supports such a view, saying, 'Muslim sexuality is territorial'. That means that the ideological framework of gender in Islam is organised along strict spatial boundaries that divide the society in two spatial sub-categories. Firstly, the male space, which includes the *umma* (community), the world religion and power, and, secondly, the female space, which includes the domestic world, sexuality and the family (Mernissi 1987, 138). Such a division of the public space, where the ideology of gender is organised around the very notions of the public, and the private sphere, where access to the public is simply non-existent, is not restricted to patriarchal interpretations of Islam. As Partha Chatterjee ([1999] 2006, 119–21) contends, colonialism and its ensuing nationalism in India have used the same spatial and ideological division. Whereas the colonisers pointed to women's suppression within the domestic sphere – in order to justify their presence in the subcontinent – native Indian nationalists relegated women to the private sphere as markers of tradition and symbols of cultural authenticity that have to be exempted from the claims of Western modernisation.

4. Interview with Shehnaz Sidrat, Lucknow on January 16, 2010.
5. Interview with Shaista Amber, Lucknow on December 15, 2009.
6. Interview with Shaista Amber, Lucknow on December 15, 2009.
7. As mentioned in the introduction, Shaista Amber, Shehnaz Sidrat, and Naish Hasan all see themselves as activists rather than feminists. Although acknowledging the fact that a lot of their activism corresponds with Islamic as well as liberal feminists' endeavours to further women's participation in the spheres of politics and law, they strongly feel that a feminist label could discredit their community membership. Moreover, as Naish Hasan tells me in a personal conversation, the upper caste and upper class women in India who call themselves feminists are out of touch with poor women's struggles such as poverty and hunger.
8. Interview by the author with Naish Hasan, Lucknow on January 26, 2010.
9. Of course, within an orthodox and conservative institutional environment, Hasan subjects herself to criticism on the part of mainly the ultra-orthodox Muslim clergy. For example, in April 2010 the orthodox seminary *Darul Uloom Deoband*, India, issued a controversial and highly criticised *fatwa* (legal opinion), which forbade women to work in the public sector and enter politics without wearing the full-body veil (*hijab*). Also see, Yoginder Sikand's discussion on the Darul Uloom's *fatwa* (http://www.countercurrents.org/sikand140510.htm, accessed November 11, 2012).
10. Interview with Noor Khan, Lucknow on November 10, 2009.

11. One reason for my focus on India's English language press is that it is, compared to local Hindi and Urdu newspapers, easily accessible. Nationally and internationally well-respected newspapers such as *The Times of India*, *India Today*, *The Hindu*, or *The Telegraph* are readily available online. Another reason for focusing on India's English language press is the fact that all three activists discussed in this paper were eager to explore the possibilities that national and international reportage offered for their activism beyond their locality. Often, Sidrat, Amber, and Hasan pitched their stories to both the national English and local Urdu and Hindi press so as to maximise their outreach, and strengthen the voices of women's activists in India and abroad. It is, however, important to keep in mind that such exclusive focus on English sources comes with certain limitations. First, it narrows the scope of my analysis to the reportage produced for India's English-speaking elite. Second, such reportage tends to follow Western opinion-making – reproducing modernist liberal perceptions of Islam and women. During my research I have also collected and translated Hindi and Urdu newspaper articles which have appeared between 2009 and 2011. These reportages, mostly concerned with the various rallies, workshops, and seminars that have been organised by Sidrat, Amber, or Hasan, were very useful for analysing some of the contests and dissensions that exist amongst Muslims in Lucknow regarding issues of gender-related religious practices and ideologies.
12. For instance, postcolonial scholars such as Homi Bhabha (1984), Talal Asad (2009 [1986]), and Chandra Talpade Mohanty (1988) decried Western Orientalist representations of the non-West as a strategy which establishes and normalises the dominance of 'the West' over 'the East'.
13. The women's, or *Zenana* Park is a piece of land in the heart of Old Lucknow that was allotted by the city to the then newly-formed *Bazme Khawateen* in 1934.
14. AIMPLB member Ateeq Qasmi, interview by author, Lucknow on March 3, 2011.
15. See: http://articles.timesofindia.indiatimes.com/2004-10-31/lucknow/27159961_1_muslim-women-offer-prayers-bazme-khawateen (accessed April 15, 2012).
16. For more information on the women's mosque see: http://sports.rediff.com/news/2004/aug/11muslim.htm (accessed September 26, 2012) and http://www.outlookindia.com/printarticle.aspx?224749 (accessed September 26, 2012).
17. See: http://www.dnaindia.com/india/report_clerics-rattled-over-namaz-by-women_1163193 (accessed 15 April 2012); http://www.hindu.com/2008/05/07/stories/2008050753660500.htm (accessed April 15, 2012); http://www.indianexpress.com/news/begum-has-many-aces-under-her-veil/449378/ (accessed April 15, 2012); http://www.siliconindia.com/shownews/Women_offer_prayers_at_mosque_defy_seminarys_edict-nid-41858-cid-3.html (accessed 15 April 2012); http://wunrn.com/news/2008/05_08/05_19_08/051908_india.htm (accessed April 15, 2012).
18. The orthodox clergy's opposition to Amber's, Sidrat's, and Hasan's notable interventions within the public space was most explicitly expressed through political debates. However, all three activists state that they have experienced actual threats by individual Muslim representatives over the phone. These verbal harassments ranged from simple defamations to actual threats of bodily harm and even death.

19. Interview by the author with Shaista Amber, Lucknow on December 15, 2009.
20. See: http://www.hindu.com/2008/05/07/stories/2008050753660500.htm (accessed September 26, 2012).
21. See: http://www.telegraphindia.com/1080507/jsp/nation/story_9236894.jsp (accessed 15 April 2012); http://www.dnaindia.com/india/report_clerics-rattled-over-namaz-by-women_1163193 (accessed April 15, 2012);http://www.hindu.com/2008/05/07/stories/2008050753660500.htm (accessed September 26, 2012); http://twocircles.net/2008sep02/women_pray_along_men_lucknow_mosque.html (accessed April 15, 2012).
22. Interviews by the author, Lucknow on March 10, 2011.
23. The phrase 'big big jewellery' used by Hasan indicates the heavy and opulent bridal jewellery worn by Muslim women in India. This includes finger rings, bangles, a big nose ring, a heavy choker necklace, earrings, a *tikka* (forehead jewellery), and a waist belt. For Hasan, this kind of bridal jewellery signifies women as mere objects within marriage rather than active agents. Naish Hasan, interview by author, Lucknow on January 22, 2010.
24. *The New York Times* termed the BMMA marriage contract as a means 'to seek gender equality in marriage'. See: http://www.nytimes.com/2012/04/25/world/asia/25iht-letter25.html?pagewanted=all&_r=0 (accessed September 19, 2014).
25. The AIMPLB did not entirely oppose Hasan's marriage being solemnised. Many clerics believe that a marriage can be solemnised without the presence of a *qazi*. As according to the Islamic scripts, the approval of the bride and groom to the marriage and the public announcement of the wedding to the wedding guests is enough for the marriage to be considered valid. Naseema Ali Ikhtedar Khan in Lucknow, interview by author on February 13, 2011.
26. Naseema Ali Ikhtedar Khan, interview by author in Lucknow, February 13, 2011.
27. Fauzia Naseem, interview by author, Lucknow, February 9, 2010; Rukhsana Lari, interview by author, Lucknow on February 9, 2010.
28. See: http://today.msnbc.msn.com/id/26263977/ns/today-weddings/t/women-led-muslim-wedding-sparks-debate-india/#.T47tLIuRBvw (accessed April 18, 2012).
29. See: http://www.telegraphindia.com/1080813/jsp/frontpage/story_9686772.jsp (accessed April 18, 2012); http://www.hindu.com/2008/08/13/stories/2008081360251400.htm (accessed April 17, 2012); http://www.rediff.com/news/2008/aug/12up.htm (accessed April 18, 2012); http://articles.timesofindia.indiatimes.com/2008-08-13/lucknow/27920567_1_triple-talaq-nikah-woman (accessed April, 18 2012); http://indiatoday.intoday.in/story/Married+to+controversy/1/13563.html (accessed April 18, 2012).
30. See: http://www.youtube.com/watch?v=g35Lhqmsc7k (accessed April 17, 2012).
31. See: http://www.hindu.com/2008/08/13/stories/2008081360251400.htm (accessed April 17, 2012).
32. Here it is worth noting that groups like the Leadership Conference of Women Religious, a progressive association of American nuns in the US, or groups seeking to ordain women to the priesthood in Christian denominations and Mormonism,

such as the Mormon women's organisation Ordain Women (http://ordainwomen.org/ accessed December 16, 2014), also work within the framework of piety. Similar to the Muslim women's activists discussed in this article, these women use the strategy of appearing devout and committed to the faith, a discursive strategy designed to protect the movement from (the plentiful) accusations of apostasy.

Chapter 4

Vying for a Gender Just Islamic Marriage Contract

Women's Legal Spaces[1]

In 2008 and 2009, the All India Muslim Women's Personal Law Board (AIMWPLB), *Bazme Khawateen*, and the *Bharatiya Muslim Mahila Andolan* (BMMA) decisively destabilised patriarchal ideas of women's responsibilities and rights within marriage and the family with the release of their own versions of the Islamic marriage contract (*nikahnama*). Religious talk about marriage and the family pervades and informs Muslim women's sociolegal spaces in Lucknow. Moreover, public talk about conjugal rights and duties within Muslim marriage characterise, to a large extent, Muslim women's political interaction with hegemonic religious bodies such as the Islamic seminaries *Darul Uloom Nadwatul* and the *Firangi Mahal* (see Chapter 2). Within the last few years, Muslim women's rights activists from Lucknow have become an integral part of the politics that have surrounded the debates about the conjugal relationship in postcolonial India. 'If we get married there should be a proper *nikah* and there should be proper rules about *mehar*, *talaq*, maintenance. . .everything should be there', says Naish Hasan (BMMA). Shaista Amber (AIMWPLB) sounds a similar note: 'Often people don't know what the *Shariat* and the *Quran* say on women's rights and duties within marriage. One of the goals of the All India Muslim Women's Law Board is to make people aware of these rights and to teach them that Muslim women in fact have rights – unlike in the opinion of the clergy'. Similar to attempts made by Muslim women lawyers, activists, and scholars in Egypt, Morocco, and Iran (Abu-Lughod 2010; Mir-Hosseini 2006), Hasan and Amber currently seek to navigate the complex terrain of sociolegal reform with the production of a tangible document – the marriage contract. Their ultimate goal is to infuse popular and formal discourse on marriage with 'women-friendly' messages on conjugality. The goal is to destabilise entrenched patterns of gender inequality within state and non-state law and in everyday life. An analysis of these documents, therefore, allows accounting for the heterogeneity of positions that exist within the fierce debate on women's rights in Islam, as well as to draw attention to the ambivalent position of the state in this regard.

Between 2005 and 2008, the debate on a gender-just formulation of the *nikahnama*, or Islamic marriage contract, made waves amongst the Muslim communities in India. Within only three years, women's organisations like the AIMWPLB and the BMMA contested women's position within the family by attempting to formulate a gender just model-*nikahnama*. The goal was to oppose, for the first time, versions of the *nikahnama* endorsed by the men-dominated religious institutions such as the orthodox, conservative Sunni All India Muslim Personal Law Board (AIMPLB) and the conservative All India Shia Personal Law Board (AISPLB), both of which re-emphasised their own version of the *nikahnama* in the same time span.

The fact that all these institutions proposed their own version of the model marriage contract in a matter of only three years shows that there are significant differences of what is to be considered as the 'correct' interpretation of Muslim marriage laws and who can legitimately set the parameters of the conjugal relationship. Not surprisingly, each organisation has claimed its own interpretation of the contract to be the right one and has dismissed the others as 'un-Islamic' and/or 'irrelevant'. A common feature of all the endeavours to formulate a model marriage contract has been the assessment that the marriage contract must be beneficial to Muslim women who are often subject to discriminatory interpretations of *Shariat* laws. Hence, the top priority of all the versions of the *nikahnama* was to address the women's position vis-à-vis men as defined in the *Quran* and the *Hadith*.[2] These four documents are thus the result of a complex series of public negotiation and reasoning over the way the Islamic conjugal family is administered and adjudicated in state courts and in a multiplicity of societal legal sites such as the *Shariat* court, the mosques, and the offices of women's organisations in Lucknow. In this regard, these different interpretations of the conjugal relationship do not coexist peacefully but clash, causing ruptures and tensions within the sociolegal arena – and within the Muslim women's activism. Hence, the story about the competing model-*nikahnama* is a story of institutional conflict and struggle for religious and legal authority and power. This is a story that once again reminds us of the sensibilities and dynamics that are at work amongst Muslims themselves and within the contested polycentric landscape – calling for an understanding of Muslim laws as shaped by and constitutive to India's complex legal landscape of interlegality (Santos 1987, 2002).

Santos (1987, 294) has described institutional conflicts that happen within the legally pluralistic landscape as a phenomenon that is very likely to occur between what he calls 'geocentric' and 'egocentric legality', meaning between the nation state and legal particularism (that is, codes of ethics of multinational organisations). However, a look at the complex pluralistic legal landscape in Lucknow, and the ways the authority of 'lawmaking' and the 'correct' interpretation of Islamic laws are contested within the context of the model-*nikahnama*, reveals a scenario of conflict that is not staged between the state and non-state legal institutions but mainly in the social arena *amongst* India's Muslim communities. Although these institutional struggles take place outside the confines of state jurisdiction, the state is not irrelevant to these struggles. Muslim women's rights activists' attempt to re-articulate gender justice within the framework of Islam particularly reveals international and state-led legal discourses as crucial in shaping the sociolegal opportunity structures. In fact, Muslim women's activists are looking for state support in order to propose an interpretation of religious law nearer to 'modern' principles of gender justice. The idiom 'modern' here is closely associated with the idea of 'differentiated citizenship right' (Young 1990). This is women's incorporation into the political as well as the religious community.

The paradoxical result of such processes, one could say, is that women address the state as a guarantor for their authority in interpreting religious law texts while operating outside of the realm of the state. In the context of contemporary India, however, little academic attention has been paid to the complex modalities by which Muslim women's rights activists mix and combine different legalities in their projects for justice in the shadow of the state. Surprisingly, scholarly debate in the area of political science and law on the reform of Muslim family law on the Indian subcontinent tends to ignore the complex social and ideological realities on the ground. This chapter fills a gap by addressing this shortcoming through a careful empirical scrutiny of the institutional and discursive complexity that shapes Muslim women's struggles for justice on the ground. To this end, this chapter explores some of the legal dimensions within which transnational, national, and customary laws entangle and overlap – in terms of interlegality – in activists' attempts to establish gender justice. In the process, I lay the groundwork for an understanding of the permeability of state and non-state legal boundaries and secular and religious institutions as visible in current grassroots struggles on gender justice. It will be illustrated that these specific women's legal spaces are characterised by cross-fertilisation of different state-led and societal discourses on gender justice within the domestic sphere. In this regard, perhaps, a generalisable lesson that can be drawn from this chapter is that the process of 'vernacularisation' (Merry 2006), this is the manner in which local actors merge and translate different legalities for local contexts, is a crucial element in socio-legal reform-processes at the grassroots.

The Islamic Marriage Contract (*Nikahnama*)

In Islam, marriage is a religious contract (*nikahnama*) that can be oral or written. The written form of the contract becomes valid with the signature of the groom, the bride, the bride's guardian, and the witnesses to the wedding. The required signatures exemplify that marriage (*nikah*) in Islam is viewed as the contractual agreement between the groom, the bride, and the bride's guardian.[3] In practice, the marriage contract is a highly controversial document, whose use and philosophical underpinnings have been reinterpreted and challenged in contemporary Muslim societies by fundamentalists, traditionalists, and reformists alike. As Mir-Hosseini (2003, 10–11) shows, contemporary interpretations of the marriage contract by theocratic nation states as well as non-state religious actors tend to adopt an outlook on marriage (*nikah*) that is based on the premises of women's moral and social subjugation. The rationale for this kind of subjugation is found in the theory of the difference of female and male sexuality. Mir-Hosseini (ibid., 10) summarises these differences as follows: God gave women greater sexual desires than men. This is mitigated by men's sexual honour and jealousy and women's modesty and shyness. The conclusion Sunni and Shia jurists draw from such a theory, according to Mir-Hosseini (ibid.), is that if women's sexuality is left uncontrolled by men it will pose a great threat to the societal order. While scholars and Islamic feminists – such as the Pakistani-American theologian Riffat Hassan (1995), the American scholar Amina Wadud (2009), the Pakistani scholar Asma Barlas (2004), and the Moroccan feminist Fatima Mernissi (1987) – have successfully shown that such interpretations of women's sexuality are pre-Islamic and negate the very spirit of humanity and equality the *Quran* propagates, such interpretations yet dominate the legal consciousness of contemporary Muslim jurists. Moreover, they are considered the blueprint of Islamic knowledge and practice, and hence unchangeable. The juristic basis for this kind of women's subjugation is provided by the marriage contract as being defined as a contract of sale. According to classical *fiqh,* the marriage contract in Islam marks the acceptance of the marriage offer by the woman or her guardian. The sexual relationship between the spouses becomes legal (*halal*) after the groom has transferred the agreed amount of *mehar* (dower) to his wife.[4] The dower or the *mehar* can be a sum of money or any valuables the husband pays to the bride at the time of the wedding in exchange for her sexual availability.[5]

Common jurist interpretation of the marriage contract, according to Mir-Hosseini (2003, 11), reflects the uneasiness of many contemporary classical jurists to fuse *Quranic* ideals with social reality. Defining marriage as a religious duty (*ibadat*), the scope of interpretation and rationalisation is limited. *Nikah*, however, as Mir-Hosseini (ibid.) writes, is one amongst the only few contracts in Islam that is not concerned with the relationship between God and the worshipper in the sphere of the social (*ibadat*), but regulates the relationship between humans in the private sphere (*muamalat*). This distinction is important, since the realm of the private (*muamalat*) is, in contrast to the realm of the social (*ibadat*), open and allows for new interpretations and rational consideration with almost no restriction. Mir-Hosseini (ibid., 12) laments that although classical jurists showed their cognisance of this by placing marriage into the realm of the private, their conception of gender relations is based on judicial interpretations where traditional and conservative *Shariat* ideals (for example, women need to be protected by men, women's sexuality constitutes a potential danger to societal order, marriage as a contract of sale, etc.), are ascribed permanent validity. Reformists and feminists refute such limiting and allegedly unchangeable notions of conjugal gender relations by pointing to the variety of definitions of marriage that are possible within the realm of the private (*muamalat)*. For instance, Islamic feminists such as Amina Wadud (2009), Asma Barlas (2004), and Riffat Hassan (1995) claim their right to *ijtihad* asserting that the *Quran* and the *Shariat* are flexible and open for interpretation. They contend that gender relations are neither created by the ruling of the *Shariat* nor by divine law. In contrary, gender relations have to be constantly reformed according to time, space, and experience. It is only by means of such adjustments that the principles of the *Quran* – justice and humanity – can be guaranteed. In this regard, gender relations are not treated as immutable but as a social practice in need of change.

From such a perspective, the Islamic marriage contract has a rich sociolegal life. It can be amended and altered according to Islamic school, religious practice, individual needs and expectations, or time and space. The Islamic marriage contract is proven in practice to be not a static and unchangeable document, as often theorised in scholarship on Islam, but subject to processes of interpretations and transformation. For example, Quraishi (2008, 89) illustrates that in Egypt the economic and social constellations of gender have been constantly altered and reinterpreted through the Islamic marriage contract from medieval to contemporary times. In this context, the question of whether or not these stipulations were 'Islamic' or 'un-Islamic' was less relevant than the realities on the ground. Also, the civil laws or personal laws of countries such as Bangladesh, Pakistan, Sudan, Algeria, Iran, and Tunisia reflect, although only partially and selectively, the flexibility of this document. The law of these countries recognises the right of the spouses to negotiate the terms of the marriage as long as they are not contrary to the textual sources of Islam or to the very meaning of marriage. These couples have the option to include a wide range of conditions to the marriage in their marriage contract. This could include maintenance (*nafaqa*), employment options, educational options, freedom to travel or visit relatives, division of household responsibilities, standards of living, breastfeeding options, control and share of property, restrictions on polygamy, divorce options, and conditions of the husband's emotional treatment of his wife. Moreover, a woman can negotiate the place of residence so as not to be too far away from her family.

In order to ensure that the bride and groom can legally enforce the terms of the marriage contract, these countries ask for the registration of the marriage on the basis of the marriage contract. Acknowledging the fact that women's rights within matrimony are often not as well protected as those of men, these countries consider the registration of marriages as important. This is because it provides women especially with the necessary documentation they need to access the judiciary system in case of a marital infringement. This requirement for registration is in line with transnational women's rights agendas such as that of the Convention of the Elimination of all Forms of Discrimination against Women (CEDAW). With the goal to place women in a better legal situation in case the marriage breaks down, Article 16 of CEDAW mandates the registration of all marriages in an official registry. Many theocratic nation states endorse such a stipulation. For instance, Muslim laws in Bangladesh and Pakistan regard the person who solemnised the marriage and who signed the marriage contract as responsible for the official registration of the marriage (Pearl and Menski 1998, 334–475).[6] However, as Mir-Hosseini (2003, 24) points out, registration alone is not sufficient to secure women's rights within marriage. She asserts that the stipulations in the marriage contract can only be effective if they are automatically inserted into the marriage contract by the state and if they are unconditional.

Unlike in many Muslim societies, Muslim (and Hindu) marriages in India remain by and large unregistered. For instance, the Family Court in India considers a Muslim marriage as valid if it is based on a binding and fully valid contract (*nikahnama*) and consented between persons of sound mind (Pearl and Menski 1998, 176; Solanki 2007, 91). Most of the Muslim marriages in India are solemnised in an informal way. This could be at home, in a mosque, or in the office of a women's organisation. According to a *Maulana* from Lucknow, the marriage contract was until a few decades ago primarily oral. As he said, people back then were God-fearing people and there was no need for a written contract with extra stipulations in regard to conjugal duties and rights. However, today in the context of the debates around registration of marriages the contract is in most cases a written one.[7] As Hamza Abidi, a Shia advocate in the Family Court in Lucknow, told me, the formal registration of Muslim marriages is not necessary. He explained that unlike a Hindu marriage, which lacks a written document to prove the marriage, Muslim marriages are usually registered with the *qazi* who has solemnised the *nikah* (marriage). In this case, a copy of the *nikahnama* is kept in the registrar of the *qazi's* office. Further, it is the right of the groom and the bride to have a copy of the *nikahnama* as a proof of their marriage. So, if the case arises where one of the party disputes the validity of the marriage in court and where a copy of the *nikahnama* is not available then the *qazi* can be approached for verification. In case the *qazi* cannot be reached then the party who maintains the validity of the marriage will have to produce evidence of the matrimonial bond. This could be by means of testimonies to the wedding ceremony, children as a proof of the consummation of the marriage, joint bank accounts, a ration card, photographs, etc.[8] A consensus regarding the stipulations in the marriage contract and an authority to enforce these very stipulations does not exist. The *nikahnama* is a flexible document, which is, if at all, registered in the various local mosques and offices of *qazis* and *maulanas*. From a legal perspective, the Muslim marriage contract is more a symbolic document than legal reality.[9]

In Lucknow, as elsewhere in India, the most widely used form of the marriage contract is simple and contains no more than the name and the signature of the couple and the guardian of the bride, the witnesses to the ceremony and the *qazi* who has solemnised the marriage. In some cases, it lists the amount of money (*mehar*) awarded to the bride at the time of the marriage. This form of the written marriage contract can be purchased in the markets of old Lucknow for Rs.10–50 (approximately US $0.25). Such a basic model of the Islamic marriage contract leaves ample room for the implementation of idealised and orthodox-conservative conceptions of marriage that stress the sexual, economic, and social inferiority of women on the one hand and of the husband's control over his wife on the other. In contrast to other Muslim countries and communities, the standard form of the marriage contract as common in India does not take into account women's and men's right to negotiate the terms of the marriage. Lucknow-based Muslim women's activists have tried to fill this lacuna by stressing the capacity of the marriage contract for flexibility and re-alignment in conjunction with different religious ideologies and practical circumstances. They refer to the possibilities such a contract offers for women to negotiate issues in regard to lifestyle, money, and property as well as conditions of divorce. Therefore, I will now examine the Islamic marriage contract as an important document that allows for individuals – whose rights are infringed upon by the religious leadership's current attempts to legal self-reform in the area of marriage and the family – a resistance strategy to respond to the government's attempt to regulate personal laws (see Introduction).

Gender Just Model-*Nikahnama*

Muslim women's public struggles and contestations around the formulation of an appropriate version of the Islamic marriage contract (*nikahnama*) are not a recent phenomena but can be traced back to colonial times. Already at the beginning of the twentieth century, upper-class Muslim women activists in India sought to challenge orthodox interpretations of Islamic marriage by reinterpreting female subjectivity within conjugality. In so doing, they felt that the written *nikahnama* offered a viable avenue through which problems of unilateral divorce, maintenance (*nafaqa*), polygamy, and property could be tackled (Kirmani 2011b). Later, in the 1930s, activists argued for the expansion of women's options for divorce and for the curtailment of the husband's unilateral right to divorce. For instance, the non-sectarian All India Women's Conference, spearheaded by its Muslim President Sharifa Hamid Ali, prepared a draft of a Muslim marriage contract containing stipulations that allowed women to divorce under certain conditions in 1940 (Minault 1998a, 150). However, such early legal mobilisation by women's activists in colonial India failed to garner support for actual 'legal consciousness',[10] most probably due to women's lack of experience with the law and the court system – experience that would be necessary to reinforce such consciousness (Merry 2003, 344).

While law reform concerning conjugality alone is not sufficient to change Muslim women's everyday realities, public debates around the *nikahnama* have shed light on the insecure position of women within and outside of marriage. The government-funded Sachar Committee and Ranganath Misra Reports as well as the non-governmental Seema Kazi Minority Report note that Muslims in India are behind other religious groups (Hindu, Sikh, Christian, Parsi, and Buddhist) in terms of education, economy, and employment – 59 per cent of Indian Muslims are illiterate, 37 per cent of urban Muslims live below the poverty line, with a monthly income of Rs. 150 or less (approximately US $2.30), and 50 per cent of Muslims in India are unemployed (Ranganath Misra Report 2007; Sachar Committee Report 2005). The Seema Kazi report (1999) shows that Muslim women bear the brunt of Muslim's overall socio-economic ostracism. In comparison to other religious groups, Muslim women show the lowest work participation and literacy rate.[11] A recently published volume edited by Laurent Gayer and Christophe Jafferlot, *Muslims in Indian Cities* (2012), bolsters such reality. Drawing on ethnographic analysis, the contributions in this volume blatantly reveal the processes of 'ghettoisation' of Muslims in different Indian cities including Lucknow, Ahmedabad, and Mumbai. As it evinces from my own research, Muslim women's lack of education and economic autonomy results in a marginal presence of Muslim women in public life and a high degree of women's dependence from their conjugal and/or natal family.

Struck by the continuing desolate socio-economic status of especially Muslim women in India, Muslim women's rights activists began to amplify their voices for legal reform and gender-just interpretation of Islamic family laws in the 1990s. This is to gain greater economic independence for women from their husband and greater freedom within the private and the public sphere For example, urban Muslim women's organisations and networks, such as the Muslim Women's Rights Network, the Muslim Women's Forum, the *Awaaz-e-Niswan,* and STEPS Women's Development, to name a few, demanded extensive changes in Muslim Personal Law in regard to gendered relations and practices. One of their strategies was to demonstrate that they could engage in process of *ijtihad* (legal reasoning) regarding textual sources of Islam such as the *Quran*, *Hadith,* and the *Sunnah*. Here the act of *ijtihad*, legal reasoning with the aim to reform religious thought and practices, is central to women's claim to authoritative lawmaking. In this respect, Muslim women's activists publicly reasoned that *nikah* is not an act of worship (*ibadat*), an area where the scope of what can be interpreted and rationalised is limited. Rather, they argue, marriage falls into the realm of the private (*muamalat*), an area within which the relationship between humans is regulated and not between them and God. The realm of the private, women's activists assert, therefore remains open to *ijtihad*. The textual sources of Islam are hence subject to interpretation and are changeable rather than absolute (Kirmani 2011b; Mir-Hosseini 2003; Subramanian 2008; Vatuk 2013). Through extrapolation they demonstrated their right to engage in lawmaking itself, through the formulation of their own *nikahnama*.

In line with Islamic feminists around the world, Muslim women's rights activists in contemporary India argue that Islam is dynamic and that its textual sources have to be interpreted by taking into consideration the social, cultural, and political reality of those it seeks to affect. Many Muslim women's activists thus feel that the religious ideals, formulated by male scholars and jurists, do not correspond with the reality of many Muslim women. They hold that there is a tension between Islamic family laws, permeated with religious ideals and ethical values, and the social reality of marriage as experienced by individuals. For instance, Naish Hasan (BMMA) says in a conversation,[12]

> Even very big *mullhas* don't know what exactly our [women's] issues in the *bastis* [slum] and in poor localities are. The majority of Muslims are poor. . . . Our major issues are education, livelihood, employment, and security. Islam is not the main issue. It is not enough to just preach Islam. The *mullhas* come and preach in the *bastis* about what Islam is and what it is not. Women are not interested in their preaching because they have to think about what they will cook in the evening. They have no money; they have to think about how to earn money and of how to get the family going. In this situation, they are exposed to a lot of insecurity and domestic violence. Therefore a model-*nikahnama* has to respond to these very practical issues rather than to a conservative Islamic ideology.

Activists in Lucknow, therefore, view it as essential to formulate a marriage contract that includes and considers the everyday experiences, problems, and aspirations of Muslim women and men. As actors in the middle, or knowledge-brokers as Merry (2006) terms them, who understand both the *Quranic* texts and the social reality, Muslim activists such as Naish Hasan feel the necessity to reconcile social reality and religious ideology. That means that their version of the *nikahnama* has to respond to daily matrimonial realities that are imbued with financial and social uncertainties, violence, restrictions, and sacrifice, such as for example those voiced by these lower middle-class Muslim women.

> **Umar Jahan, divorced, does embroidery, Sunni, 43 years** – My in-laws were not happy with the dowry (*dahej*) and they tried to find a reason to blame me all the time. I had problems in my marriage. At my in-laws' place I did not get a place to sit, there were no bed sheets and no one gave me drinking water. I lived there in this manner for two or three years and a son was born to me. My son must have been around two-and-a-half years old when I came to my natal place [the place where she was born]. My in-laws had kicked me out and had

not allowed my son to come with me. They troubled us a lot. At my natal place a girl was born to me in 1983. Also in my natal house I had to face a lot of problems. Only my father supported me. My husband divorced me when my daughter was three years old. At that time I didn't know about my rights – I didn't know what to do.

Group discussion, married housewives, Sunni, 45–60 years

Woman 1: In our religion women are not important. Women serve their husband for their entire life but once your husband says the word *talaq* thrice your whole life is completely ruined.

Woman 2: He can say it anytime…

Woman 3: Yes, for men it's not a big problem because they can easily go for the next marriage and they can easily get a bride, but for women it is difficult. Nowadays women are being tortured at their in-laws'. If they are not educated how can they know about their rights? If they didn't study how can they know about their duties and rights and about human and women's rights?

Mehrun, married, housewife, Sunni, 43 years – My life is full of sacrifices. I started sacrificing since the day I got married and I don't know when this sacrificing will come to an end. I also do some social work as well as religious work. I worry a lot about the marriage of my daughters. I don't have any support from anybody except Allah. If I want to write about my life I could write a lot but I don't want to think about my life all over again. I left everything on Allah. Every woman in the world is in trouble. There are some women who are troubled more than me. I am fine in comparison to them. My husband is better than those who beat their wives in a state of intoxication. But if I left him, where would I go with my children? What would other people think of me? So, women have to adjust. This is the way it works here.

In a context where the great majority of Muslim women depict matrimony as a place of insecurity, violence, and despair rather than love, security, and protection, Muslim activists point to the flexibility of Islam and the Islamic marriage contract. They univocally argue that the document of the marriage contract has to resonate with women's complex day-to-day realities in order to improve their life conditions. Deploying an 'interpretative methodology', to borrow from Mirza (2008, 30), these activists destabilise the myth of Muslim law as homogenous and immutable. In so doing, they advocate for reform in regard to divorce, marital property, custody, and inheritance. The four marriage contracts analysed in this chapter illustrate the ways in which Muslim women's activists currently decentre hegemonic discourses about marriage and the family by softening and/or disrupting legal boundaries of both state and non-state laws.

Competing Model-*Nikahnamas*

A Mumbai group that includes lawyers, academics, and NGO representatives made the attempt to draft and disseminate a women-friendly model-*nikahnama* in the early 1990s. The new model contract, which tackled problems such as polygamy, maintenance, and divorce, was presented to the AIMPLB in 1994 but without success (Kirmani 2011b, 58; Hussain 2006, 4; Subramanian 2008, 658; Vatuk 2008, 505–6). The AIMPLB did not embrace the document due to internal disagreements among board members regarding the interpretation of triple *talaq* (Hussain 2006, 4). Despite the AIMPLB's rejection of this women-friendly contract, the clerics began to acknowledge the nascent legal mobilisation of Muslim women and their growing engagement in the area of lawmaking. The AIMPLB started to pay more attention to reforms in the area of Muslim family law so as not to forfeit its legal authority and monopoly of religious interpretation. In the late 1990s, the AIMPLB launched a reform movement in order to purge Islam from un-Islamic practices such as dowry and caste endogamy. As Subramanian (2008, 657) has argued, in a political climate where the respect for Muslims by non-Muslims, notably Hindu nationalists, was decreasing on the one hand and the Muslim community increasingly suffered internal fractures on the other, influential Muslim religious scholars formed the Islamic Fiqh Academy in 1989.[13] The members of the Fiqh Academy reintroduced the practice of *ijtihad* (the interpretation of Islamic laws in view of contemporary circumstances) in order to build a loose consensus on socio-religious practices and adjudicative approaches within the Muslim community (ibid, 658). Moreover, the AIMPLB began to demand that all Muslim women be given inheritance rights involving agricultural land, as well as a share in agricultural income. The Board also published a booklet specifying the forms of Islamic family life (ibid.). So, as part of the AIMPLB's effort to minimise the legal mobilisation and intervention by the fast-growing urban Muslim women's organisations and networks, the Board published a model marriage contract in 2005. The initial draft of this contract followed some of the suggestions made by Muslim activists. It gave women a number of rights, such as the right to unilateral divorce (*talaq-e-tafweez* or *khul*), the right to live separately if the husband marries someone else, the right to retain all gifts that the couple received during marriage, and a voice in regard to polygamy. The final document, however, does not include these stipulations. This is, as Subramanian (ibid.) notes, due to internal disagreement in the Board, particularly that both male and female members did not approve of the wife's right to divorce.

Establishment of a normative discourse on marriage: AIMPLB's interpretation of marriage in Islam

The model-*nikahnama* that was finally released by the AIMPLB in 2005 is a small document of four pages in Urdu. One of the authors of this document, the *qazi* of the *Darul Qaza* in Lucknow, describes this *nikahnama* as a 'good improvement. It encourages the bridal couple to solemnise their marriage in written form and keeps in mind the benefits (*phaida*) of men and women within conjugality'.[14] However, the guidelines stipulated in this document are not mandatory and there is no mechanism to enforce them. Like all the other *nikahnamas*, this document consists of multiple sections. One is the actual *nikahnama* that mandates the signature of the bride, the groom, and the father or guardian of the bride. The second part of the marriage contract is called the *iqrarnama* or agreement, where stipulations regarding the process of dispute settlement, financial transactions at the time of the wedding, property, inheritance, divorce, etc., can be made. The third section, called the *hidayatnama*, lists the guidelines for the marriage under *Shariat*-law.

The document prepared by the AIMPLB adopts a view on law that is strongly image-based, and that describes the matrimonial relationship in terms of metaphors.[15] Moreover, the document represents a style of law that is large-scale and symbolic, and talks about social responsibilities and duties rather than rights. In so doing, this *nikahnama* integrates and even dissolves the social with the legal representation and privileges a description of reality that is symbolic and informal. Drawing on the textual sources of Islam, it describes marriage as a 'gift from God' or a 'service to God'. It holds that the conjugal relationship rests 'on mutual love, mercy and respect' and that the spouses are 'each other's garments'. This contract stresses the difference in nature between women and men and their respective and specific duties and responsibilities, and it attaches importance to the wife's moral behaviour and sexual conduct.[16] For example, the *hidayatnama*, which sketches the guidelines of a Muslim marriage, declares that it is the wife's duty to duly 'obey' and 'honour' her husband. It requires that the wife seek her husband's permission to step out of the matrimonial home, although it 'allows' the wife to visit her parents and relatives and holds that the husband should safeguard her 'honour' and 'respectability' when the 'need' arises. He, on the other hand, has to assure financial security, including food, clothes, and shelter, for his wife. This contract establishes an ideal of the conjugal relationship that rests on a conservative interpretation of the *Quran* and the *Hadith*. Thereby, the husband and wife relationship is structured by means of a discourse that stresses the wife's moral duties within conjugality rather than her individual rights.[17]

The AIMPLB's version of the *nikahnama* only introduces minor reforms. For example, it mandates a strict procedure of dispute settlement to prevent rushed divorces, the requirement of a written record of all marriages and their copies to be given to the bride, the groom, and the office at the *Shariat*-court, and the mandatory presence of parents and guardians at the marriage in order to prevent forced marriages. It does not provide any safeguards against men leaving their wives without sufficient maintenance, and it ignores issues such as marriage of minors, polygamy, and the woman's right to divorce either by *khul* or by the delegated right to divorce (*talaq-e-tafweez*). It only mentions that triple *talaq* is 'avoidable'.[18] Nevertheless, this *nikahnama* does put forward some reformist features, such as requiring the husband to give the *mehar* to the bride at the day of the wedding and in tangible assets such as jewellery, gold, or silver so as to avoid inflation.[19] Although the AIMPLB did not bring its limited reformism, to bear on adjudication, it approached the government of Uttar Pradesh, and then the Indian government, in 2006 to give all Muslim women the rights to inherit agricultural land and to a share in family agricultural income. However, no pressure was exerted to materialise such demands (Subramanian 2014, 226).

The dominant Islamic discourse in the AIMPLB's *nikahnama* that constructs the husband as the provider, protector, and guardian has been mimetically extended to the relationship between the AIMPLB and the wider Muslim community as such. The *iqrarnama* says that in case of conjugal infringements the couple is subject to the exclusive arbitration of the *Darul Qaza*. In other words, this section forecloses the couple's option to address the state courts if a dispute arises.[20] The judge of the *Darul Qaza* explains such stipulations by saying: 'Unlike the state courts, where decisions are often fraudulent, *Shariat*-courts provide a good option for Muslims to get real Islamic justice. A true Muslim', he continues, 'would not dare to tell lies in the court of *Allah*, but settle the dispute in an amicable way'.[21] This contract is hence a reflection of the clergy's current efforts to keep state law and state courts, which they consider 'un-Islamic' and as a threat to Islamic identity – and where perjury is permissible – at bay. Similar to what Stowasser (1998) has argued in the context of the Middle East and Patricia Hill Collins (2000) in the context of the United States, conservative movements often strategically deploy the rhetoric of family for their own political agendas. In this respect, the AIMPLB's model-*nikahnama* is a perfect example to illustrate how issues around women's rights provide an excellent site for conservative Muslim leadership to strengthen the continuity and stability of the

Muslim community. More recently, in July 2012, the AIMPLB compounded its demand for legal self-regulation with an effort to obtain government marriage registrar status for the *qazi*. This request is a response to the Supreme Court's verdict for compulsory registration of marriages.[22]

A Shift toward a Rhetoric of Rights within the Dominant Islamic Discourse

Other men-dominated religious establishments have also supported gender reforms by means of the *nikahnama*. In November 2006, the Shia Personal Law Board (AISPLB) released its own version of the model-*nikahnama* as formulated according to the Shia school of jurisprudence. The result is a ten-page document available in Urdu and English. Apart from a media statement by the AIMPLB that declares this version as 'irrelevant', the release of the Shia-*nikahnama* has otherwise been received quietly.

The incentive for the president of the AISPLB, *Maulana* Mirza Mohammed Athar, to draft a new *nikahnama* was to, first, offer a specific Shia version of the contract and, second, to tackle malpractices in the area of marriage. The latter item, he contends, compromises women's dignity. Athar holds that women in Islam are often tortured by their husbands, who deprive them of maintenance and reject them by making use of cruel divorce practices. 'Marriage', the *Maulana* asserts, 'often degrades Muslim women to mere servants or even slaves that are held on a tight rope just like animals'.[23] However, it seems that the goal of establishing a specific Shia version of the marriage contract is given priority over the cause to better women's situation within marriage. The obvious story the document tells is patriarchal – framing women's identity as relegated to the home and the family. The power of such hegemonic conjugal ideals lies in the fact that women are left with relatively little room for negotiation of their rights without violating the meaning of the 'Islamic family'. Throughout, the contract stresses the wife's obedience, devotedness, and naiveté and establishes the husband as her protector and provider. Let me illustrate: the foreword of the English version of the contract reads as follows,

> Prophet Mohammad has said that it is obligatory on [the] wife to obey her husband. Never disobey him, keep watch in his house and not give even '*Sadqa*' from husband's money without permission. Likewise *Hadith* also ordains that it is imperative on [the] husband to provide good food and clothes to [the] wife and to forgive her if she makes any mistakes unknowingly.

The most important advancement made by this *nikahnama* was to delegate the right to divorce to the wife under certain circumstances (*talaq-e-tafweez*). These are: if the husband fails to provide maintenance for longer than four months during the subsistence of the marriage, if his whereabouts are unknown over a time period of four years, if he mentally and physically tortures his wife, or if he forces her into sexual relations with other men. Moreover, this Shia version further curtails the husband's right to unilateral triple *talaq* in one sitting, a practice that the Shia consider un-Islamic and unconstitutional due to its discriminatory effect on women. It also advocates that divorced women should receive alimony beyond the period of *iddat*, until they are able to support themselves. *Maulana* Athar explained to me that although the latter stipulation corresponds with the contested Section 125 of the Criminal Procedure Code, wherein the woman is entitled to maintenance even beyond the period of *iddat*, it has also been brought into accordance with the 'Islamic concept of humanity'. This is by appealing to the husband's responsibility as a protector and provider toward his former wife.[24] 'This way', Athar says, 'I can avoid the critics of the clergy who reject state-regulated Muslim Personal Law as the official legal position'.[25] Here, the Shia *nikahnama* cautiously softens the boundary between the secular state and informal law by dragging state law into societal laws. However, the gender-friendly advancements brought forward in this *nikahnama* are not binding – the *nikahnama* declares that it is not mandatory for the parties to accept the conditions laid down for the groom and bride in its own pages. This stipulation is not only a reflection of the absence of an authority to actually enforce the stipulations made in the contract, but, moreover, it indicates the political implications of this marriage contract. From a perspective of politics, the question of whether or not the stipulations made in the contract are actually enforceable might be less pertinent than the fact that the contract constitutes an inherent part of the political debates around marriage and the family in Islam.

Disappointed by these male versions of the model-*nikahnama*, and in particular by the one drafted by the AIMPLB, two Muslim women's rights organisations (AIMWPLB and BMMA) challenged the clergy's interpretation of the religious texts, as well as their authority to make laws, with the release of their own model-*nikahnamas*. In their view, the pre-existing documents failed to address such issues as – the exclusive right of the husband to ex-judicially divorce his wife by simply uttering the word *talaq* thrice in one sitting, the prohibition of polygamy, and verification of the couple's age at the time of marriage for prevention of child marriage (Hussain 2007, 4; Vatuk 2008,

505–7).[26] Moreover, Muslim women's activists in Lucknow felt that their identities and rights as citizens were seriously jeopardised by such patriarchal interpretations of matrimony. In this regard, they claim that their activism is crucial for building awareness among Muslim women and men, which, they hope, will eventually result in sociolegal change.

Muslim women's activists' interpretations of the Muslim marriage contract

Against the backdrop of such rather patriarchal constructions of conjugality, the question of how Muslim women's activists square entrenched patterns of gender hierarchy with principles of gender justice comes to the fore and will be discussed further.

Muslim women's rights activists in Lucknow contend that a model-*nikahnama* drafted entirely by women was necessary in order to question the clergy's discriminatory way of interpreting the textual sources of Islam. In line with Muslim feminists active in the United States, Iran, Egypt, Indonesia, and elsewhere, these activists hold that the *Quran*, the *Shariat*, and *fiqh* are not one single legal code but a variety of positions of Islamic jurisprudence. In a situation where the orthodox clergy sets the discursive stage for the understanding and implementation of 'God's law' women confront them on their own turf. They argue that the relationship between God and the believer is a direct and personal one. 'God's law' is therefore a product of the reasoning of the individual with her own beliefs and religious ideologies.

In their own interpretation of the textual sources of Islam they posit their quest for gender justice neither within an orthodox Islamic nor a liberal discourse of marriage and gender with its idea of total equality between the sexes. Rather, they exhibit an approach that strives to maintain the balance of their identity as 'good Muslims' on the one hand and Indian citizens on the other. These Muslim women activists command an eloquent knowledge about Islamic laws as well as state-governed Muslim Personal Law, Criminal Law, the Indian Penal Code, and international human and women's rights.[27] Hence, these activists are fluent in a variety of legal languages, which they combine, fragment, and hybridise in order to decentralise widely accepted assumptions of the working of gender within the intimate sphere of marriage. I understand these very processes of vernacularisation and hybridisation as a form of 'subaltern cosmopolitanism' (Santos 2002) geared toward centralising alternative conceptions of the Muslim marriage within a limited and constraint discursive field of power.[28]

Muslim women's rights activists in Lucknow, which are placed at the margin of state and community justice systems, create a complex legal space that allows for a conceptualisation of the *Quran*, state administered religious laws, and the Indian Constitution not as opposites, but in terms of their synergies through which they can work for gender justice (for example, equality, dignity, equal legal protection by the state, and anti-discrimination on the grounds of sex). In their opinion, these legal frameworks are not mutually exclusive but complementary. So, rather than having to opt for one or the other, both Muslim women's organisations, the AIMWPLB and the BMMA, consider the *Quran* and the Indian Constitution as two different formulations of the same object – human dignity. This approach, common amongst Islamic feminists and activists from divergent schools of thought, is geared toward overcoming the apparent 'liberal dilemma' (Nussbaum 1999) where the principle of the right to religious freedom clashes with women's constitutional rights to freedom of movement, freedom of equal treatment under the law, and freedom of equal political participation, etc. For example, Shaista Amber (AIMWPLB) says,

> I think that Islamic laws are universal and provide women with all the rights – even the Constitutional rights are enshrined in the *Quran*. The *Quran Sharif* is not only a religious book – it is a Constitution for the human being and the ultimate source of justice and equality. It is a guide book that tells us how to live our life.

In a similar manner, Naish Hasan (BMMA) contends: 'There should be a gender-just law based on the *Quran* that takes into consideration the legal principles of this country. We don't have this right now. So, we have to fight for a gender – just law on the basis of the *Quran*. Then the *Quran* is like a Constitution or human rights declaration – it is universal'.

As shown by such statements, both organisations, the AIMWPLB and the BMMA, view the *Quran* and the Indian Constitution as both expressing different avenues to achieve human dignity. The only notable difference between these two representations of human dignity is, in their view, language and not content. To revisit Islamic scripture in a manner termed 'democratisation of *ijtihad*' (Mirza 2008, 30) challenges not only conservative representations of women as spiritually inferior to men, but further undoes, to some extent, the boundaries between formal human rights, state laws and informal interpretations of the religious scripts. Such approach thus reveals legal boundaries as fuzzy and unclear, and subject to different legal perspectives.

The AIMWPLB's version of the Islamic marriage contract

In March 2008, the AIMWPLB released its own model-*nikahnama*, which is a seven-page document available in Hindi and Urdu.[29] Shaista Amber, the president of the AIMWPLB and the author of the document, has argued that in a country where most Muslim women are not educated and do not know about their rights, and where the clergy is busy re-establishing patriarchy by seriously curtailing women's conjugal rights, a *nikahnama* that stipulates the rights and duties of husband and wife as according to the *Quran* and the *Hadith* is needed. In order to make sure that women can legally enforce the rights set forth in this *nikahnama*, Amber lobbies the state to recognise this document.[30]

The release of a modelmarriage contract entirely drafted by lay-women and not the clergy has created much stir among Lucknow's Muslim community. Whereas the *nikahnama* has been welcomed by women's rights organisations all over the country, the clergy has deemed the document as a 'joke' and a 'public stunt'. They have publicly defamed Amber as a *kafir* or non-believer who lacks the religious knowledge and authority to formulate a *nikahnama* that is in accordance with *Shariat*-laws.[31] Considering this harsh public critique, the dissemination of this women-friendly document turned out to be rather difficult. Amber's attempts to have her *Shariat-nikahnama* sold in local stores in the old part of Lucknow failed. As she said, the vendors were afraid that the Muslim clergy would exercise repression. So for now, the *nikahnama* can be downloaded from the Board's website and is distributed among members of the AIMWPLB.[32]

This reactionary stance of the *ulema* toward alternative formulations of the model-*nikahnama* poses a great challenge for Muslim women activists, who have entered and operate within a sociolegal space hitherto reserved exclusively for men. Hence, the AIMWPLB has been wary not to step outside the line of 'the acceptable' with their own formulation of the model contract. Their strategy is not to directly confront the dominant discourse on gender and Islam, but rather to gain recognition and acceptance within existing constraints. Without rejecting state interference into Muslim marriages, Amber believes that working for gender justice from within an Islamic framework is indispensable. Stepping out of the framework of Islam would, according to her, render their efforts for legal mobilisation irrelevant to the majority of the Muslim community and lay them open to the alleged charges of being 'irreligious' and of 'undermining Islam'. Their *nikahnama* can therefore not be understood simply as an open claim for secular women's rights but, as Amber has put it, as a contract that 'cunningly hides' the fundamental Constitutional rights it confers (for example, age of consent and a woman's right to legal protection and to live in dignity). What Amber calls 'hiding' is actually a process of vernacularisation wherein constitutional values are merged with religious knowledge, idioms, and practices. It allows Amber to minimise the criticisms of the conservative clergy and its supporters, who draw a sharp line between secular and religious laws. So, in a context within which women's legal mobilisation is constrained, the conceptualisation of gender justice as brought forward in this *nikahnama* cannot be understood within stereotype Western liberal parameters. Rather, the analytical eye has to adopt what Santos (1987, 288) calls a 'large-scale' or 'microscopic view' of the law in order to appreciate the subtle advancements concealed within seemingly normative formulations of Muslim women's rights.

In its introduction, the AIMWPLB *nikahnama* advises the couple on how to lead their conjugal lives and encourages Muslim to duly follow the rules set forth in the *Shariat*, listing crucial *Quranic* textual sources on a woman's right to *mehar*, property, maintenance during *iddat*, polygamy, and divorce. At first glance, Amber's vision of the conjugal relationship as set forth in this *nikahnama* does not seem to substantially differ from conservative conceptions that emphasise conjugal duties over rights. Similar to conservative versions of the marriage contract, this *nikahnama* adopts an image-based approach, which stresses two separate sets of rights for men and for women in marriage. The *hidayatnama* says,

> Husband and wife are supposed to respect and support each other. The husband cannot take his wife as a housekeeper because she likes him. He is also the master of the house and thus he must not overburden her with work. She too deserves respect. Likewise the wife must also respect and honour her husband. Both should be loyal to each other and must not cheat on the other partner.
>
> It is his duty of the husband to look after the welfare of his wife. He is to provide for her shelter, food, clothes etc. He is to do so to the best of his abilities.
>
> Both of them must treat each other well and happily. It is not right that when the wife goes out she dresses to her best but when the husband returns she meets him in her dirty clothes.
>
> The woman who loves her husband and is more ready to solve problems rather than creating them, and can apologise when she commits some mistake is surely someone who deserves paradise.

To outside eyes, such language is indiscernible from traditional conservative marriage contracts. Women are prompted to create a domestic environment of love and harmony and men are responsible for their financial welfare. However, in contrast to male-formulated versions, here women's subjectivity is not conceptualised in terms of her duty to obey her husband; rather, this *nikahnama* appeals to the bridal couple to respect and honour each other. This discourse on respect and honour, as employed in this *nikahnama*, allows a woman to demand certain obligations from her husband, such as for example to not force her into domestic labour, to provide for her financial maintenance, to remain faithful, and to mentally support her. Like Muslim women's rights activists working in other parts of the Muslim world, Amber sees no problem in fighting for gender justice within a discourse on gender that stresses their biological and social differences (Badran 1991; Foley 2004; Hassan 1995; Hatem 1998; Mir-Hosseini 2003; Moghadam 2002; Tripp 2003; Wadud 2009).

This discourse on mutual respect and honour penetrates the sociolegal imagery of the conjugal relationship throughout the whole document. For instance, the section that lays down the conditions under which a woman has the right to initiate a divorce reflects such a discourse. Since husbands often divorce their wives over trivial matters and even from afar, the AIMWPLB has included a clause in the section on *talaq* that prohibits triple *talaq* through email, SMS (short message service), phone, and videoconferencing. In case the husband divorces his wife in such a disrespectful manner, the *nikahnama* stipulates the wife's right to take *khul*. This is to separate from her husband extra-judicially. Furthermore, the *nikahnama* asserts that the divorce is only valid after it has gone through a mandatory process of arbitration over a time period of three months, as per *Shariat*. This includes the practice of *talaq-e-bain*. This requirement aims to prevent desertion of women and to give the couple a chance to reconcile. The third *talaq*, however, is final. Once the divorce is pronounced, the husband is obliged to give his ex-wife 'a warm farewell' and the *talaqnama* (decree of divorce) must be read aloud by a *Maulana* or scholar in the presence of two witnesses.[33] In the absence of a divorce, any woman can opt for separation if the whereabouts of her husband are unknown for the duration of four years, if he tortures her, if he commits adultery, or if he refused to disclose human immunodeficiency virus (HIV) status at the time of the marriage. Amber states that the latter stipulation is a reference to a *fatwa* (legal opinion) issued by the Islamic Fiqh Academy which stated that women have the right to unconditionally divorce their husbands who were HIV-positive at the time of marriage.

Furthermore, the section that stipulates the financial rights of the former wife is couched within language that stresses the notion of respect. This section mandates the husband to treat his former wife kindly and respectfully after the divorce. In this manner, the husband cannot deny shelter to his ex-wife in the matrimonial home during the period of *iddat*, nor has he the right to claim her property. Conversely, it is the husband's duty to pay her *mehar* to the best of his abilities. Although the *nikahnama* encourages the husband to financially support his wife beyond the *iddat* period in order to protect her from destitution, it is not a declared mandate. This also reflects the common practice of the High Courts in India that tend to interpret the terms 'fair' and 'reasonable' in the related provision of the Muslim Women (Protection of Rights on Divorce) Act of 1986 very broadly. Due to such an interpretation, Muslim women are entitled a one-time payment from their husbands during and beyond the time of *iddat* that could be worth *lakhs* (hundreds of thousands) of rupees. These amounts clearly exceed the meagre amount of money women tend to get under Section 125 of the CrPC. However, in cases where the ex-husband cannot financially afford to support his ex-wife after a divorce, 'fair' and 'reasonable' means that the wife is only eligible for a minimal amount in a lump-sum payment – if at all.[34] The terms 'fair' and 'reasonable' mentioned in this *nikahnama* have thus to be understood against the backdrop of these current court practices.

In contrast to the *Shariat* law, this *nikahnama* advises against polygamy and reminds the husband only to take a second wife if he is able to afford her and if the first wife agrees on the marriage. Further, this *nikahnama* includes two important stipulations which, as Amber explained in an interview, both reflect the efforts of the AIMWPLB to harmonise with secular state laws and to bring marriage and the family under the legal auspices of the state. The first one prohibits the marriage of juveniles. This *nikahnama* is the first to mention the age of consent otherwise not codified in Islam and may reflect the fact that there have recently been changes in Indian child marriage law. Traditionally, women are considered ready for marriage once they have reached so-called 'physical maturity', which usually means the beginning of menstruation. This leaves ample space for misuse and clashes with the formal state law that suggests a minimum female age at marriage of 18 years. The second stipulation declares the registration of marriage as mandatory. International policymakers and modernist thinkers have considered registration as most important in order to end discrimination against women and prevent forced child marriages. Registration of marriages grants legal approval to the marriage and further authorises the bride or the groom to claim the property and investments of the spouse in the case of his or her death or disappearance. Both stipulations regarding the age of consent and registration are in accordance with the secular Special Marriage Act of 1954.[35] In order to facilitate registration, the *nikahnama* suggests incorporating photos of the bride and the groom and their registered address, dates of birth, occupations, and nationality. Three forms of the *nikahnama* should be completed: one for the couple, one for the state marriage bureau,[36] and one for the *qazi* who has solemnised the marriage.[37]

This *nikahnama* constitutes a crucial counter-hegemonic voice in the debates on women's rights in South Asian Islam. It clearly challenges the clergy's stance of strict separation between the state and the Muslim community and between secular state law and religious family laws by creatively vernacularising state law with religious idioms and language. This contract facilitates a space of women's semi-autonomy in the shadow of the state within which normative discourses on the ideology and practice of the conjugal relationship are challenged and the legal authority of the Muslim leadership is fractured. In asking the state to support this version of the Muslim marriage contract, it seems that the AIMWPLB seeks to produce a hybrid form of legal authority through which women, backed by the state, could become authorised to interpret Islamic texts in order to define new rights for women within Muslim family law. However, such endeavour reveals Amber's acknowledgement that hermeneutics alone is not enough to correct harms that have been done in the name of conservative interpretations of the religious scripts. Without the backing of the state and its law enforcement, mechanisms that protect citizens hermeneutics is very limited. I believe that Amber's ideas are similar to those of feminist scholar Valentine Moghadam (2002, 1160) who asserts in the Iranian context,

> [A]lthough religious reform is salutary and necessary, it is important to acknowledge its limitations. Women's rights and human rights are best promoted and protected in an environment of secular thought and secular institutions, including a state that defends the rights of all its citizens irrespective of religious affiliation, and a civil society with strong organizations that can constitute a check on the state.

The idea that legal reform within the framework of Islam can only be achieved through the state legal framework is firmly advocated by Muslim women's rights activists in Lucknow that work in close proximity with the state, such as Naish Hasan (BMMA). While Amber and Hasan agree on the necessity of a re-reading of the *Quran* in the area of the family, Hasan, unlike Amber, not solely focuses on theological arguments but on socio-economic and political realities that structure state legal and political systems.

A Secular Reading of the Islamic Marriage by the BMMA

In an effort to further stretch this space of legal autonomy vis-à-vis the Muslim leadership, the BMMA released a so-called 'secular' version of the Islamic marriage contract in November 2008. This contract is subject to the exclusive jurisdiction of the court – and hence renders Muslim marriage subject to state control. This *nikahnama* has to be understood as a part of a larger project of the BMMA that seeks to codify Muslim Personal Law, which is then entirely administered by the state. This project of the codification of Muslim Personal Law is supported by a variety of secular Muslim women's groups all over India and organised under the auspices of the eminent scholar Asghar Ali Engineer, former head of the Centre of Islamic Studies and the Centre for Study of Society and Secularism, until his death on May 2013. The BMMA continues its collaboration with the Centre for Study of Society and Secularism for the codification of Muslim marriage laws to this day.[38]

The reason for the need of such a secular *nikahnama* is, according to Naish Hasan, twofold. First, it seeks to curtail the control of the Muslim leadership and its freedom to interpret Islamic laws. Second, it seeks to launch a thorough codification of Muslim Personal Law on the level of the state. This would, in her opinion, help to bring the Muslim community under the umbrella of state law in the area of the family and prevent the discriminatory ways in which Muslim Personal Law is currently adjudicated and interpreted by judges and advocates in the lower district courts. In order to initiate a process of codification of state-administered Islamic Laws, the BMMA engaged in a dialogue with lawyers and eminent scholars of Islam who Hasan calls the 'educated type of *qazi* and *Maulana*'.[39] However, as already mentioned above, such a strategy to expand state control over Muslim family laws will be hardly accepted by the Muslim majority, who tend to advocate for a separate legal space within which Muslim law is articulated and adjudicated. This is even more so given the resurgence of communal violence and the Indian state being unable to protect minority communities through the law (see Introduction).

This version of the contract is grounded in a discourse that envisions women's rights in terms of the complete equality of the sexes. Such an interpretation vehemently rejects concepts of biologically-based mental or emotional differences between men and women, and holds that they are equal. *Equal* here means that men and women share the same rights and duties and are valued equally in all areas of life. Contrary to all other versions, the *quranic* stances which establish the wife as the embodiment of love and honour and the husband as her 'provider' and 'protector' are nowhere mentioned in this *nikahnama*. Instead, Hasan, co-drafter of the contract, explains that their interpretation of the *Quran* takes into account the socio-economic situation of men and women in contemporary India. From such a perspective, Islam is reinterpreted in a manner that fits the contemporary daily realities of Muslim women. Nevertheless, due to their engagement with the Islamic texts and with their own faith, members of the BMMA do not see themselves as falling out of the Islamic framework with the formulation of a secular marriage contract. The first two *quranic* stances cited in the afterword illustrate nicely the BMMA's idea of social and economic gender equality in Islam:

> The rights of the wives (with regard to the husband) are equal to the (husband's) rights with regard to them (HQ 2:228)
>
> Men shall benefit from what they earn and women shall benefit from what they earn (HQ 4:32)

Within the paradigm of gender equality, this *nikahnama* dismisses all kind of unilateral and extra-judicial divorces, including the husband's rights to triple *talaq* and the wife's right to *khul* and *talaq-e-tafweez*. In so doing, the *nikahnama* establishes divorce as a right that is shared equally and only becomes valid with the agreement of both parties (*mubarat*). Polygamy, according to this *nikahnama,* is prohibited. The age of consent is 18 for the bride and 21 for the groom, as per the Prohibition of Child Marriage Act 2006. Note that this Act only applies to Hindus, Christians, Jains, Buddhists, and those who are non-Muslims in India. Muslim marriages are governed under the Muslim Personal Law (Shariat) Application Act of 1937, which does not restrict the age of marriage but merely asks for parental or custodial consent for marriage. Needless to say that while child marriages still exist among non-Muslim groups in India, the absence of a law that regulates Muslim marriages leaves ample room for misuse in this regard.

Given Muslim women's overall weak economic position within the family/conjugality, this *nikahnama* also focuses especially on the financial rights of the wife with regard to *mehar*, marital property, gifts, and maintenance. As Hasan explains, these financial rights are formulated in accordance with state-regulated Muslim Personal Laws such as the Dissolution of Muslim Marriages Act of 1939 and the Muslim Women (Protection of Rights on Divorce) Act of 1986, as well as with secular provisions such as Section 125 of the Criminal Procedure Code. The *nikahnama* itemises and registers the amount of *mehar* in cash or kind, such as gold, silver, fixed deposits, land, or cheques, and stipulates them as the sole property of the wife. As announced on their website, the *mehar* amount stipulated for marriages performed under this *nikahnama* range from Rs 5,000 (approximately US $97) up to Rs. 100,000 (approximately US $2,000).[40] This stands in sharp contrast with the majority of Muslim marriages, where women either 'forgive' (*maph karna)* their *mehar* and receive nothing or receive only a minimal amount. Very often, the dower, or *mehar*, is considered more a symbolic than a real matrimonial right.[41] In a separate annexure, the *nikahnama* lists the financial and material transactions that take place at the time of the wedding. This includes gifts received by the bride from her parents and relatives or from the groom's parents and relatives, as well as the articles received by the groom from the bride, his relatives, and friends. Both the bride and the groom sign the annexure.

The *nikahnama* further insists on women's right to equal share in all property acquired during the time of the marriage. In case of a divorce, the husband is obliged to financially maintain his former wife with a reasonable and fair provision (*mattaa*) that equals the amount of ten-year maintenance. *Mattaa*, as referred to in the *Quran*, delineates that maintenance for divorced women should be provided on a reasonable scale. This stipulation reflects the wording of the Muslim Women (Protection of Rights on Divorce) Act of 1986, according to which Muslim women are entitled to a 'fair' and 'reasonable' provision by their ex-husbands. Given that the amount of *mattaa* remains unspecified in the *Quran*, the Indian Muslim women's movement interprets the line so as to give adequate maintenance for the divorced woman even after the period of *iddat*. The activists involved in the drafting process of this *nikahnama* have hence decided on the 10-year limit. Such an interpretation stands in clear opposition to most the clergy's understanding of the term. As per classical law, under the *Hanafi* law position, maintenance payment beyond the *iddat* period is not permitted. *Mattaa*, in contrast, is a provision or maintenance referred to in Chapter II in the *Quran*, which is paid to the destitute ex-wife as a lump sum after the time of *iddat*. Hasan states that this provision of *mattaa* aligns the (ex-)husband's duty to pay maintenance with the secular Section 125 Cr. Pr. C., from which Muslim women are theoretically exempt, and with the Muslim Women (Protection of Rights on Divorce) Act of 1986, which was basically reiterated in the Danial Latifi case verdict from 2001 (see Introduction). There the husband is once again obliged to pay a 'fair' and 'reasonable' provision to his ex-wife after the divorce.[42] Further, the woman is now granted the right to reside in the matrimonial home during the subsistence of the marriage as well as after a divorce. This is in accordance with one of the most important features of the more recent Protection of Women from Domestic Violence Act of 2005. This Act, which is a general law and thus also applies to Muslim couples in India, provides for women's right to reside in the matrimonial or shared household, whether or not she has any titles in the household. This right is secured by a court-issued residence order.

In order to ensure the implementation of the financial rights and to prevent unilateral and instant divorces, this *nikahnama* provides for all the necessary documentation needed for governmental registration as per the Special Marriage Act of 1954. It mandates photographs of the bride and groom, a wedding invitation card (if available), a copy of the passport or any other identity card, a copy of the ration card, proof of employment, and, in case of an earlier divorce or a widowing, a divorce decree or death certificate. Apart from the address, date of birth, and marital status, the bridegroom is obliged to give information about his current occupation, his income, and the particulars of his property (self-acquired and inherited). Three forms have to be filled out, one for the bride, one for the groom, and one for the marriage solemniser. Moreover, this *nikahnama* affords the couple with the opportunity to add further stipulations as long as they do not violate the provisions of the original contract.

This *nikahnama* marks not only a change in the discourse of the conjugal relationship, but an important shift in terms of the language – a shift away from a religious cadence toward a judicial one. For instance, metaphors and references to religious sources in the contractual language have been omitted, while the phrasing has been brought into accordance with the judiciary style common to state law. It is only the afterword of the document that contains a set of *quranic* stances on maintenance, polygamy, *mehar,* and the ideal of a matrimonial relationship. The BMMA hence places its own formulations of gender equality and justice within this highly competitive legal and political landscape by appropriating the legal jargon of the state legal system. Doing so, the BMMA seeks to remove the regulation of Muslim marriages from the penumbra of the state by asking the state to integrate their proposal into its legal apparatus. This is to create a democratic legal space within which Muslim women's rights are articulated on the premises of the secular values of the Constitution and human rights. The Constitution and human rights thus appear, as Yüksel Sezgin (2013) states in the context of India, as a 'testing ground' for measuring and re-evaluating women's level of participation within the public and private sphere. In this case, to measure Muslim women's rights against national and international legal standards might not necessarily result in radical change, but enhances the BMMA's capacity to challenge existing power relations. Discourses on the Constitution and human rights are thus of political value even though the Indian state's enforcement of the same is rather lax.

Both the AIMWPLB's and BMMA's *nikahnamas* exemplify the fact that both religious and secular discourses of gender justice stand not in opposition, but merge within the localised discourses on women's rights and Islam – creating new forms of law within newly designed legal spaces. So, rather than being caught between the discursive strategies of a liberal versus religious discourse on equality and women's rights, both organisations claim that the Indian Constitution, the state-administered Muslim Personal Law, other secular laws, and the *Quran* are all sources of synergy and not conflict. It is thus the *in*clusion rather than *ex*clusion of modern secular legality, within local interpretations of Islamic laws, by which Muslim women's organisations stake their claim for participation in the lawmaking process. Such modes of legal 'translation' and 'vernacularisation' on the part of Muslim women's activists often leads to a 'shift in subjectivity', as theorised by Merry (2006), where the language of conjugal duties and responsibilities is – at least to some extent – replaced with a language on rights. This allows for the creation of a non-antinomic legal space of new interpretations and productions of Islamic laws within the context of Indian citizenship and the specific day-to-day realities of Muslim women in India.

However, I note that while these two versions of the model Islamic marriage contract have been successful in shaping discourses around marriage and Islam, they are not yet a part of legal reality. Be it out of ignorance of the contract, or fear of incurring the wrath of community and family authorities, Muslims in Lucknow hardly use the women-friendly versions of the *nikahnama*. In an attempt to increase the use of these documents the AIMWPLB and the BMMA have launched public campaigns and identified moderate *qazi* who agree to perform weddings on the basis of these alternative versions of the *nikahnama*. For example, Amber promotes her version of the *nikahnama* through her activity as a legal counsellor. In June 2009, she, together with her supporter *Maulana* Abdul Kayum, solemnised the remarriage of a couple. The couple had lived separately for fifteen years after the husband pronounced *talaq* twice upon his wife on the phone. Considering a marriage dissolved by *talaq-e-bain*[43] as revocable and a divorce pronounced over the phone invalid, Amber encouraged the couple to remarry using her model-*nikahnama*.[44] The BMMA, on the other hand, performed forty marriages in Juhapura district, Gujarat as a part of their activism, using their model-*nikahnama*.[45] Notwithstanding the practical limitations of these contracts,[46] I agree with A. Suneeta (2011, 59–60), who conceptualises these marriages contracts as important voices from within the community in contested debates on issues regarding marriage in Islam. These women-friendly contracts are thus a community reform launched by grassroots Muslim women's activists, rather than Western-thinking feminists or international women's rights advocates.

Transforming Normative Ideas of the Islamic Marriage and the Family

How do Muslim women's activists in Lucknow convincingly demonstrate that Islamic laws are not static doctrines but an ideology susceptible to ideas around human and women's rights? In this chapter, I predicated my analysis on two women-friendly versions of the marriage contract in order to illustrate the manners in which discourses on gender justice in Islam get fragmented within a politically and ideologically contested legal setting. To counter static and subjugating discourses on women's rights in Islam with the release of a women-friendly *nikahnama* is a well-chosen strategy. Instead of chiming in with liberal feminist struggles on women's rights within the private sphere, Naish Hasan and Shaista Amber challenge the clergy on their own turf: religious family law. These bold strides into debates about Islamic family laws – debates usually discussed within the triangle of the orthodox religious clergy, the state, and liberal feminists – sparked new controversy within the community, particularly amongst the AIMPLB-affiliated clergy. What exactly are women's duties within marriage? And what are their rights?

The four different versions of the marriage contract discussed in this chapter give insight into the heterogeneity of positions in the fierce debates on Muslim women's rights and their ambivalent relation with the state. Especially, the two women-drafted versions of the contract evince the tangled web of interrelationships between formal and informal discourses and legalities on women's conjugal rights in Islam. This is to say that the legal landscape in the city of Lucknow is complex: different legalities do not merely coexist but entangle and overlap in debates on marriage and gender in Islam. More often than not, women's activists establish their meanings and position on women's rights by drawing together legal discourses emanating from state legal institutions, quasi-judicial bodies such as the *Shariat*-courts, and international organisations such as women's rights organisations and the UN. The contracts scrutinised in this chapter illustrate that grassroots activists do not merely 'replicate' different legalities so as to get their point across, rather, they engage in processes of 'hybridisation' and 'vernacularisation' (Merry 2006). This is to draw on idioms, practices, and realities that structure everyday people's life in order to render their proposals of family law socially intelligible. In short, these contracts reveal a great deal about the complexity of the legal landscape. Santos (2000, 1987) theorised such complexity with the concept of 'interlegality' which he describes as 'a highly dynamic process because the different legal spaces are non-synchronic and thus result in uneven and unstable mixings of legal codes' (1987, 298). Within such an intricate legal landscape, women's rights discourses travel through institutions, documents, and activists' public actions and are appropriated by and mixed into both formal and informal sites of justice. Thus, the sociolegal spaces carved out by means of these contracts foster legal conceptions that allow for the formulation of positions on religion and gender that take into account both women's identity as members of the Muslim community as well as their rights as citizens.

It seems that it is precisely this very complexity of the legal field that opens up room and possibilities for Muslim women' rights activists to work toward gender justice beyond the normative dichotomies of the state/community and women's rights/religion. Destabilising both the state's patriarchal legal discourse as well as the Sunni clergy's mysogynist interpretations of marriage, these women-friendly versions of the Muslim marriage contract illustrate the paradoxical dynamic of centralisation and decentralisation of law allowing for spaces of legal transformation and pluralisation. Gender equality in this context emerges as uneven and complex and indicative of a multi-layered process of negotiation on knowledge and legal authority within the broader landscape. I therefore apprehend the polycentric legality in the area Muslim family law as a factor that facilitates Muslim women activists' efforts to destabilise, negotiate, and re-articulate notions of the family, gender, and religion. In what follows, I will step out of the elite discursive world of institutional politics and focus on the manners in which female litigants and activists navigate legal realities on the ground.

Endnotes

1. An earlier version of this chapter was published in the *Journal of Law and Social Research*. I am grateful for all the comments and suggestions made by the anonymous reviewers on previous drafts.
2. I have collected all versions of the model-*nikahnama* discussed in this paper. The *nikahnamas* unavailable in English haven been translated from Hindi and Urdu into English. The contracts are available in the Annex.
3. For a Muslim wedding to take place, the bride and her guardian must both agree on the marriage. Should either the girl or the guardian disagree on the marriage, it may not legally take place. In short, a father cannot force his daughter to agree to a marriage, but he can stop her from marrying someone he considers an unsuitable match. In Islam, the minimum requirements and responsibilities for a marriage are that the groom provides living expenses (food, clothes, housing, and maintenance) and

the bride, in return, has the responsibility to raise the children to be proper Muslims. In accordance with these basic requirements, other rights and duties such as property, inheritance, custody, and divorce can be stipulated. After all the parties have signed the contract in the presence of at least two male witnesses and the requisite words have been cited in front of a *qazi*, the marriage becomes valid. Right after the *nikah*, there is a feast, which is given by the bride's family. This feast is an indispensable part of the entire wedding (*shadi*) ceremony. The wedding is then publicised with a wedding banquet or *walimah*, which is the second feast, this time given by the groom's family. This *walimah* usually takes place in the same night as the first feast, after the bridal couple has gone to the groom's house, where the bridal bed is set up. But sometimes the consummation of the marriage does not take place right away because the couple is either considered too young or not ready yet for other reasons. In that case, the *walimah* may be delayed and only held after the bride has moved to the groom's house in a ceremony called *rukhsati*. The *walimah* takes place on the day after the couple has consummated the marriage to announce that this final step has been taken. (Interview with the AIMPLB executive committee member Begum Naseem Ali Ikhtedar Khan in Lucknow, February 13, 2011.)

4. The feminist and political scientist Carol Pateman (1988) has established the term 'sexual contract' to illustrate that the marriage contract is in its essence not an agreement between two individuals but a re-establishment of the asymmetric relationship between the sexes. She says: 'It is sexual in the sense of patriarchal – that is, the contract establishes men's political right over women – and also sexual in the sense of establishing orderly access by men to women's bodies' (1988, 2).
5. Similar to classic *fiqh*, there is a tendency in anthropological scholarship to focus on marriage as a system of exchange, or trafficking, of women between men in order to build alliances (Lévi-Strauss [1949] 1969; Rubin 1975). Maybe the most popular proponent of such an approach is the structuralist Claude Lévi-Strauss, who captured marriage as a system of exchange, wherein rights, goods, and persons are exchanged in order to build alliances between kinship groups. In his account, women are the most valuable gift of exchange between male kin. Building on Lévi-Strauss's definition of marriage as a system of 'exchange of women,' the feminist and anthropologist Gayle Rubin (1975) conceptualises marriage as 'a traffic in women', whereby women are transacted as passive objects between men. Women are thus considered as a conduit for the establishment of relations among men rather than partners. Rubin contends that it is this very asymmetry in the process of transaction at the time of marriage that establishes a gendered relation, wherein men are bestowed with certain rights over women. It is then this social transaction that is the locus of women's oppression (Rubin 1975). The anthropologist Marilyn Strathern (1984) has carefully rethought these concepts of marriage as an exchange or traffic of women. In so doing, she criticises the conception of marriage as a system of dual exchange, meaning the exchange or trafficking of women (brides) versus things between 'takers' and 'givers'. Drawing on Comaroff (1980) and using her own empirical material from Melanesia, Strathern (1984, 44) recasts marriage as a system that establishes social relations wherein the

actors formulate and pursue certain interests that might not be purely economical. Consequently, Strathern stretches Lévi-Strauss' and Rubins' conception of marriage by theorising it as a process of 'societal regeneration'. In other words, Strathern points to the aspect of the gendered motivations within marriage and the way agency is allocated differently within this scenario. She thereby shifts our attention away from women as objects of exchange to the possibility of agency that opens up for women within that very process. In her view, despite their value in marital transactions women are not denied agency. Rather, women too participate in creating networks and formulating their specific interests in this process.

6. Moreover, in Pakistan and Bangladesh, under the Muslim Family Law Ordinance, not only marriage but also the process of divorce is legally regulated. Under the ordinance, men may seek divorce by pronouncing *talaq* and giving written notice (*talaqnama)* to the chairman of the Matrimonial and Family Law Court and a copy to his wife (Pearl and Menski 1998, 334-335). With the divorce being officially registered, women can (theoretically) make effective their rights to maintenance, marital property, and custody after the divorce as stipulated under the Muslim Family Law Ordinance. However, Pearl and Menski (1998, 337) also point to the fact that despite the regulation of the conditions to the marriage by means of a standard *nikahnama*, there are substantial gaps in the Pakistani and Bangladeshi Muslim Family Law Ordinance, which makes it difficult to strictly implement the laws as set forth in regard to marriage and divorce (e.g. no limits are laid down by the Pakistani and Bangladeshi law about when to give the notice of divorce). Moreover, the lower courts often disregard gender-just stipulations made under the Muslim Family Ordinance legal practice in Pakistan and Bangladesh.
7. Interview with *Maulana* Dr. Abdul Kayum in Lucknow on February 19, 2011.
8. Interview with Hamza Abidi, Advocate at the Family Court in Lucknow, February 13, 2011.
9. India signed CEDAW on July 30, 1980. There, the state made a reservation stipulating that given India's vast population the registration of marriages was difficult to achieve in practice.
10. Merry (1990, 5) understands legal consciousness as "the way people conceive of the 'natural' and normal way of doing things, their habitual patterns of talk and action and their common–sense understanding of the world" in terms of the law.
11. 60 per cent of Muslim women are self-employed – mostly working from home. In urban areas, 15.7 per cent of Muslim women work as compared to 27.7 per cent for Hindu and 51.5 per cent for Christian women. Similarly, roughly 60 per cent of Muslim women in urban areas are illiterate. This is compared to 22.2 per cent of Christian and 25.3 of Hindu women. The female literacy rate among India's Muslims is a shocking 28.1 per cent (Seema Kazi Report 1999, 25).
12. Interview with Naish Hasan in Lucknow on January 22, 2010.
13. The Islamic Fiqh Academy initially emerged from conservative groups such as the Darul Uloom Deoband and the Darul Uloom Manzar-e-Islam, which all operate under the umbrella of the AIMPLB. Despite the fact that the Islamic Fiqh Academy came into existence in 1989 through the efforts of these conservative *ulema*, it now represents

a departure from orthodoxy in favour of a more flexible approach to Islamic law that allows for the reinterpretation of the textual sources of Islam (*ijtihad*), a practice that has been neglected by most Sunni *ulema*, who previously had largely relied on authoritative commentaries on the *Quran* and the *Shariat*. For a more detailed discussion of the Islamic Fiqh Academy see Narendra Subramanian (2008, 657–658).

14. Interview with Ateeq Ahmad Qasmi in Lucknow on February 12, 2011.
15. Such a rich and metaphoric legal language has been termed by Santos (1987, 295) as the 'biblical style of law'. He explains the concept of the biblical style of law as an approach to law which 'presupposes an image-based legality characterised by preoccupation with inscribing the discontinuities of legal interaction into the multi-layered contexts in which they occur, and with describing them in figurative and informal terms, and through iconic, emotive and expressive signs'.
16. The socio-economic relationship between husband and wife, as constructed in these different marital contracts, will be analysed with the help of the categories of equity and equality – a categorisation made by Foley (2004, 59) in her discussion on Muslim women's rights activism in Malaysia. Foley has argued that the strategies for the interpretation of the textual sources of Islam in regard to women's rights can be divided in two: equity and equality. Whereas equality rests on the premises of equal rights of men and women in a classical liberal sense, the notion of equity describes the strategy that envisages women's rights as rights due to them as wives and mothers. I draw on Foley's categorisation of equity and equality to unravel the plural notions of the conjugal relationship, gender, and religion across legal spheres.
17. Such an approach to law that deploys symbols and metaphors rather than traditional abstract legal language is also reflected in the rhetoric of two female members of the AIMPLB's executive committee who were both involved in the drafting of the new model-*nikahnama*. In an interview, Rukhsana Lari, a teacher at a Muslim Girl's college in Lucknow, describes marriage as a 'necessary union' that is essential in preventing 'social evil' (prostitution). Within that union, the woman is physically weaker and she is thus not 'made' to go out and work. But she is the 'queen of the house' and it is her duty to look after the children, house, and the husband's physical and emotional 'needs'. Women can only take up a job if it is for the 'betterment of society' (for example, if her husband is sick and unable to work or if she is doing charity work). It is in this respect Lari describes men and women as 'each other's garments'. Along similar lines, Fauzia Naseem, a professor of chemistry, expressed to me her views of married women as the 'guardians of good society' and as the cornerstone of 'Islamic' ideology. Within such an explanatory framework, the construction of female duties and rights is intimately linked with notions of purity (*halal*) and impurity (*haram*). Sexual purity prior to marriage is portrayed as the idealised requirement for Muslim women. In contrast to unmarried women, who are viewed as a potential danger to the social order, married women embody purity and act as the symbol of a 'good' society. For women, premarital, extramarital, or any other sexual expression outside of marriage (*zina*) is regarded as sinful, shameful, and immoral. Female sexuality needs thus to be vigilantly controlled and 'protected' prior to marriage and becomes only

legitimate within matrimony. Drawing on these two narratives, the theological, legal, and social assumptions brought forward in the AIMPLB's version of the contract (for example, women's need of men's protection, control of women's sexuality, women's inferiority to men) are broadly supported by orthodox Muslim women.

18. The judge of the *Shariat*-court in Lucknow offers an explanation to these omissions. In a personal conversation, he argued that the inclusion of the issue of divorce in a marriage contract draws a veil of negative sentiments over the otherwise happy occasion of the marriage. In his opinion, to think or talk about divorce at the time of marriage is not only rude and inauspicious but entirely inappropriate and causes the marriage to break more easily. In his opinion it is the duty of the *Shariat*-court to solve problems, in case there are any. Hence there is no need to make any extra-stipulations in the marital contract. Thus, unlike men, women are left with only little room to negotiate a divorce without the interference of the *qazi* or a lawyer. Shehnaz Sidrat (*Bazme Khawateen*) raises the same objections. She considers any extra stipulations in regard to divorce in the marriage contract as inauspicious for the marriage. In her opinion, such a stipulation is only necessary where the groom's family has doubts about the bride and her family, as is the case in marriages where the families do not know each other very well, in other words where there exists no established relationship of trust. The elderly female executive member of the AIMPLB, Begum Naseema Ali Iqtedar Khan, explains the neglect of the contract to include stipulations about divorce, saying that divorce among Muslims was rare. Having built a home and family, she says, a husband does not leave his wife easily. In her opinion, it is only after months and years of quarrel and discrepancies that the marriage is finally ended by unilateral *talaq*. Such statements reflect a highly idealised conceptualisation of marriage rather than social and legal reality.
19. However, the stipulation about the *mehar* has to be read carefully. It does not say anything about the amount that has to be paid as dower. The judge of the *Shariat*-court in Lucknow, for example, has told me in an interview that he had paid his wife a *mehar* of a hundred and seven rupees. This amount was fixed according to the amount that was given to Mohammed's daughter Fatima at the time of the Islamic revelation. This amount, however, does not protect a woman from financial despair after divorce.
20. Flavia Agnes, lawyer and women's activist, has described it as 'really unfortunate' that the AIMPLB discourages people from using the state courts. There are, however, several cases where women got justice from the *Darul Qaza* courts in regard of divorce and maintenance. See: http://www.frontlineonnet.com/fl2211/stories/20050603003303600.htm (accessed April 30, 2012).
21. Interview with Ateeq Ahmad Qasmi, *qazi* in the *Darul Qaza* in Lucknow on December 12, 2009.
22. See: http://www.indianexpress.com/news/aimplb-to-seek-marriage-registrar-status-for-qazis/972052/ (accessed August 26, 2012).
23. Interview with *Maulana* Mirza Mohammed Athar in Lucknow on February 24, 2011.
24. Though not mentioned by *Maulana* Athar, this stipulation of the *nikahnama* also corresponds with the Muslim Women (Protection of Rights and Divorce) Act of

1986. In 2001 the Supreme Court heard arguments concerning Section 3(1)(a), which stipulates the ex-husband's responsibility to pay his former wife a 'fair' and 'reasonable' provision of maintenance in terms of Article 14 and 15 of the Indian Constitution. There the Supreme Court held that a fair and reasonable provision extends through the period of *iddat* and until she remarries. See Danial Latifi vs Union of India: http://www.legalserviceindia.com/article/l141-Danial-Latifi-v.-Union-of-India.html (accessed August 23, 2012).

25. Interview with *Maulana* Athar in Lucknow on February 24, 2011.
26. For the reactions of Muslim women's groups and women's networks on the release and content of the AIMPLB's *nikahnama*, see: http://www.frontlineonnet.com/fl2211/stories/20050603003303600.htm (accessed April 30, 2012).
27. Despite the fact that these Muslim women's rights organisations use a discourse of human and women's rights they are not necessarily interlinked with transnational feminist movements, organisations, and networks. For instance, the AIMWPLB is, despite its generous use of discourses on human rights, not related to any other local, national, or transnational women's organisation – be it secular or religious. The BMMA in contrast actively networks with transnational development agencies such as UNICEF, USAID, and UN Women. The BMMA, moreover, receives funding from USAID.
28. Santos' (2002, 472) idea of subaltern cosmopolitanism highlights the ways in which the oppressed articulate their own conceptions and concerns about equality and difference. However, since alternative views have to be formulated within the limits and constraints of the discursive field, Santos describes legal hybrids as phenomena that mix heterogeneous legalities by means of disintegration and fragmentation.
29. This document is not available in English and has thus been translated by an interpreter. The original version in Hindi can be downloaded from: http://www.muslimwomenpersonallaw.com/index.html (accessed May 18, 2012).
30. Until today, the possibility for Muslim women to approach the court in case of a marital dispute has been restricted due to the lack of codification of Muslim family laws and peoples' general unawareness of their legal possibilities (Pearl and Menski 1998; Solanki 2007). For instance, under the Muslim Women (Protection of Rights on Divorce) Act of 1986, an unhappy Muslim woman is guaranteed access to the courts the moment the *iddat* period is over and she is dissatisfied with the arrangements made by her ex-husband. Since most Muslim women do not know about this, this Act is hardly used for the negotiation of financial and social arrangements *after* divorce. Additionally, the majority of Muslim marital cases are mediated and negotiated outside of the state legal system. A lot of cases are resolved either within the family or brought to the attention of a religious scholar (*alim)* who advises the couple and their families on how to proceed.
31. For a good discussion of the responses that have surrounded the release of the All India Muslim Women's Personal Law Board's version of the *nikahnama* see: Venkitesh Ramakrishnan, *Frontline*, April 11, 2008, http://pay.hindu.com/ebook%20-%ebfl20080411part2.pdf (accessed April 19, 2011).

32. The *nikahnama* is posted on the AIMWPLB website at http://muslimwomenpersonallaw.com/aboutus.html (accessed January 10, 2012).
33. In contrast to the Shia practice, Sunni jurisprudence does not declare the presence of witnesses as mandatory for a divorce to become valid. This way of interpreting *Shariat*-laws facilitates the husband to divorce his wife anytime and anywhere. In many cases, women do not even know about the divorce and might come to know about it through a third person.
34. In legal practice Muslim women are often granted substantially more money under the Muslim Women (Protection of Rights on Divorce) Act of 1986 (MWA) than under Section 125 of the CrPC. A female advocate at the Criminal Court in Lucknow explained to me that it was often more difficult to demand monthly payment, as granted under Section 125 CrPC, than the one-time payment Muslim women are entitled to under the MWA. (Interview with Risha Syedi, advocate at the Criminal Court in Lucknow on January 20, 2010).
35. The Special Marriage Act of 1954 is a secular piece of legislation that is not a part of the personal laws. It is applicable on all Indian citizens irrespective of their religion, but is hardly used by anyone. The Act provides for inter-faith marriages and the formal registration of marriages. The marriage performed under this Act is a civil contract and there is no need of rites or a ceremony. The Act considers a couple as eligible for marriage who have reached the age of consent (groom 21 and bride 18), who are monogamous, who are mentally competent to be able to give valid consent to the marriage, and who are not within the degree of a prohibited relationship. However, the Special Marriage Act also conflicts with the Prohibition of Child Marriages Act from 2006 and Muslim law as it considers marriages that have been solemnised between two parties who have not reached the age of consent as void. Under the Prohibition of Child Marriages Act of 2006, however, all child marriages are, although voidable and punishable, still not void. The *Shariat* recognises all marriages contracted with the consent of two parties who have reached puberty as valid. The stipulations set forth in this version of the *nikahnama* are further congruent with the Convention on the Elimination of all Forms of Discrimination Against Women, a transnational piece of legislation. As an attempt to end discrimination against women, CEDAW stipulates the right of women and men to choose their spouse, to share the same responsibility within matrimony, and to decide on the number of children as well as the spacing between them (Article 16). This convention states that child marriages should not have legal effect and that all marriages must be put into a register. India signed the convention on July 30, 1980. However, the Indian state made a declaration saying that given its vast population the registration of marriages was not a viable practice. Considering registration of marriages as the best strategy to prove that the marriage is valid, the AIMWPLB *nikahnama* would overturn the state's reservation toward registration and aligns its wording with secular national and transnational legislation.
36. *Marriage bureau* is the term Shaista Amber uses for the state registrar office.
37. Here it is important to again note that these stipulations are idealised expectations and not actually letters of the law. In India, the law declares the customary ceremony,

here the *nikah*, and not the actual act of registration is the dominant piece of evidence for the marriage. Although the spouses could register their marriage with the district registrar, most marriages in India remain unregistered. The reason for the high number of unregistered marriages among Muslims (and Hindus) could be a reflection of the fact that state intervention in the area of Muslim marriage is not acceptable to most Muslims. If this impression is true, then the AIMWPLB's strategy to selectively include state and law into societal laws will most likely remain an ideal rather than becoming socio-legal reality.

38. The BMMA's draft of The Muslim Family Act, a document that sets out the guidelines for the codification of Muslim Personal Law, can be downloaded here: http://bmmaindia.blogspot.com (accessed June 23, 2015).
39. Here, Naish Hasan uses this terminology of the 'educated type' in order to contrast those clergy who support the agenda and activities of the BMMA with those who reject it by arguing that the interpretation and administration of Islamic laws fall into the purview of male clerics and not 'lay' women.
40. See: http://bhartiyamuslimmahilaandolan.blogspot.com (accessed December 8, 2011).
41. Dower or *mehar*, signifies the husband's responsibility to pay a fixed amount of money to his wife at the time of the wedding (*nikah*). In practice, *mehar* is rarely given to the woman at the time of the marriage. Most of my female informants, belonging to a variety of educational and economical groups, have stated that they have not received any amount of *mehar*, even after having been in the marriage for decades. Whereas women from a privileged background have felt that the *mehar* was an outdated and old-fashioned practice that reduces women to mere objects of trade, women from less privileged backgrounds often find it as disturbing to ask for their dower. Moreover, it is common sense among Muslims in Lucknow that *mehar* is a financial right that becomes effective at the time of divorce, not the time of marriage. For example, at the Family Court in Lucknow I have interviewed six Muslim women who have all approached the state legal system to make effective their financial rights according to the *Shariat* and Muslim Personal Law. All of them were either separated or divorced from their husband and none of them had received their *mehar*.
42. Today, the Muslim Women (Protection of Rights on Divorce) Act of 1986 basically says the same as Section 125 of the CrPC. Risha Syedi, the feminist and advocate at the Criminal Court in Lucknow, explained to me that in fact Muslim women are often granted larger sums of money from their ex-husband under the Act from 1986 than under Section 125. This is because it was easier to secure the lump-sum payment, which could be as high as Rs. 90,000 (US $1,650) from the ex-husband, than to claim the monthly payments that could be as low as Rs. 500 (US $9). Moreover, Syedi argues, husbands would often stop paying after a few months.
43. *Talaq-e-bain* is a term indicating that if the husband has pronounced *talaq* only twice before deciding to remain in the marriage, the couple can be remarried in the presence of a *Maulana*.
44. Images of this marriage are posted on her website: http://muslimwomenpersonallaw.com/news5.html (accessed January 31, 2013).

45. See their website: http://bhartiyamuslimmahilaandolan.blogspot.com (accessed May 29, 2012).
46. Sabiha Hussain (2006/2001) and Sylvia Vatuk (2013) have both argued that these model-*nikahnama* are elitist. According to Hussain (2001, 145), the *nikahnama* is a document that is mostly in use among certain sections of upper–class Muslims in India, with poor and illiterate Muslims hardly making any use of it. According to my data, this assumption is not entirely true. Most of the poor Muslim women I have interviewed in the Family Court, stated that their marriage has been solemnised with a written *nikahnama*. However, the fact that this document is in many cases not in their possession renders it difficult for them to produce it in court as an evidence of their marriage. Evincing from my data, only well-educated Muslim women from a wealthy background have stated that they have inserted clauses such as their right to pocket money (*kharacha-e-pandan*) or *talaq-e-tafweez* (delegated right to divorce) in their *nikahnama*. For example, Fatima, which is a fictive name to protect her anonymity, the daughter of a well-known heart surgeon in Lucknow, has divorced her estranged husband by drawing on her right to *talaq-e-tafweez* that was enshrined in her *nikahnama*. (Interview with Fatima in Lucknow on October 10, 2009).

Chapter 5

Legal Realities

Doing Gender Justice from Below

'In the state courts, the truth of the cases remains hidden behind the lawyers' interests. There, women are just puppets in the hands of men. You only get justice if they consider you 'good'. Also in the *Darul Qaza*, the *qazi* is more interested to demonstrate his religious authority than in the lives of women'. This voice belongs to a young Muslim woman, whom I call Nisha. Nisha is a victim of domestic violence and a recent divorcee. For more than two years, she unsuccessfully sought to obtain maintenance for her daughter and herself in the Lucknow Family Court. Despite having spent all her saving money on court and lawyer fees, she has not 'found justice' or, '*insaaf nahi milla*', as she says. As it emanates from Nisha's narrative, the state legal system's approach to women's rights is neither context nor value free. Instead, the formation of legal subjectivity, and thus women's access to 'justice', is more often than not shaped by the court's concern to uphold standards of 'ideal feminine behaviour' – rather than egalitarian notions of citizenship. Similarly, the *qazi* of Lucknow's *Darul Qaza* is, according to Nisha's portrayal, not inclined to prioritise women's lives over often – orthodox interpretations of the religious scripts.

Finding herself in great financial despair and with no support from her natal family or community members, such as the religious authorities who run two *darul qazas* in the city or the *Maulana* from the local mosque, Nisha sought help and support with *Bazme Khawateen.* Shehnaz Sidrat has opened the doors of her office about a decade ago to Muslim women litigants who wish to solve their family disputes apart from the men-dominated state and *Shariat*-courts. The All India Muslim Women's Personal Law Board (AIMWPLB) also offers legal counselling and support for those who wish to solve their disputes in a cheap and efficient manner. As Shaista Amber told me, there was an urgent need for a women-friendly legal forum in the city of Lucknow, where women's problems and concerns were taken seriously. Both Shehnaz Sidrat and Shaista Amber lament the absence of any progressive women-friendly clergymen in the city. They both state that the clergy in the city is more concerned with establishing and demonstrating their socio-political authority – locally and nationally – than with the concern of women. In fact, during the nine months of fieldwork in Lucknow, I learned that these informal mediations and counselling centres are often the only place where especially poor women's concerns in regard to domestic violence, marital rejection, polygamy, child custody, property, and maintenance are heard and taken seriously.

Based on semi-structured interviews with litigants in the Family Court, judges and lawyers and non-participant observation in the *Darul Qaza*, the offices of *Bazme Khawateen* and the AIMWPLB, this chapter aims at providing ethnographic snapshots of the processes of dispute settlement within Lucknow's polycentric legal context. These snapshots are intended as a lens through which to capture the particular logic of dispute settlement within a specific context. While such non-longitudinal approach based on non-participant observation limits, at least to some extent, the dialogue as well as the intersubjectivity between participant and observer, it nevertheless allows for a context-sensitive and comparative approach to dispute settlement in the city. So, in this chapter, I am not aiming at offering an extended-case analysis as for example theorised by (Burawoy 1998).[1] Rather, the goal is to dismantle some of the logics that structure imaginations of the family, marriage, gender, and religion in the context of dispute settlement within a variety of sociolegal settings. My analysis of these snapshots that constitute the cases brought to the Family Court and the offices of Muslim women's rights organisations in Lucknow is thus based on discourse analysis of the dialogues and narratives from within these forums. For analytical purposes I define a case as a dispute that is either ongoing or resolved.

The first part of this chapter looks comparatively at the manner in which women's subjectivity is constructed within the Family Court and the *Darul Qaza*. Such analysis augments our understanding of how class, race, gender, and religious affiliation structure processes of legal marginalization in the area of family law within Lucknow's men-dominated legal landscape. Drawing from these insights, this chapter then explores in a second part the opportunities the offices of Muslim women's rights organisations provide for the articulation of legal subjectivity in the area of the family for subaltern (Muslim) women. This chapter theorises these women's offices as elastic epistemological spaces within which meanings of womanhood, freedom, egalitarianism, and equality are revised and re-configured beyond the citizenship-Islam dichotomy.

Rights and Subaltern Legal Subjectivities

Throughout this book, my analysis of the manners in which Muslim women's activists in the city of Lucknow negotiate Muslim women's rights illustrates the plurality of sociolegal constructions of Islam, marriage, and the family that influence ideas of gender justice in institutional struggles over legal authority. Moreover, such analysis brings to the fore that the categories of rights, justice, religion, and Islam are neither static nor hermeneutically sealed, or clearly defined. Instead, I argue, these very categories are shaped by the competing forms of knowledge and power that structure current ideological and political struggles on legal authority in the city of Lucknow. Such findings mark a departure from mainstream scholarship on Islam in South Asia where the discursive plurality in the area of family and marriage all too often remains eclipsed by an understanding of the Muslim community as homogeneous and highly conservative. In this chapter, I will thus take this discussion a step further by focusing on how the tensions around the constitution of the subject and the meaning of justice and equality are crystallised in the process of dispute settlement within the family court, the *Darul Qaza,* and the offices of Muslim women's rights activists.

Let me start with a discussion about some of the sociolegal dilemmas that structure women's rights positions and legal subjectivities on the ground. As discussed in Chapter 1, the Indian Constitution is a liberal document that reflects an Enlightenment approach to abstract equality where all citizens are entitled to the same rights and legal protection under the law – regardless of their race, caste, gender, and religion. However, the manner this liberal document was adapted in the Indian context illustrates the successive governments' intent to forward the rights claims of minority groups and the idea of group-differentiated citizenship. In so doing, the postcolonial Indian state adopted a dual approach to equality: this is an approach that establishes formal equality within the public sphere and guarantees religious freedom and the protection of minority rights within the private sphere (Narain 2013, 95). Feminist scholars have argued that such dual approach to justice, which establishes a sharp distinction between the private and the public sphere, renders women vulnerable to discrimination in the area of the family that is regulated by religion-based personal laws (Kapur and Cossman 1996; Hasan 1999, 1998; Narain 2013; Sunder Rajan 2003). In this respect, since the state's guarantee of equality does not extend to the family, women in India are simultaneously included and excluded from equal citizenship (Narain 2013, 95).

Notwithstanding feminist criticism, however, it is important to note that the Indian Constitution also leaves room for transformation in favour of social equality. For example, taking Article 15 which prohibits any form of discrimination on the grounds of religion, caste, race, and sex, or place of birth seriously, the Indian government has set up a statutory body called the National Commission on Women under the National Commission for Women Act 1990, implemented programs and schemes in favour of women, and is signatory to all principal international covenants and conventions including the Declaration of Human Rights (1948) and the UN Convention on the Elimination of All Forms of Discrimination Against Women (CEDAW) (1979). Furthermore, since the 1990s, the Supreme Court has shown some enthusiasm in reaching decisions in favour of equality rights within religious personal laws. For example, in the case of *C. Masilamani Mudaliar & Ors v. Idol of Sri Swaminathaswami Thirukoil & Ors*, Supreme Court, India, 30 January 1996, the Supreme Court ordered that women in fact are entitled to full property left to them in a will. To not do so would constitute an infringement on Article 2 and 16 of CEDAW.[2] Recently, in October 2015, Supreme Court Justices Anil R. Dave and Adarsh Kumar Goel took a decisive step back from the Shah Bano ruling of 1985, as discussed in the Introduction, by asking for a Public Interest Litigation to be registered to examine whether the discrimination suffered by Muslim women in matters of marriage, polygamy, and divorce infringes on women's Constitutional rights as enshrined in Article 14 (equality clause), Article 15 (anti-discrimination), and Article 21 (protection of life and personal liberty), as well as in international conventions and covenants.[3] Such advance on the part of the judiciary to deal with issues of rights that discriminate against Muslim women has unsurprisingly sparked opposition on the part of the Muslim clergy, in this case the Jamiat Ulama-i-Hind, who feel that their freedom to religion is infringed upon.[4]

So, while the Indian government in the 1990s has taken programmatic steps to improve women's access to justice and the Supreme Court is currently engaging in deliberations on the future of Muslim women's rights in the area of the family, the legal realities of especially poor Muslim women on the ground has hardly improved. The lack of effective legislation in the area of especially Muslim family laws combined with structural inequalities that contribute to Muslims overall low socio-economic status – 50 per cent of all Muslims in the subcontinent live below poverty line with a monthly income of Rs. 150 (US $2.19) (Kazi Seema Minority Report 1999) – negatively affects women's rights position on the ground. In fact, the great majority of Muslim women litigants I have interviewed at the Lucknow Family Court and in the offices of Muslim women's rights organisations hailed from the lower and lower-middle class. The plot of their collective stories is similar: the majority of them had been thrown out of their marital homes or divorced by their husband against their will. Their (ex-) husbands were employed in a range of low-paying jobs. These included work as manual labourers, tailors, traders, or owners of small businesses. Some toiled in low-ranking office and government jobs, or as car and bicycle mechanics. The women, who found themselves with no financial means to support themselves after the marital rejection by their husbands, had returned to their relatives' homes, or their natal place, where they then resided. Such a return, however, is inextricably coupled with the loss – for the women and for their natal family – of social reputation and honour. Moreover, these women deeply felt the financial burden that they imposed upon their relatives. In India, in lieu of any functioning welfare system, divorced women and their children often rely financially upon their relatives. In light of this, women tend to prefer to stay in dysfunctional or abusive marriages rather than lose their social and economic footing. Generally, the episodes of violence were linked to dowry demands, the failure of the woman to conceive, or the general dissatisfaction of the husband with his wife.[5] In all scenarios, the husband had either already remarried or expressed his desire to do so in the near future.

The stories above bolster the insight offered by Indian postcolonial and feminist legal scholars such as Nivedita Menon (1998) or Ratna Kapur (2014a, 2013) who argue that there exists a discrepancy between rights, law, and legal subjectivity. Both, Menon and Kapur, challenge the very core assumption of the liberal project that more laws equal more rights and a steady forward path to social equality, as opposed to being a governance project that creates gendered in- and exclusion as outlined above. In fact, as the narratives above show, women's lack of economic resources and the possibility of social stigmatisation in case of a divorce prompt many women to stay in an abusive relationship rather than to opt out. Needless to say that women in this context are not merely citizens unfettered by their familial and community ties as a classical liberal reading of the Constitution suggests. Instead, these stories illustrate that 'the abstract subject [is] not standing separate from the particular and local', as the feminist Leti Volpp (2001, 1201) puts it. In line with critical legal and postcolonial feminist scholarship, these narratives expose the gap between what should be generally assumed when we talk about the protection of women's rights through the law and of how rights and access to justice derives from specific moral norms and values that are placed outside the monolithic liberal rights discourse. Drawing from these narratives, I borrow from Ratna Kapur (2014a, 28) and argue that while these stories might indicate the limitation of the pre-given liberal subject, it does by no means mark the death of the subject. Then for example, Locke's idea of the value-free and universal liberal subject, in fact, consists a moot point when considering the many circuits of power that structure subjects' actions, desires, and imaginations on the ground. So, I contend, these narratives are indicative of the production of subaltern (legal) subjectivity.

The term subaltern, which in broad terms refers to the lower and voiceless class/individual of society, was initially coined by Antonio Gramsci in his prison notebooks. The term was then re-appropriated by the Subaltern Group[6], a group of Indian postcolonial scholars, as a response to the underrepresentation of non-Western voices in political, legal, and historical scholarship and discourse. This line of scholarship draws our attention to the hegemonic power inherent in establishing and legitimising the interests and superiority of the socio-economic elite that then appears as normal, normative, and ideal. In regards to law, subaltern studies defy the idea of law as a neutral entity and as a universalising force that necessarily results in social equality and justice (Bhabha 1990; Chakrabarty 1996; Spivak 1988). Such subaltern approach has influenced critical feminism (Mohanty 1988) and race theory (Collins 2000, 2015; Crenshaw 1991) that examine the dominance of men, and especially white men, who control the production of knowledge and epistemologies that underpin political, social, and economic interests. Knowledge validation processes, they argue, thus reflect the interest of the dominant group (Collins 2015, 271). However, the process of creating hegemonic domains of naturalised men-dominated power, critical feminist/race scholars argue, does not deprive dissent and oppressed groups, in this case (black) women, of agency. Instead, an analysis of the hegemonic function of social, political, and legal organisations allows for an exploration of the possibilities for counter-hegemonic struggles of resistance and transformation (Mohanty 1988; Spivak 1988).

This is precisely what this chapter intends to examine. Borrowing from such anti-essentialist approaches to social and political processes of marginalisation and hierarchy, I use the concept of subaltern legal subjectivity so as to understand the manners in which Muslim women litigants, and especially those hailing from lower socio-economic background, are positioned within the processes of dispute settlement in the Family Court and the *Darul Qaza*. Drawing from the shared experiences of Muslim women litigants, this chapter aims at providing a better understanding of how women's subjectivities in the process of dispute settlement are constructed and deployed against the background of normative ideas of justice and equality in the area of the family. Referencing the above-mentioned postcolonial and critical approaches that examine how subjects placed on the margins conform and/or resist dominant ideas of social, political, and economic organisation, I will focus on how litigant Muslim women's understanding of the legal world – their 'legal consciousness' (Ewick and Silbey 1992) – shapes their actions under the law. In so doing, this chapter does not primarily ask about the efficacy of women's rights discourse. Instead, it examines the manners in which Muslim women litigants from different socio-economic and ideological backgrounds submit, reproduce, or disturb the apparent normalcy of orthodox and patriarchal ideas of gender relations within Lucknow's family court, the *Darul Qaza*, and the offices of Muslim women's rights organisations.

In so doing, I ask: How do women litigants' differing identities as mothers, wives, and Muslims combined with their structural position in terms of class and education contribute to their marginalisation within Lucknow's two most dominant arenas of dispute settlement in the area of Muslim family law? How do these identities intersect and shape multiple dimensions of women's experience under the law? To what extent do women litigants placed on the margins challenge dominant epistemologies on gender relations within marriage and the family?

Constructing Women's Legal Subjectivity within the Family Court and the *Darul Qaza*

Doing justice in the Lucknow Family Court

Lucknow's intricate sociolegal landscape in the area of Muslim family law is comprised of the police, the Uttar Pradesh State Commission for Women (*Rajya Mahila Ayog Adhiniyam*),[7] the Family Court, the Criminal Court, and the offices of Muslim women's rights activists (see Chapter 2). The Family Court is Lucknow's most widely used institution for the adjudication of Muslim family law. The Family Court in Lucknow is a bustling place – especially between 11:30 in the morning and 4 o'clock in the evening when the judges (if present) hear cases in the two hearing rooms, with sessions interrupted by a one-hour lunch break. On average, a judge hears between 60 and 80 cases in three hours, allotting less than three minutes per case. At my visits, the judge had already assessed eight cases within the first ten minutes of hearings. These cases included: three cases for *dawa rukhsati*, one case for maintenance in which the man claimed not to have sufficient financial capacity to maintain his four children,[8] one case for divorce by mutual consent, and three cases for maintenance, which were filed under Section 125 CrPC. In all, just over one minute was invested per case in reaching the day's rulings.

Many litigants I have interviewed were deeply frustrated with the manner in which their cases were cycled through the process of adjudication in the Family Court rooms as well as the manners in which their cases were handled by their advocates. For example, Salma, a young and childless Sunni Muslim woman who was married at the age of 16 and divorced by triple *talaq* one-and-a-half years later, says,

> He pronounced *talaq* in a quarrel with me. But I didn't hear him saying *talaq*. The things were like this. First of all he beat me and then he threw me out of his house. He just left me after our fight and got married to another woman. When we came to know that my husband got married again, my lawyer advised me to file under the Dowry Act in order to make my case stronger. I have changed my lawyers a lot. My husband bribes them. My current lawyer is also not working well. Nothing happens here in the court.

Similarly, the seamstress Sahar – a 34-year-old Sunni who was divorced by her husband of whom she has one daughter, laments,

> My husband has given me *talaq*. I didn't want the divorce. I wanted to live with him. He came to me and gave *talaq* in written form in front of so many people. I felt so humiliated. I filed under the Dowry Act and for maintenance under Section 125 for my daughter. I wanted to stay with my husband, but he divorced me. What else could I have done? I want justice and my rights. I want him to pay maintenance for my daughter and me. But the advocates do not take my case seriously and the judges never take time to actually look at my case.

Yet another litigant, the 20-year-old Ayesha childless and Sunni whose husband physically abused her before he finally threw her out of the matrimonial home argues,

> He troubled me a lot. He used to beat me. He wanted money from my father so that he could start his own business. Two *lakhs* [US $3,700]. My parents have five daughters. How can they help him? I have filed under the Dowry Act and for maintenance [Section 125 CrPC]. Nothing has happened so far. They [in-laws] come to the court irregularly. So we got one date after the other. My case has been going on in the court for about two years. The lawyers make a fool of us people. I have changed my lawyers four times. And the judges just don't care![9]

The portrayals of the Family Court by these three Muslim women litigants resonate with critiques of the Indian courts offered by Indian feminists and political scientists as slow, inefficient, corrupt, and not interested in the grievances of litigants and of especially litigants belonging to the lower socio-economic echelon. So, despite the fact that the Family Courts in India established under the Family Courts Act in 1984 were intended to grant easier access for especially marginalised women to deal with cases regarding divorce, maintenance, adoption, and custody (see Chapter 2), these narratives show that women are often at the mercy of judges and advocates who have little, or no interest in women's actual lives. The Family Courts initially being inaugurated as a cheap legal forum that encourages self-representation so as to avoid costly advocates, especially women from lower socio-economic background with minimal education do more often than not lack confidence for self-representation. As Solanki (2011, 94) writes in the context of the Mumbai Family Court, such privilege is reserved for women with high school level education and above. Moreover, as Indian feminists such as Ratna Kapur and Brenda Cossman (1996), Srimati Basu (2012), and Veena Das (2008) point out, the courts in India do 'not necessarily provide a supportive atmosphere free from expectations of conventional gendered behavior (Basu 2012 476)'.

For example, during my research, I collected and analysed six Family Court rulings on petitions filed under Section 125 CrPC. As shown in these documents, Muslim women were most likely to obtain a judgement in their favour if they could successfully reiterate their subjectivity as a 'good wife', 'good mother', and 'good daughter-in-law'. The court rulings in favour of women produced the plaintiff as a person that is 'doing her duties as a good wife', 'observes *purdah*', 'gave birth to her husband's children', and that 'fulfils her husband's demands'. So, the 'good litigant' is not a woman who expresses her autonomy and self-interest in court, but one who tells her story as one of devotion to her in-laws, children, and husband. As shown in these documents, advocates and judges at the Family Court in Lucknow tend to construct the social problem through a patriarchal legal discourse that stresses women's submissiveness and propriety over men's material and social responsibilities within marriage and the family.[10] In this respect, as argued by Indian legal feminists such as Srimati Basu (2006), Zoya Hasan and Ritu Menon (2005), Rajeswari Sunder Rajan (2003), Nivedita Menon (2002), or Ratna Kapur and Brenda Cossman (1996), the formal Indian courts all too often perpetuate, rather than abolishes, oppressive values and practices in regard to gender and class. This is further strengthened with the ongoing process of informalisation of the Family Courts in India, where substantive laws tend to be sidelined and where perceptions of lawyers and judges play a large role in the process of dispute settlement. However, as Solanki (2011) points out, while courts can be gender-unjust, it is more complex. Solanki further argues that the presence of pro-active, creative, and legally-well-versed judges, informal and formal networks and exchanges between social workers, academics, feminist activists and lawyers, NGOs and women's groups, as well as court personnel – judges, lawyers, and social workers of the Family Court – coupled with individual legal mobilisation are some factors changing and challenging institutional and legal patriarchies in the Family Court. While the courts are without a doubt an important avenue for initiating and implementing sociolegal reform, this is a sluggish process.

This line of scholarship ties in with the feminist critique of the Indian state offered for example by the eminent legal scholar and activist Flavia Agnes. Her work on anti-violence against women laws reveals the inefficacy of these laws to actually change attitudes toward women within marriage and the family. Instead of actually protecting women from violence, Agnes argues, the Indian state has successfully strengthened its authority and power to define and control ideas around family and marriage (Agnes 1992). Agnes' work as well as more recent feminist legal studies (Basu 2015; Solanki 2011; Subramanian 2014) theorise the Indian state as an authority that all too often establishes, rather than challenges, mechanisms of marginalisation and hierarchy in terms of gender, class, religious affiliation, and race by deploying marriage laws as a norm to establish community values. In this scenario, the Indian state seems more concerned with upholding and protecting 'traditional' ideals of womanhood rather than implementing a more inclusive civil rights framework. Such approach has most recently become blatantly visible in the series of rape cases that have created international uproar. While the Indian government has reformed its penal code, extending the definition of rape and providing for the death penalty in cases of non-marital rape after the 2012 Delhi rape case where a 23-year old woman was gang raped on a bus after coming back from the movie theatre with her male friend, the current Indian government under Prime Minister Narendra Modi has failed to effectively address and tackle structural issues of violence against women (Roychowdhury 2016).

However, notwithstanding the fact that the formal legal system and law reinforces relations of subordination through gendered legal discourse and practice, the formal legal system nevertheless provides space for resistance. While most Muslim women litigants I have interviewed at the Lucknow Family

Court have addressed this formal legal institution with great reluctance – fearing the social and the material damage that a court procedure might inflict – they do not necessarily engage with this legal authority to negotiate claims within the purview of the law. In fact, two out of six litigants I have talked to on the Family Court premises stated their hope to restore societal respect and honour through the formal courts.[11] The 20-year old divorcee Ayesha whose husband swiftly re-married after having refuted her, says: 'He got married to another woman. I want everything back so people respect us again. I don't know what to do. My husband won't keep me'. Or, the 34-year-old Salma whose husband has failed to pay maintenance for her and their daughter after the male-initiated unilateral divorce states,

> I want justice and my rights. I want him to pay maintenance for my daughter and me. He is a government employee. I want my share in his income. I want to re-install my and my family's reputation in society. I am not giving up. So far, I have spent about two lakhs [US $3,700] or even more than that. You can imagine how much money you spend in the court in twelve years!

Both, Ayesha and Salma have filed cases under Section 125 CrPC in the Family Court. This secular section allows divorced and married women to claim maintenance for themselves and for their children. While Salma and Ayesha use the space created by this legislation to reclaim the money and the jewellery that their parents gave them at the time of their wedding, their legal claims are not exclusively economically motivated. More pressing is the position of societal disgrace in which the women who have been repudiated – as well as their birth families – invariably find themselves. Spending more money on court fees than a positive maintenance order would ever afford them, these women use the space provided by the legislation to negotiate societal respect and honour. These examples show that while these women might not necessarily trust the formal courts as an avenue to get justice in the strict legal sense, they strategically involve the Family Court as a means to urge their husband and his family to get exposed and ideally humiliated through the formal court system. To this end, I argue, Ayesha and Salma's tactical engagement with this formal institution affords them agency through the symbolic power the formal court and laws represents in people's everyday life. This is to say that despite the state's patriarchal management of marriage and the family and officials' disparaging interpretation of Muslim Family and criminal laws, this formal institution nevertheless affords room for women to contest gender relations and kinship – even if outside the purview of the law (Holden 2008; Solanki 2011;

Vatuk 2005). To this end, the state appears as an incoherent and multifaceted ensemble of power relations that allows for both – domination and resistance.

So, despite the Family Court being the most widely used legal institution among Muslims in Lucknow, the number, in fact, culled from a statistic provided to me by AALI, a Lucknow-based feminist advocacy and legal initiatives group, shows that cases filed under Muslim Law in the Lucknow Family Court between 2006 and 2010 are significantly lower than the number of cases filed under the Hindu Marriage Act. For example, between 2006 and 2010, 564 cases were filed under the Dissolution of Muslim Marriage Act (DMMA) (1939). This is in comparison to 4160 cases filed under the Hindu Marriage Act (HMA) (1955) during the same time period.[12] These numbers, however, are not representative of the divorce rates or even legal mobilisation among Hindus and Muslims in the city. Gopika Solanki (2011) and Livia Holden (2008) both show that Hindu divorce and other marital issues that fall under the HMA are negotiated across a broad institutional spectrum ranging from the Family Court over notary offices and caste *panchayats* to women's organisations and political parties. Similarly, a large portion of Muslim divorces is not brought to the courts. This is firstly due to the reason that Muslim men can easily repudiate their wife by means of triple *talaq*, which does not require court intervention. Muslim women, however, can challenge triple *talaq* in courts through Section 125 CrPC. Secondly, while Muslim women can file for *khula* in the Family Court, they can also negotiate a divorce (*khula* and *faskh*) in the *Darul Qaza*, the offices of women's organisation, or through a *Maulana* of the local mosque. In fact, especially Muslim women from lower socio-economic backgrounds interviewed in the Family Court and in the offices of Muslim women's organisations in Lucknow stated their mistrust in the formal legal system, which not only is costly and sluggish, but also once involved leaves very little room for reconciliation within their marriage.[13] Moreover, as stated above, these women feel that the courts and court officials are not interested in their marital problems. While most of the women I interacted with stated that they had before filing a case in the court tried to solve the quarrel internally through family meetings, some women stated that they had additionally engaged in dispute-settlement processes guided by the *Maulana* in their local mosque or the *qazi* in one of Lucknow's two *darul qazas* (see Chapter 2).

In fact, the withering reputation of the Family Court amongst Muslims in the city of Lucknow prompted the *qazi* affiliated with the Deoband seminary Darul Uloom Nadwatul to call for a 'revival' of community justice in the city of Lucknow – and elsewhere in India. In a personal conversation in December 2009 he stated, 'The state courts are not making good decisions (*faisla*) for Muslim women. We from *Nadwa* know how to interpret the *Quran*. The *Darul Qaza* is a very women-friendly place. We work toward the well-being of Muslim families, and this concerns women in a very important way'. According to him, the court of *Allah* provides women with the opportunity to fully vent their grievances *vis-à-vis* a trustworthy and knowledgeable member of the community.[14] In order to get a more comparative perspective of the manner in which legal subjectivities are constructed in the Family Court and the *Darul Qaza*, I will in the following section discuss a case negotiated in the *qazi*'s courtroom.

Adjudicating marriage in the *Darul Qaza*

In February 2010, I was able to observe a dispute settlement where a young and well-educated Muslim woman, I call Sabiha, from Lucknow sought to obtain *faskh*[15] from her estranged husband Raoul.[16] Sabiha approached the *Darul Qaza* hoping that the *qazi* would support and understand her quest for a divorce from the perspective of Islamic law and practice. The hearing of Sabiha and Raoul took place in a large room set up with astounding similarity to the hearing rooms of the state courts. The judge's cumbersome semi-circular wooden table and his large black faux-leather armchair dominated the room. The plaintiff and the defendant sat at each corner of the table in front of the *qazi*, who was flanked by his secretary, who was tasked with recording the hearing in Urdu. On each side of the room sat a few benches for onlookers such as family members and religious scholars (*ulema*). The day of the hearing, the plaintiff and the defendant appeared in front of the judge without their family members.[17] Each was granted enough time by the *qazi* to elaborate in depth about their side of the dispute.

Sabiha was 26-years old and from a middle class background. She married Raoul, a 27-year-old contractor belonging to Lucknow's lower socio-economic class, four-and-a-half years earlier. The couple remained childless. After the wedding, Sabiha moved to her in-laws' house where she lived for one year. In her written application to the *Darul Qaza*, Sabiha stated that she was pressured financially and suffered physical torture at the hands of her in-laws, specifically her mother- and brother-in-law. She argued that the cruelty that she endured in her matrimonial home was mostly related to dowry. To illustrate, Sabiha described how her in-laws forcefully confiscated the jewellery she had received at the time of the wedding when she announced, after one year, that she would return to her natal family. In the *Darul Qaza*, Sabiha pleaded for *faskh* – a divorce initiated by the *qazi* – or for triple *talaq* – initiated by her husband. Her motives were clear: in the case of a woman-initiated divorce (*khul*), the claimant loses not only her right to maintenance during *iddat,* but to her *mehar* and to the jewellery and the money that she received at the time of the wedding. Raoul, on the other hand, desired to re-establish their marriage, fearing the loss of social reputation for both himself and his family should his wife obtain the divorce.

At the time of the hearing, Sabiha and Raoul's dispute had already undergone a lengthy legal process in Lucknow's Family and Criminal Courts, where, for more than two years, Sabiha attempted to negotiate a divorce. She first lodged an FIR (First Information Report) in the police station, which resulted in charges against her husband under Section 498A IPC (Indian Penal Code) in the Criminal Court. Shortly after, she filed under the Dowry Prohibition Act of 1961 in the Criminal Court.[18] As a result of these petitions, her husband was incarcerated. By enlisting the criminal legal system against her husband, Sabiha hoped to pressure Raoul to pronounce *talaq* upon her. However, her husband's family bailed him out of jail and upon his release he promptly filed for restitution of conjugal rights.[19] His aim was to reinstate his damaged social respect and honour. However, the case was still pending in the Family Court at the time of the hearing in the *Darul Qaza*. Usually, the *Darul Qaza* in Lucknow does not entertain cases that have already been adjudicated in the state courts. This is due to the *qazi's* conviction that couples that have brought their disputes to the state legal system are most likely unwilling to reach an amicable consensus.[20] The *qazi* tells me that he has made an exception because the woman seemed really desperate for a divorce. However, disappointed with Sabiha and Raoul's unwillingness to comply in the *Darul Qaza,* the *qazi* dropped the case after the first hearing.[21] Regardless of the fact that the case was never resolved in the *Darul Qaza*, this first hearing provides valuable insight into the ways gendered subjectivities are constructed in the process of dispute settlement. I note that I did not have the opportunity to personally talk to Sabiha and Raoul. My analysis below is thus solely based on discourse analysis from the court hearing.

The marital dispute from the wife's perspective

Sabiha was the first to present the marital conflict to the *qazi*. In her indictment, she justified her quest for a divorce by citing Raoul's failure to provide her with a protected marital environment characterised by economic stability, affection, and piety. Based on their different educational and class backgrounds, Sabiha furthermore questioned the compatibility between her and her husband.

Coming from a well-educated religious family, Sabiha complained about the lack of piety in her matrimonial home. She described her husband and his family as uneducated, ignorant about Islamic life and practice, and quarrelsome. She complained that he and his family did not pray or fast during the month of *Ramadan*. Despite her efforts to remind her in-laws about the importance of an Islamic lifestyle, they would not change. Sabiha lamented that co-habitation with Raoul and his family was characterised by intimidation and by verbal and physical violence over the issue of dowry. Her mother- and sister-in-law instigated fights daily, finding fault with everything Sabiha did. She affirmed that all efforts to improve her relationship with her husband and in-laws – by means of intra-familial mediation – were unsuccessful. Moreover, her mother-in-law, a financially challenged widow with daughters engaged to be married, made further claims for dowry, specifically, a car, a refrigerator, and more cash. Sabiha's parents, who at that time faced financial problems themselves, were unable to comply with these stipulations. In response, her mother-in-law restricted Sabiha's right to visit her natal family and threatened her with a court procedure. Sabiha condemns Raoul for not 'protecting' her from the verbal and physical onslaught of his mother and siblings. Instead, Raoul demonstrated disinterest in their marriage, accepting no responsibility for Sabiha's financial or social well-being. For example, she lamented that Raoul failed to pay for her doctor and hospital visits when she fell severely ill, providing her only with minimal pocket money. Daunted and quite certain that the relationship with her husband and in-laws will not improve, Sabiha now came before the *qazi* requesting divorce by means of *faskh*. *Faskh,* however, often comes with a certain price. Apart from the immediate material concerns involved, Sabiha's narrative in the *Darul Qaza* alludes to the impending damage to her and to her family's social reputation, to the fact that a divorce will deprive her of becoming a mother, and to the resulting low prospect for marriage faced by her three younger sisters a divorce would bring.

In the *Darul Qaza,* Sabiha's claim for a *qazi*-initiated divorce in the absence of physical torture and neglect, however, was met with confusion.[22] The *qazi* sceptically asked her: 'If you didn't have any real problems related to food, pocket money, or severe violence, what is it that makes you asking for a divorce from your husband? What? Why exactly don't you want to live with him? What is the reason? Tell me the reason!' Sabiha's answer was simple: 'He doesn't understand me. I don't want to live with him, that's all. They are not educated people. They believe in *taziya* and *Muharram* and they go to *martam*.[23] I don't believe in these things. They force me to do all those religious things I don't believe in'.

Incompatibility between spouses that prevents a harmonious marriage, as portrayed by Sabiha, is recognised as a valid reason to dissolve a marriage under Islamic law. The *qazi* himself in fact reiterated directly to me that this was reason enough for him to grant a divorce – since there was no point in upholding an unhappy marriage. In this specific case, however, the *qazi* was unwilling to dissolve the marriage on the grounds of educational and ideological differences. This was because, as he said in a personal conversation, Sabiha prioritised her own feelings and desires over her marriage.

The marital dispute from the husband's perspective

Shy, nervous, and with a soft voice, Raoul countered his wife's accusations, stating: 'These allegations against me do not reflect the truth or reality. I won't lie in the court of *Allah*. I never ignore religion and education. I always donate to the mosque and the *Madrasa* according to my income'. Raoul's strategy in the *Darul Qaza* was to reinstate his reputation as a pious and good husband. He claimed that he had always supported his wife in every possible way: lending her father money to pay the moneylender or constructing a separate house for her. Painting an image of himself as supremely generous, Raoul contradicted Sabiha's allegations regarding dowry, querying: 'How can I ask for dowry while paying my father-in-law's debt?' Raoul also refuted Sabiha's depiction of his family as quarrelsome and violent, describing his mother, brothers, and sisters as peaceful and understanding. In contrast to the image of his peace-loving family, Raoul constructed Sabiha as a bad housewife who is both demanding and nosy.

Given the negative image that Raoul conjured of Sabiha in the *Darul Qaza*, his plea for reconciliation and for the re-establishment of his marriage came as somewhat of a surprise. Raoul explained to the *qazi* that he feared social humiliation should his wife be granted a divorce – either through the state courts or in the *Darul Qaza*. He argued that Sabiha brought shame to his otherwise respected family by having him incarcerated. Raoul felt that he could regain his social reputation only if he wins the case for restitution of conjugal rights in the Family Court. Raoul's strategy of keeping his otherwise neglectful and insubordinate wife for the sake of his and his family's reputation sparked some incomprehension with the *qazi* as well. Sceptically, he asked: 'Is it great-heartedness or something else that you want to live with her? I would like to ask you, how could you expect good things from the person who has sent you to jail? Would you give her *talaq* if she excuses her *mehar*?'

The decision

After having listened to both parties, the *qazi* assessed Sabiha and Raoul's marriage as an irreparable failure. In his opinion, the only way to end the dispute was by means of divorce. However, in the absence of sufficient evidence of systematic physical torture and financial neglect, the *qazi* could not comply with Sabiha's request for a divorce initiated by him (*faskh*).[24] In a lengthy debate, the *qazi* attempted to convince Raoul to either divorce his wife by unilateral triple *talaq* or to grant her a female initiated divorce (*khul*). Since Raoul was not ready to compromise, the dispute was left undecided.

Drawing from this snapshot of dispute settlement, one can conclude that only obedient, moral, battered, and materially neglected women are deemed worthy of the *qazi*'s support. In this regard, the *Darul Qaza* in Lucknow is similar to the state-administered Family and Criminal Courts as the decisions passed down in the *Darul Qaza* evoke standards that stress the prerogatives of men and the obedience and propriety of women within marriage. Along these lines, Sabiha was denied *faskh* because she did not fit the conservative standards of female morals and submissiveness and because she could not prove material neglect and physical torture. In the eyes of the *qazi,* she did not entirely qualify as a 'good litigant'. Both these formal and informal bodies of justice in Lucknow apply an adjudication framework wherein the granting of women's conjugal rights is dependent upon the establishment of their submissiveness and propriety.[25] The transcript of the one-and-a half-hour-long hearing illustrates, in fact, that the *Darul Qaza* and the Family Court are similar in terms of how normative models of the family are shaped, imagined, and debated. Both institutions distinguish between the 'good' and 'bad' litigant. In other words, the privilege of justice is reserved to those women who, in the eye of the judge or the *qazi*, qualify as 'good' Muslims, wives, mothers, and daughters-in-law – or in other words – to women whose subjectivity is constructed outside the realm of the sexual as sexually unavailable. So whether it is paternalistic liberalism or religious ideology, the protection promised by both ideological strands to women seems to be seriously hampered once women deviate from normalised codes of women's behaviour within marriage and the family. In this regard, seeking legal remedy within marriage and the family in the Family Court as well as the *Darul Qaza* means to adhere to the paternalistic rules and standards set by court officials and advocates rather than to the black letters of the law.

However, despite these institutions being instances where the strategies and techniques of male power can be traced, they also constitute – even if only limited

– sites of resistance and subversion. For example, some women litigants use the Family Court and/or the *Darul Qaza* as a forum where they have the authority to speak and to narrate their experiences around expectations around marriage and the family. Being aware of the limitations of the law as implemented within the Family Court and the *Darul Qaza* to actually transform misogynist ideas of the family on the ground, some women litigants decide to use these institutions to negotiate their position within marriage and/or re-instate the honour of themselves and their family. In this scenario, I hold, women are not merely subordinates and powerless dependents of their protectors in the guise of the state, community, or their family but, in fact, they strategically and cunningly craft their subjectivity at the margins of the law revealing the articulation of subaltern agency.

Another instant of subaltern agency can be traced in the offices of the All India Muslim Women's Personal Law Board (AIMWPLB) and *Bazme Khawateen*. Taking advantage if the state's 'fractured sovereignty' (Randeria 2007) in the area of marriage and the family, Muslim women's rights activists in the city have taken on the task to challenge some aspects of the historically shaped power structure that allows for the domination of 'masculinist power' (Brown 1992) in the area of (Muslim) family laws. Aware of the fact that women's experience and concerns tend to go unnoticed within the Family Court and the *Darul Qaza*, Shehnaz Sidrat (*Bazme Khawateen*) and Shaista Amber (AIMWPLB) have both set up their *own* mediation and counselling centres in Lucknow.[26] Pushing towards the democratisation of the public legal space, the presidents of *Bazme Khawateen* and the AIMWPLB seek to engender alternative legal spaces from where to tackle the continuing social, educational, and economic marginalisation of Muslim women in the subcontinent.[27]

Female Sites of Justice: The Offices of Muslim Women's Rights Activists

The offices of both the AIMWPLB and the *Bazme Khawateen* are informally organised. There is no designated hearing room, no hearing committee, and no judge. Neither organisation keeps meticulous records of their cases. Most women who address these forums are poor, hardly educated, and often arrive in need of instant advice and help. As victims of domestic violence as well as sudden marital rejection, these often socially isolated women seek the help of Muslim women's rights activists for mediation and legal advice. Both Shaista

Amber and Shehnaz Sidrat informed me that the most common disputes that appear in these offices are related to domestic violence, marital rejection, and maintenance. The majority of women who arrive there have been married at a fairly young age and are therefore vulnerable on multiple levels. Firstly, their early marriage often deprives them from basic education and exposes them to early and unwanted pregnancies.[28] Secondly, women are vulnerable to a wide range of capricious justifications for marital rejection by their husbands. For example, a man may reject his wife for birthing a girl instead of a boy, or if she is 'unable' to properly perform her marital duties (for example, cleaning, cooking, looking after the children, and performing her sexual obligations), or, if he simply has doubts about her chastity. After a marital rejection, these women are often left with little or no support from their natal family, the community, and the state. These informally organised offices, therefore, offer women a space within which they can vent their most intimate grievances, find support for dispute settlement, and receive legal advice. In fact, the complainants with whom I spoke emphasised the solidarity and empathy that they encountered within women-led legal forums. 'Here we can speak the truth', says one woman whom I met in the office of *Bazme Khawateen*, or, 'here they work for the benefit of women', says another. The women I encountered in the office of the AIMWPLB explained their motivation for choosing this women-led sociolegal forum of dispute settlement along similar lines: For example, a female member of the AIMWPLB in her mid-thirties says: 'Women are not toys in the hands of men. The AIMWPLB gives good Islamic justice by referring to the *Quran* and the *Hadith* from a women's perspective'. Another woman in her sixties who reached a divorce from her abusive husband, an alcoholic, with the help of the AIMWPLB states: 'I had a very bad experience at the Family Court and the police abused me. [...] Here, my case was settled in six months! I got a divorce and my ex-husband pays some maintenance'. Or, Nazia, a 30-year-old mother who has been unilaterally divorced by her husband – a pilot in the Indian army – and has so far not received maintenance for her and her son, says,

> In the *Firangi Mahal* and the *Darul Qaza*, they say that if a husband thinks in his dream that he has given *talaq* to his wife, it is valid. *Firangi Mahal* does not support girls – no woman goes there. They are not cooperative. If a woman approaches them for *khul*.... If she wants to leave her husband, she will have to prove that her husband is bad. This is very difficult and they won't believe her. In contrast, the husband does not have to prove anything. They can give *talaq* at anytime and anywhere. The courts do not accept the *fatwas* released by the *Firangi Mahal* and the *Darul Qaza*. I don't know whether or not Shaista

> Amber can actually change something, but she listens to both parties and tries to reconcile. She wrote a document for me regarding the validity of my *talaq*. She helped me to submit the *talaqnama* in the Supreme Court and I am waiting for the decision. Amber has her own way of helping that is different from the court. That's why I came here to Shaista Amber to ask for help in securing an order for maintenance.

Forms of Islamic community justice in the area of family law in the subcontinent, however, has been disparaged by feminists, political scientists, and legal scholars alike who fear that these forums further marginalise women and contribute to the exclusion of women from a state-led civil rights framework. Notwithstanding the limitations a fractured state such as India for women's access to justice yields, the fact that this also allows for possibilities for social justice is, in my opinion, a highly positive implication. My analysis evinces how women litigants, as law-navigating *subjects* (Solanki 2011, 47) strategically utilise the support of Muslim women's rights activists in the city to negotiate their positionality within marriage and the family. Through the analysis of three specific instances of dispute resolution, I examine the manner in which situational conceptualizations about rights, justice, and religion get fragmented and pluralised within these women-friendly counter-hegemonic sociolegal spaces.

The questions that guide this inquiry are: How are the parameters of women's subjectivity within marriage and the family constructed in informal discussions between Muslim women's activists and the complainants? What levels of law do such discussions entail? And finally, what opportunities for gender-justice do these informal women's offices open up within an otherwise patriarchal polycentric legal landscape? My analysis engages with these questions, revealing the offices of Muslim women's rights activists as interactive and elastic epistemological spaces within which meanings of womanhood, freedom, egalitarianism, and equality are revised and re-configured.

The office of *Bazme Khawateen*

As a result of the growing afflux of especially poor Muslim women seeking informal and affordable support for dispute settlement, Sidrat has turned the office of *Bazme Khawateen* into a temporary mediation centre. It is organised to function very informally. There exists no case register. Since the disputes are resolved orally, the verdicts are often not written down. However, in order to bring a dispute for mediation to *Bazme Khawateen*, the complainant is strongly advised to fill out an application.[29] Sidrat estimates the number of resolved dispute resolution cases as of 2010 to be between 800 and 850. Most are solved within the office of *Bazme Khawateen,* without the involvement of legal professionals or the clergy, but Sidrat strategically utilises her familial connections with the clergy of the *Firangi Mahal* for disputes requiring their authority. These are more complicated scenarios, in which the 'aggressor' does not want to comply with a decision made by Sidrat, or where she requires a notarisation. For example, if the *Bazme Khawateen* president dissolves a marriage by means of *faskh,* she will have a divorce decree (*talaqnama*) issued by the *Firangi Mahal*. Such a decree might also prove important in the case that her client, in a further step, wishes to claim her material rights – i.e. to maintenance, property, or inheritance – in the state courts.

I will first analyse a dispute of adultery that was brought for mediation to *Bazme Khawateen*. This dispute concerns a middle-aged and impoverished Muslim woman, I call Farwa. Farwa lives together with her husband, a tailor, at his family home. Her husband is having an extramarital affair (*zina*) with her sister-in-law, who lives in the same house. Farwa claims that her husband makes no secret of his affair. She laments that he arrives home late at night, following no routine for breakfast, lunch or dinner. In this manner, she argues, it is hard for her to fulfil her conjugal duties such as preparing food and maintaining a sexual relationship. Farwa further states that her mother-in-law became upset and began troubling her once she brought these problems to light; finding fault with everything she did, including her nightly reading of the *Quran*. When she confronted her husband, his response was that *she* must 'adjust' to his 'lifestyle', or he would divorce her. Farwa additionally complains that her husband confiscated and sold all her jewellery, which was a wedding gift from her parents and that he physically and verbally abuses her.[30] In this difficult situation, Farwa finds herself left with only little support from her biological family. Her father passed away a few years back and her brothers seem unconcerned with their sister's marriage. The only family member supporting her is an older sister. In the office of *Bazme Khawateen,* she expresses her helplessness, asking: 'How can I continue to live in this house where everybody is unhappy with me and mistreats me?' Shehnaz Sidrat, *Bazme Khawateen's* president, suggests the following: 'Go together with your brothers to your husband's house and ask him what he wants. If he doesn't want to be your husband then you can leave him'.

Sidrat's advice to return to a cruel and estranged husband seems counterintuitive from a rights-perspective. According to the Dissolution of

Muslim Marriage Act, 1939, physical cruelty combined with adultery in the conjugal relationship is reason enough to ask for a divorce. However, regardless of the domestic violence and adultery present, Sidrat is reluctant to suggest divorce as an instant remedy for her client. Knowing that divorce would leave the woman destitute and publicly shamed, Sidrat encourages her to seek reconciliation instead. Therefore, although the victim's vaguely expressed desire for justice alludes to a marital separation, Sidrat recommends that she give her marriage one more chance. Sidrat's underlying articulation of justice in this instance is coloured by her desire to provide women with the 'safety' and the 'protection' offered in marital/familial relationships. Rather than rushing to a divorce or to a legal battle with family members, Sidrat seeks to (re-) establish women within the safety-net of social relationships. In conversation, Sidrat explains that the strength of this approach lies in the fact that through it, she may take advantage of existing social and kin networks. This dispute illustrates nicely the *Bazme Khwateen* president's endeavour to open up possibilities for agency through the very discourse that frames women's economic and social dependency within and outside of marriage – a phenomenon that Kandiyoti (1991b) has so eloquently described as 'bargaining with patriarchy'.[31] Sidrat contents that in a context where a state-administered social welfare system is absent and where the state is often unable to enforce legal maintenance verdicts, the safest course for Muslim women is to re-integrate within the system of social relationships. As she tells me: 'Once a woman is divorced, she loses everything. Her respect, economic security, and a sense of belonging. And more often than not', she adds, 'women have no income on their own to support themselves and their children. I only suggest a divorce if the husband is unwilling to consider reconciliation'.

So, while the law might empower women as legal subjects, state laws such as the Dissolution of Muslim Marriage Act, 1939, may have little relevance in a context within which Muslim women – and especially those from lower socio-economic background – have literally nowhere to go once they exit the space of marriage. In fact, as already mentioned above, according to a statistic on Family Courts in Lucknow, the Dissolution of Muslim Marriage Act, 1939, constitutes only a small percentage of the overall number of cases filed. Expectations of justice in the office of *Bazme Khawateen* are hence coloured by Sidrat's desire to secure at least minimal economic and social security within the space of marriage for her litigants. So in a context where the Indian state is not able to 'protect' female citizens from destitution after the marital breakdown, Sidrat's shifts women's legal subjectivity from the state legal system to the sphere of the family and community. These two rights position, however, do not have to rub against each other. Instead, I argue, such decision illustrates the flexibility and uncertainty of the legal subject as well as the contested meanings of freedom and justice on the ground.

The disputes discussed below, shows that in fact, Sidrat has little empathy for women who refute to turn their story of suffering within marriage into one of emancipation and happiness. As I will show below, Sidrat's idea of freedom and ultimately happiness '[…] can be anchored in a non-liberal metaphysical system and delinked from the epistemological and metaphysical trajectories of the liberal tradition', as Ratna Kapur (2014a, 41) has so succinctly argued. In other words, subaltern subjectivity does not deprive women from happiness and freedom. Sidrat's strategy reflects such position, as she aspires to reconstitute women's happiness within the very constraint of hegemonic ideas of marriage and the family. However, in cases where the woman refuses to submit to such enterprise, Sidrat, in fact, withdraws all support. This was the case with a young woman who arrived, together with her older sister, at *Bazme Khawateen* because her marriage of three years was failing. Two-and-a-half years earlier, her husband threw her out of their marital home where the couple lived along with his parents, two brothers, and their respective wives. The reason for the marital rejection was her husband's suspicion that she was having an extramarital affair. As it emerged from the conversation between Sidrat and her client, the husband took strong issue with his wife's mobile phone conversations. Lengthy calls to unknown numbers led the husband to assume that she was engaged in 'sex-talk' with other men. His suspicion was confirmed in his view when one day he caught her in conversation with an unknown young man in a public park. Based on this, she was thrown out of the house. For two years, he refused to take her back.

The wife, on the other hand, suspected her husband of infidelity with their sister-in-law. Similar to the dispute above, she accused him of spending the nights with the woman instead of with her. In addition, the relationships between the wife and her mother- and sister-in-law were tense, with little to no verbal communication. After several unsuccessful efforts at intrafamily mediation with the goal of reuniting with her husband, this young woman approached Sidrat for help, asking her to intervene in her marital dispute. In the office of *Bazme Khawateen* it was agreed that the husband would take back his wife under the condition that she would no longer use her personal mobile phone. Apparently, the wife did not follow Sidrat's instruction and was caught four days later secretly talking on the phone underneath her quilt. The wife explained that she had to call her mother who was sick at that time. In a rage, her husband submerged the phone in a glass of water and once again threw her out of the house.

Sidrat was outraged to learn that, against her advice, her client had once again used her phone to make 'secret' calls. Consequently, she refused to further offer mediation. In her opinion, the wife was at fault. As she stated: 'No husband tolerates his wife talking and roaming around with other men. Our culture does not allow such a thing. Also, if she wants to talk to someone, she should use her husband's phone'. The in-office conversation between Sidrat and her litigant was intense and fierce. While the wife tried to convince Sidrat to mediate one last time between her and her husband, Sidrat vehemently rejected re-intervention, arguing that she had no time to waste counselling women who are clearly not interested to work toward harmonising familial and marital relationships. Sidrat sarcastically advised the wife to leave her husband and go for a second marriage, given the many men she could choose from. The manner in which this dispute was approached demonstrates again Sidrat's strong determination to work within a framework of marital preservation. Within such a framework, Sidrat ascribed the failure of the marriage to the wife's lack of effort to 'adjust' to the new circumstances of her conjugal home, as well as to her unwillingness to 'obey' her husband. Along these lines, Sidrat seemed to attribute the marital conflict, as well as the husband's promiscuous behaviour, to the wife's failure to unconditionally 'love' and 'care' for him. Arguing that her intentions are to 'fix' and not to 'break' marriages, Sidrat withdrew all empathy.

Sidrat's socially conservative approach toward happiness and freedom reveals the very paradox that marks the above-cited women's struggles for justice. On the one level, there is this desire to leave the marital union and thus detach the self from the marital union that renders them – to some extent – dependent from their husband and his family. On another level, both women are well aware of the social and economic implications of a marital separation and of the possible stigma a divorce might inflict on them and their families. Given the lack of financial support for divorced as well as widowed women from the state and the community, Sidrat's strategy is thus geared toward complying with normative ideas of women's subjectivity within marriage. She does so by supporting women's struggle for happiness by appealing to the principles of Islam according to which the husband's responsibility is to 'protect', maintain, and 'care' for his wife. In order to claim these rights, however, Sidrat strongly advises women to 'adjust' to the life as a married woman. It is through this form of pious obedience, Sidrat tells me, that women create a space of empowerment – or agency – within marriage. Borrowing from Saba Mahmood, I argue that although the subject of freedom in the office of *Bazme Khawateen* is constituted through the very discourses that constitutes its subordination – Sidrat's strategy provokes a 'shift in social relations of power that influence the resisters as well as those who dominate' (Mahmood 2005, 9) – allowing for the creation of a space for the cultivation of women's consciousness. Similarly, the office of the AIMWPLB also provides women with the opportunity to disclose their intimate and private conflicts – away from the men-dominated state and community courts.

The office of the AIMWPLB

The president of the AIMWPLB, Shaista Amber, launched its mediation centre in February 2005 in presence of the media.[32] Every Friday, Muslim women and men were welcome to approach Amber directly in the AIMWPLB office, located on the premises of her mosque just outside Lucknow. Amber asserted that she had mediated hundreds of cases over the last few years. Her case file, however, consisting of loose papers sporadically pinned together and randomly stored, makes it difficult to verify such numbers. If the complainant wished for mediation, Amber advised her (or him) to write an application. The application, which was written either in Hindi or Urdu, included the contact information of the complainant and the defendant, as well as a short synopsis of the case. Based on that application, Amber summoned both parties for a hearing. If the 'aggressor' refused to respond to the summons, she would often visit him (or her) at home. Most of the cases that reached the office of the AIMWPLB pertained to matters of rape, property, domestic violence, divorce, polygamy, and custody.

Amber's endeavour to offer Muslim women a legal space in which their problems can be assessed from 'a women's perspective on the *Quran*' has received support from legal professionals and the moderate Muslim clergy. Amber works in cooperation with an advocate who offers pro bono or low-cost legal support to AIMWPLB members. She also receives support from the Lucknow-based moderate *Maulana* Abdul Kayum. *Maulana* Kayum offers his services as a *qazi* and advises Amber in questions concerning interpretation of the *Quran* and of the *Hadith*.[33] In order to create more public awareness of her activities as a legal arbitrator and counsellor, Amber regularly ventured into remote villages in Uttar Pradesh. Therefore, the complainants who I met at the office of the AIMWPLB usually came from the poorer echelons of society within the region's rural areas, who had travelled from small villages one to two hours by bus. Middle-class clients typically arrived from as far away as New Delhi and

Chandigarh (Punjab). They learned of the AIMWPLB through television or through newspapers.

One of the women who approached Amber for help and support is Ayesha. Ayesha is in her mid-sixties and has been abused by her husband over decades. He – an unemployed alcoholic from a poor economic background – began physically torturing Ayesha shortly after the wedding. He would beat Ayesha, throw hot food at her and douse her with hot cooking oil. Ayesha gave birth to five children under very difficult social and economic circumstances. In order to feed her husband and the children, she began working as a seamstress from home. Her husband's alcoholism consumed almost her entire salary, as well as the little extra money that she received from her parents. There was hardly anything left for the family. In response to such economic constraint, her husband attempted to sell their thirteen-year-old daughter to a 'friend'. When Ayesha found out about his plans, she left with her children and came to Lucknow to live with her brother. But her husband would not let her live in peace. Shortly after her escape, he came to retrieve her. Ayesha felt unable to successfully leave her husband. None of her relatives would provide shelter for her and her children and she could not afford a place on her own. Therefore, she eventually went back to him. Already in her sixties, Ayesha's husband finally repudiated her. With no money and no place to go, her sister advised her to seek help from the AIMWPLB.

In view of women's financial vulnerability, Amber states that she strongly deplored the existing reality in which men may repudiate with ease their wife often of decades by means of triple *talaq*, with no accountability or responsibility for the woman's further well-being. Invoking the Islamic principle of mutual respect – with its indirect implication that women and men share equal value – Amber profoundly questions the moral justification of such repudiation, declaring,

> We from the AIMWPLB have argued that Ayesha devoted her entire life to her husband. She worked her entire life to earn money for her family and her husband. But in the last phase of her life, when she was in need of support and help from her husband, he gives her *talaq*. This is against the Islamic principle of respect. The least he can do after a divorce is to make sure that the mother of his children does not starve and has a place to stay.

In line with such reasoning, Amber calls for Ayesha's right to reside in the matrimonial home and for maintenance *after* the divorce. She first tried to solve the dispute informally - appealing to the husband's morals. The husband, however, was unwilling to offer his former wife shelter and maintenance as a gesture of respect. Given the husband's refusal to assume his 'proper position' as a husband within such normative Islamic framework, Amber brought Ayesha's marital conflict to the attention of the UP State Commission for Women (*Mahila Ayog*). The UP State Commission for Women receives complaints about women's harassment and its role is to offer women legal advice, and report to the government on women development issues. With the help of the Commission, Amber secured a court order under the Protection of Women from Domestic Violence Act, 2005.[34] The order stipulates Ayesha's right to live in her matrimonial home *after* the divorce. In addition, the court ruled that Ayesha's husband must pay maintenance for her and for her children. As a consequence of the court intervention, Ayesha's husband has moved out of their matrimonial home. Today, Ayesha lives together with her children in her matrimonial home. However, two years after the verdict, her husband has still not paid maintenance. The single mother supports herself and the children with the small income she generates with embroidery from home.

This story shows again the manner in which especially poor women are prone to be alienated within their conjugal home and family and very likely to losing their financial rights after the termination of the marriage. To this extent, Ayesha's story reveals the precariousness of the female subject within such hierarchically constructed social arrangement. Amber first attempted to establish Ayesha's legal subjectivity within the normative framework of Islam. According to Amber's interpretation of the religious script, women, divorced or married, have the right to dignity in life – which begins with the basic necessities of shelter and food. In the absence of community and state material support for divorced women and because the biological families of her clients are often impoverished themselves, Amber appeals to the liability of the (ex-) husband even *after* divorce. Invoking the principle of respect as laid down in the *Quran*, Amber opens up substantial room for re-interpretation of gender relations, accentuating the *spiritual* equality of men and women within and outside of marriage.

In this respect, Amber questions the existing male prerogatives commonly propagated in orthodox and widely-accepted Islamic legal discourse that free men from responsibility toward their wives after a divorce. Countering such narrative of spousal relationships, Amber argues that women who have been in a committed marriage *deserve* to be treated with respect after a divorce. Here, the concept of respect opens up an epistemological space within which, the responsibility of the (ex-) husband to provide shelter and maintenance for his wife even *after* a divorce is envisaged as a gesture of appreciation of women's selflessness in motherhood and marriage. However, it is not before Amber links this normative epistemological space to an abstract rights discourse, which stipulates Ayesha's right to housing and maintenance under the Protection of Women from Domestic Violence Act, 2005 that her intervention becomes effective. This is through using religion instrumentally to achieve desired ends for women. Such strategy not only increases the effectiveness of her intervention, but gives her access to the state as well.

In order to successfully enforce her claims, Amber therefore must mediate between the formal and informal worlds of law, translating Islamic ideologies into the language of state law as well as vice versa. Merry (2006) uses the term 'knowledge-broker' to describe activists who translate between different legal worlds and who are fluent in a variety of legal languages. As a knowledge-broker, Amber validates her own interpretations of *quranic* laws through the secular language of state law. For the purpose of implementation, Amber leverages the police and the UP State Commission for Women. In this respect, the office of the AIMWPLB constitutes a space within which the boundaries between formal and informal institutions and legalities are crossed and fragmented. In this respect, Muslim women and men who bring their complaints to the office of the AIMWPLB do so not only because it is an affordable option by which to negotiate justice on the ground, but because the AIMWPLB could be helpful to challenge patriarchal concepts of gender relations through actively selecting and referencing international human rights norms and state and informal laws that are less controlling of women's sexuality or that provide women with more economic security and protection from unilateral divorce.

Similar to Shehnaz Sidrat, Amber's main goal is to provide economic safety to her clients and mitigate the harm done to their reputation as 'good wives'. Then to be categorised as a 'failed wife' or '*kharab bibi*' reduces women's chances for social integration and/or an eventual second marriage. So justice in the offices of Muslim women's rights activists cannot be captured with a liberal imaginary but is implicated in power relations – in a deeper reflection on systemic power relations that surface from patriarchal and orthodox constructions of marriage. So, to turn the gaze to the interstitial spaces that exist between and intersects with state and community law and legal forums offers a different epistemology within which to understand the legal longings and experiences of the women who have turned to the offices of Muslim women's rights organizations for advice. Within such epistemology, justice is context-sensitive and reveals the activists and litigants endeavour to balance a citizenship-based rights discourse with every day realities. I contend that legal subjectivity in this context cannot be subsumed under one (or even several) homogenous labels. Instead, legal subjects exist as heterogeneous and multiple creatures who, as legal agents rather than instruments, contribute to both strengthening and fragmenting normative imaginaries of women's (legal) subjectivity within marriage and the family (Kleinhans and Macdonald 1997, 36). Law and the legally pluralistic landscape in this context, I argue, are no longer a social fact, but modes of knowledge that shape litigants', activists', and court officials' self-understanding under and vis-à-vis the law.

'Doing' Justice on the Ground

In this chapter, I have proffered insight into the various ways in which justice is understood, negotiated, and articulated by litigants, activists, and judges within four different legal institutions: the Family Court, the *Darul Qaza*, the offices of *Bazme Khawateen,* and the AIMWPLB. The *behind-the-doors* snapshots of these legal institutions presented in this chapter capture the voices of the women and men actually participating in the legal reality as it unfolds. These individual perspectives afford insight into some of the modalities by which litigants use diverse sociolegal authorities and by which they recognise and react to the interrelationships that constitute these very authorities. Moreover, they allow for capturing the manner in which litigants understand themselves within such legally pluralistic context and how they use formal and social legalities and institutions so as to negotiate different versions of religion and conjugal life.

To return to the question of the beginning of this chapter: How do women litigants' differing identities as mothers, wives, and Muslims combined with their structural position in terms of class and education contribute to their marginalisation within Lucknow's two most dominant arenas of dispute settlement in the area of Muslim family law? How do these identities intersect and shape multiple dimensions of women's experience under the law? Do what extent to women litigant placed on the margins challenge dominant epistemologies on gender relations within marriage and the family?

My analysis of litigants' experiences in the Family Court shows that women's identities – and legal subjectivities – tend to be reduced to their assumed role as mothers and wives. This creates a certain amount of gender normativity within the family and marriage which functions as the benchmark for measuring whether or not the woman in question 'deserves' the rights awarded to her under the Indian Constitution and/or by Muslim family law. While gender normativity within the family and marriage in this regard without a doubt limits women's possibilities under the law, I have shown that some litigants in fact strategically use the hegemonic power of the Family Court to reinstate their and their family's respect and honour by publicising their marital dispute – and in most cases the very lack of their husband's spousal accountability – through the formal court system. The *Darul Qaza* is yet another legal forum that is used by women to pressurise their husband and his family.

Being aware of the Family Court's ignorance toward the suffering of especially poor women (and men), some Muslim women turn to the community authority of the *Darul Qaza* for dispute settlement. While the decisions made in the *Darul Qaza* have no legal standing, such forum for community justice tends to be used by women to remind their (ex-) husband of either his marital duties or to initiate a divorce with the help of the *qazi*. In this sense, the *Darul Qaza* constitutes a 'subversive site' (Kapur and Cossman 1996) for the negotiation of family ideologies within the framework of Islam. In both institutions, however, it is the women who tend to be blamed for the breakdown of the marriage. All too often, those women who step outside the normative framework of the 'obedient' wife and daughter-in-law and who claim their rights either in the Family Court or the *Darul Qaza*, tend to be disparaged as 'non-compliant' and thus as not deserving of their rights.

So, especially poor female litigants in Lucknow are confronted with a legal reality where the discourse of citizenship rights, or Islamic women's rights, often constitute a moot point and where neither the state nor the Muslim community provides financial support or shelter for them and their children. In addition, these women are often left without the support of their natal family or, frequently, their (ex-) husband. Given these sociolegal realities, I have argued that, in fact, the Indian's state's fractured sovereignty in the area of the family not only poses an obstacle to women's access to justice. Instead, such situation can also create opportunities for the emergence of legal spaces within which meanings of womanhood, freedom, egalitarianism, and equality are revised and re-configured.

The offices of the AIMWPLB and *Bazme Khawateen* in Lucknow constitute spaces of resistance within which the patriarchal-legal ideology of the orthodox religious clergy on the one hand and that of the state on the other is – although to a different extent – challenged. I have theorised the office of *Bazme Khawateen* as a space where women's legal subjectivities are grounded in Islamic ideals of marriage – an ideal that is envisaged as the locus of women's happiness, and freedom. In so doing, Sidrat strives to bridge the gulf between the Islamic ideals of marriage where women are entitled to care, respect, and protection on the part of their husband with women's all too often dire conjugal realities. Using a socially conservative approach, Sidrat strives to unearth possibilities for women's agency within a religious framework of marital duties and rights. In so doing, Sidrat deploys the ideal of the Islamic family as both legal status and potential for action that can help to reinstate women's position within marriage and the family. As mentioned above, the success of this legal space lies less in radically challenging patriarchal discourse around marriage than generating and fostering women's legal consciousness of their rights (as well as obligations) within the marital union. In so doing, Sidrat also enlists the authority of the religious clergy, the *Firangi Mahal,* to reinforce her views on women's rights within marriage.

Amber's strategy differs from Sidrat's in that she further stretches the space of women's consciousness by engaging in 'forum shopping'. Deploying the multiple legal avenues to secure Muslim women's rights within the family, Shaista Amber enlists the authority of the police, the UP State Commission, and a lawyer working at the Family Court so as to assess and solve the disputes that reach her office. So doing, she mediates between a variety of legal worlds and discourses to articulate and act upon her vision of Muslim women's rights. I argue that these very contestations over the meaning of the family, gender relations, and subjecthood evince the fluidity and the porousness of the categories of Islam and women's rights on the ground. So what do these instances of dispute settlement tell us about the feminist theorisation of women's rights on the ground?

I suggest that women's legal subjectivity is incoherent and unstable and thus cannot and should not be judged along classical liberal parameters of individual freedom, choice, and autonomy. Instead, the empirical data presented in this chapter underscores the importance of a comprehensive approach to law, which incorporates individuals' perspective of justice and that looks more closely at the manner in which women's agency is constituted on the ground. I therefore apprehend these women's legal spaces as an *opportunity* for Muslim women to negotiate and frame justice within the penumbra of the state in postcolonial India.

Endnotes

1. Michael Burawoy (1998) theorises the extended case method as a reflexive method of social research that is based on participant observation over an extended period of time. The goal of this research method is to gain insight into the working of power through the elaboration on the interconnectedness of micro level realities with macro-level structures in a specific case.

2. The specifics of the case can be downloaded here: http://indiankanoon.org/doc/1999938/ (accessed February 12, 2016)
3. See: http://www.huffingtonpost.in/2015/10/28/muslim-personal-law_n_8406562.html (accessed February 12, 2016)
4. See: http://indianexpress.com/article/india/india-news-india/court-cannot-test-validity-of-personal-law-muslim-group-to-supreme-court/ (accessed February 12, 2016).
5. The great majority of poor Muslim women I have interviewed in Lucknow at rallies, Muslim women's rights workshops, seminars, and public gatherings, were all victims of domestic violence. They have been doused with hot vegetable oil, burnt with kitchen utensils, deprived of food, or forced by their husbands to have sex with other men. The husband's intent with such an action was to demonstrate his absolute power within marriage and to humiliate his wife. Strikingly, only a small minority of abused women has taken legal steps against their husband or in-laws.
6. The Subaltern Group emerged as a collective of postcolonial historians that gathered around Ranjit Guha – the founding editor of *Subaltern Studies* – in an attempt to break with the writing of colonial Indian history as a history of the elite and as a product of Western modernity at the end of the 1970s. Partha Chatterjee (1993) and Gayatri Chakravorty Spivak (2000) for instance have criticised Indian historiography as a European product, undermining the agency and consciousness of the subordinates and thus ignoring their contribution to history. Chatterjee exemplifies his criticism of the bourgeois-influenced Indian historiography by drawing upon the peasant struggle. Doing so, he unveils the fact that the subordinates express their distinct and autonomous social identities by learning in their own ways the mechanisms of the new power system. In this respect, the subalterns have to be acknowledged as 'historical agents' and as valid historic material (1993, 167–9). Spivak (2000, 325) sees the general political importance of subaltern studies in its production of knowledge that seeks to weaken the monopoly of conventional historiography and evokes the urge to rethink the political.
7. The State Commission for Women in Uttar Pradesh was established in Lucknow under the Uttar Pradesh State Commission for Women's Act of 2004. The Commission is a quasi–judicial body that has procedural power equal to the civil courts. It takes up cases concerned with rape, domestic violence, dowry, death, and maintenance under Section 125 CrPC. The Commission does not deal with cases regarding property and divorce. The Women's Commission in Lucknow mediates cases and, if needed, cooperates with the police and advocates. The Women's Commission is further assigned to investigate instances of atrocity and discrimination against women in public (work, school, etc.), ensure the implementation of the constitutional rights for women, undertake research so as to suggest ways for women's due representation in all spheres, participate in the planning process for women's socio-economical development, evaluate the progress of women under the state (law, social, political, economic, health, etc.), and coordinate with police cells when dealing with cases related to atrocities against women and formulate an action plan. According to the

Chairperson Abha Agnihotri in a personal conversation, the success rate of this relatively new legal body is small; litigants I met at the Women's Commission in Lucknow essentially all told me they approached this body as a last resort after all efforts to resolve the case in the state courts had failed. As according to Agnihotri, it is difficult to summon the other party for mediation. Although the Commission can enforce the court summons through the police, Agnihotri laments that it is generally difficult for them to compel the other party to attend. This is especially so in cases where the husband is unreachable since he lives abroad. For more information on the State Women's Commission visit their website at http://mahilaayog.up.nic.in/index.htm (accessed October 9, 2012).

8. In the case documents related to Section 125 CrPC that I have studied, men often state their income to be minimal or purport to be unemployed. With this strategy men hope to minimise the amount of maintenance money they would have to pay to their wife and/or children. However and most interestingly, all court rulings that I have studied were in favour of the women. After the cases have been in the court for several years, these women and their children were each granted between 500 and 1,000 rupees (US $9–20) per month. This is considerably low considering the fact that in some instances the husband's income was as a high as Rs. 15,000 to 25,000. (U.S.$276–460) per month. Whether or not these women have been able to secure maintenance payments from their husbands does not emanate from these documents. However, this can be doubted. Most of the litigants I have interviewed in the Family Court stated that they have not received any payments although the decision in the court was in their favour.
9. All the names have been changed to respect the anonymity of these women.
10. Many feminists on both sides of the Atlantic disparage state legal institutions as gender-unjust. Whereas liberal feminists lament the exclusion of women from the state legal system, radical feminists such as Gayle Rubin (1993) and Catherine MacKinnon (1987) criticise the supposedly liberal and neutral state for its patriarchal interpretation of the law. Radical feminists such as Rubin and MacKinnon hold that the law reflects a patriarchal system of power that is based on male supremacy. Locating the root for women's oppression within patriarchal gender relations, radical feminists point to the role the law plays in reproducing women's oppression. Much of the insights gained and arguments made by radical feminists have found entry into anthropological studies of law and gender, such as, for example, the work of the anthropologists Mindie Lazarus-Black (1997) and Marilyn Strathern (2004). In discussing a case of child support in Antigua, Lazarus-Black (1997, 641) argues that the same state which creates legal remedy for women shapes and reproduces gender inequalities through litigation by relegating women to the home as mothers and wives. Similarly, Indian feminist and anthropological scholarship theorises formal Indian courts as patriarchal, perpetuating rather than abolishing oppressive values and practices in regard to gender, race, and class (Basu 2006; Bose 2002; Hasan and Menon 2005; Mehra 1998; Menon 2002; Mukhopadhyay 1998; Sangari 1999; Kapur and Cossman 1996; Sunder Rajan 2003). All of these perspectives criticise the law for its commitment to patriarchy and its limited remedies for women.

11. Bettina Dennerlein, however, points out that such use of the state courts does not necessarily indicate that these women disrespect those courts and their laws. Taking Algerian courts as an example, Dennerlein (2001) argues that women's expectations of the Civil Courts are often bound up in a mixture of claims to rights, social recognition, and support. Moreover, Dennerlein (2001, 256–257) suggests that the strategies used in the court by female litigants should be interpreted as 'reflexive attitudes people develop on the basis of their own understanding of their situation and their sense of justice as well as on the basis of a more technically legal knowledge provided by the lawyer'. In other words, it seems that female litigants use the legal authority provided by the state as well as their knowledge of formal law in order to symbolically as well as materially leverage social and family networks.
12. It is thus important to keep in mind that only a small number of cases regarding domestic violence, unjustified conjugal rejection/divorce, and dowry actually reach the courts. The large majority of women I have talked to in numerous informal conversations never considered filing a case either in the formal or informal court. This is either due to their lacking knowledge of the legal process and/or lack of financial means, or because they considered the dispute as a 'family matter' that should not involve people such as advocates and judges from 'outside'. Mindie Lazarus-Black (2008) uses the term 'cultures of reconciliation' to explain the fact that in Trinidad, as elsewhere, more women accommodate and endure emotional and physical abuse within marriage and the family than seek legal remedy from the outside. Lazarus-Black (2008, 40) argues that 'there is a place reserved for violence in the ideologies and practices that constitute family, gender, and work, and that these coalesce to form local 'cultures of reconciliation' that act as filters not only in between, but also within, the community and the institutions of law and the state'. In other words, a culture of reconciliation upholds hegemonic gender and power hierarchies that allow a certain space for violence that is acceptable if not even legitimised. Lazarus-Black's observation in Trinidad also applies in India. All women from the lower class that I have talked to either at the Family Court or in the offices of women's organisations were victims of domestic violence. This includes physical violence, mental violence, sexual harassment, dowry hassle, rejection, and adultery. All of these women without exception told me in conversation that their first priority was to save their marriage – not their physical or mental well–being. They all expressed their willingness to endure a certain degree of matrimonial cruelty for the sake of the marriage.
13. Sally Engle Merry (1990, 3) makes a similar argument in the context of the lower courts approached by the urban working class in the U.S. There, the plaintiffs thought that, although the law was on their side, to evoke it was a risky business and might worsen the situation rather than bring justice.
14. In contrast to the Family Court in Lucknow, where litigants are granted one to two minutes in front of the judge, the judge usually grants a considerable amount of time for each party to expound their dispute.
15. The *qazi* Ahmed Qasmi highlights *faskh* (*qazi*-initiated divorce) as a particularly women-friendly specialty of the *Darul Qaza.* However, *faskh* comes with some restrictive criteria: for a woman to be eligible, her husband must be missing, unsound

of mind, unable to have a sexual relationship with her, unable to maintain her, or threatening towards her. A Muslim woman can also file for a divorce in the Family Court under the Dissolution of Muslim Marriage Act of 1939 on the grounds that her husband has abandoned her, failed to maintain her, is insane or impotent, treats her with cruelty, or that the marriage was performed when the bride was under the age of fifteen. Under this Act her right to *mehar* and *iddat*-money remains intact. In practice however, Muslim women hardly claim for a divorce under this Act. As Hamza Abidi, an advocate at the Family Court, explains, the majority of divorces amongst Muslims are informal and initiated by the husband (triple *talaq*). And those women who want to divorce their husband look for an informal way to do so. This is so because they are not willing to wait for years, if not decades, until a divorce comes through in the official courts.

16. The names of Sabiha and Raoul have been changed to protect their anonymity.
17. The *qazi* in Lucknow prefers to listen to the litigant and the defendant in absence of their family members in order for them to be able to speak freely and without any inhibitions. In his opinion, this policy helps to prevent false statements. (Interview with Ateeq Ahmed Qasmi, *qazi* in the *Darul Qaza* in Lucknow on January 12, 2011.)
18. A First Information Report (FIR) is a written report prepared by the police which sets the criminal process in motion. After the FIR is registered in the police station, the police take up the investigation in the case. Section 498A IPC offers legal remedy for women who are subject to cruelty by their husband and/or relatives. The Dowry Prohibition Act of 1961 prohibits the giving or taking of dowry. The offenders of this law are punished with imprisonment of at least five years and a monetary fine of not less than Rs. 15,000 (US $275).
19. Although Muslims cannot ask for restitution of conjugal rights under the Hindu Marriage Act, the courts often consider such requests based on legal precedents such as the recent Abdul Moin vs Mst. Rafia Bano (2014) case where the restitution of conjugal right was interpreted by the lower court in Lucknow as a right that emanates from the Muslim marriage contract (*nikahnama).* There it was settled that the *nikahnama* was a civil contract and a suit for restitution of conjugal rights is truly speaking a suit for enforcement of certain obligations arising out of that contract. See: http://indiankanoon.org/docfragment/199308674/?formInput=suit%20for%20restitution%20of%20conjugal%20rights (accessed February 26, 2016).
20. In this regard, the *Darul Qaza* in Lucknow seems to differ from the ones in Delhi as researched by Katherine Lemons (2010). In her dissertation, Lemons argues that Muslim women in Delhi use the *Darul Qaza* often in combination with the state legal system, or after their possibilities for justice within the Family and Criminal Courts have been exhausted (Lemons 2010, 50).
21. Interview with Ateeq Ahmad Qasmi, *qazi* in the *Darul Qaza* in Lucknow on February 12, 2011.
22. Susan Hirsch (1998), who researched the *Shariat*-courts in coastal Kenya, points out that women often use the court as a public arena within which they disrupt male discourse on gender relations. She argues that whereas women are often silenced

in daily life, the *Shariat*-courts prove to be a space where they are afforded the opportunity to resist hegemonic ideals on gender through presenting their own narratives. But, similar to what I have observed in the case of Sabiha, Hirsch (1998, 33) argues that such non-hegemonic narratives are often the cause of further dispute rather than the settlement of the case.

23. *Muharram,* the first month of the Islamic calendar, is an important period of mourning in Shia Islam. As a part of that festival *taziya* is the re-enactment of the battle of Karbala and *martam* designates the congregation of men and women for the ceremonial chest beating. These are all Shia rituals usually frowned upon by Sunni Muslims in Lucknow and elsewhere. Already in the past as well as today *Muharram* has been the occasion for violent excesses between Shia and Sunni in Lucknow.
24. The *qazi* told me that he only grants *faskh* in cases where the husband has been neglecting his wife for a very long time and/or she has been tortured on a regular basis. As an illustration, he offered the story of a woman to whom he granted *faskh* because she had been living separately from her husband for twenty-seven years because he could not maintain her properly.The *qazi* considered the 200 Rs. the woman received as maintenance every month as insufficient for her to make a living. Because the husband was not willing to divorce his wife even after twenty-seven years of separation, the *qazi* nullified the marriage by means of *faskh*.
25. Katherine Lemons (2010) has made a similar observation in her empirical research on three different *Darul Qaza* institutions in Delhi. She describes the *darul qazas* in Delhi as 'ambivalent spaces' where women's success in securing justice lies in their capacity to represent themselves as 'good persevering wives, mothers and daughters-in-law' (2010, 29).
26. As mentioned in previous chapters, the fact that Muslim women are one of the most marginalized groups in contemporary India has been stated in the Sachar Committee Report, produced by the Indian government as well as independent Ranganath Misra Commission and the Seema Kazi's Minority Report.
27. I note that the BMMA has very recently, on July 6 2013, started legal aid cells called Women's *Shariat* courts in Mumbai, Pune, Ahmedabad, and Dindigul in Tamil Nadu. While these Women's *Shariat* courts, which deal with cases regarding unilateral divorce, maintenance, custody, and polygamy, deserve to be scrutinised, these extraordinary women's courts are (unfortunately) not included in my analysis. On overview of the BMMA's women's *Shariat* courts can be downloaded from their blog: http://bmmaindia.blogspot.com/p/reports.html (accessed June 23, 2015)
28. According to a quantitative study conducted amongst Muslims in India by Zoya Hasan and Ritu Menon (2004, 77–79), Muslim men and women in North India generally enter their first marriage before age sixteen. Early marriages are still very common in India amongst all religious groups despite the fact that according to Indian law the marriageable age for men is twenty-one and for women eighteen. As a result, these women are very likely to bear children at a fairly young age. Dr. Rukhsana Khan, a gynaecologist who runs a private clinic in Lucknow, explained to me that the great majority of Muslim women and men who come to her clinic refuse

to adopt permanent contraception methods such as a vasectomy or tubectomy. Rather, she says, women generally try to convince their husbands to use condoms – especially after having given birth to five or six children already. Dr. Khan explains to me that women usually pressurise their husband to use contraceptives so as to prevent sexually transmitted diseases and to minimise the financial burden of multiple pregnancies and many children. Men, on the other hand, Khan asserts, generally reject the use of condoms, or any other contraceptive, as they are more likely to consider pregnancies as 'God-given'. (Personal interview with Dr. Rukhsana Khan, Lucknow on December 29, 2009)

29. These applications, written in either Hindi or Urdu, are kept loosely in drawers or randomly amongst stacks of paper atop Sidrat's desk. I could thus not make out any logical method by which the cases are filed and stored.
30. According to informal Islamic law as well as state-administered Muslim Personal Law (The Muslim Women Protection of Rights on Divorce Act, 1986) all the gifts a woman has received at the time of the wedding and during the marriage are her property.
31. Deniz Kandiyoti (1991b) has coined the phrase 'bargain with patriarchy' to describe the ways women negotiate patriarchal conditions for their own benefit within a seemingly highly constraint social reality.
32. Amber invited the press to report about the launch of this new *Mahila Adalat* (women's court). The liberal Indian newspaper *The Hindu* depicted the AIMWPLB's first *Mahila Adalat* (women's court) as a full-blown success, reporting that 166 cases related to 'triple *talaq* and atrocities related to dowry' had been successfully processed. According to *The Hindu,* women from different districts in Uttar Pradesh flocked to the meeting in Lucknow in order to seek justice and to call alleged offenders to account (see: http://www.hindu.com/2005/02/27/stories/2005022702101100.htm, accessed January 28, 2013). However, it appears that the start of this Women's Board was not as glorious as reported by those news agencies. The former general secretary, Parvin Abidi, told me in a conversation that the convening of the *Mahila Adalat* in fact never occurred. Instead, what was referred to as *Mahila Adalat* by the media was actually a random selection of mostly poor Muslim and veiled Hindu women 'recruited' on the occasion of the inauguration ceremony of the Women's Board in order to publicly convey grassroots enthusiasm and support.
33. Dissatisfied himself with the *Darul Qaza*'s misogynist approach to Muslim family law, *Maulana* Kayum decided to support Amber in her endeavour to challenge the legal hegemony of the clergy. In conversation, Kayum explained to me one crucial shortcoming of the *Darul Qaza.* Since, as mentioned earlier, it rejects cases that have already undergone adjudication in the state courts, potential litigants are afforded very limited access to its services. On the other hand, according to Kayum, the community courts help Muslims receive prompt Islamic justice compared to the sluggish working of the state courts. Nevertheless, as a strong supporter of the state legal system, Kayum views community courts as *temporary fixes* only – to be phased out once the state legal system has become more efficient. Therefore, together with Amber, he currently

lobbies the state to set up 'Fast Track Courts' for the adjudication of Personal Law in the Family Court. Both argue that crimes committed against women should be registered there rather than in community courts. This fast track system stipulates that cases should be adjudicated within a year. It reserves a fifty-percent women-to-men-ratio seat in the parliament and makes available a female *mufti* or *alima* in the state courts, securing the implementation of women's rights under Islamic laws. In our conversation, *Maulana* Kayum envisioned Fast Track Courts as spaces within which hearings occur on a daily basis, and the judge's as well as defendant's absences are punished by fine. He further suggests that the state should increase the number of judges in these courts in order to improve efficiency (*Maulana* Kayum passed away in 2011). Amber has explicitly expressed her demand for Fast Track Courts in the area of Personal Law in a letter addressed to the President. The letter is available on her blog: http://shaistaambar.blogspot.com (accessed January 28, 2013). In India, Fast Track Courts already exist in the Criminal Courts but not in the Family Courts. In the Criminal Courts, the Indian government has established fast track courts in 2001, which were financed by the Ministry of Finance for a time period of ten years. (For further information, see the website of the Department of Justice: http://doj.gov.in/?q=node/108, accessed January 29, 2013.)

34. One of the most important provision of the Protection of Women from Domestic Violence Act from 2005 is to secure women's right to housing. As according to this Act, *every* woman has the right to reside in the matrimonial or shared household whether or not she has any title or rights in the house. This residence order is valid for all women, whether married, unmarried, divorced or widowed.

Chapter 6

Muslim Women's Quest for Justice

Theoretical Implications and Policy Suggestions

This book puts forward the claim that understanding the legal world as plural is an important starting point to think about women's access to justice. In fact, the adjudication of Muslim family law in contemporary India is not confined to the formal legal system. Rather, it often takes place in the shadow of the state: in the offices of Non Governmental Organisations (NGOs), community justice centres such as the *Darul Qaza*, the mosque, and people's homes. The potential that non-state law and practice hold for the protection of gender justice in the area of the Muslim family law in South Asia, however, is a contentious issue. There has been a highly polarised and politicised debate on the reform of Muslim family law on the Indian subcontinent. All too often the relation between gender justice and religion is reduced to one of conflict between Muslim women's rights activists and the state and/or the Muslim leadership. In the context of South Asia, the continuing controversy has thus been long on polemic and ideological positions but often short on facts. As a result, we know very little about the importance of community leaders, religious officials, and women's rights activists in Muslim women's everyday struggles for gender justice in the area of family law. Thus, the complexity of the political and sociolegal field is overlooked in scholarship that discusses Muslim women's rights in isolation – rather than inter-relation – with state and non-state legal institutions.

Muslim Women's Quest for Justice addressed this contentious issue through an empirical scrutiny of ongoing initiatives of sociolegal reform from below. It sought to fill this gap by analysing the manners in which several Muslim women's rights organisations rooted in the city of Lucknow – namely the All India Muslim Women's Personal Law Boar (AIMWPLB), the *Bharartiya Muslim Mahila Andolan* (BMMA), and *Bazme Khawateen* (Women's Club) – articulate ideas of Islamic gender justice within a complex patriarchal and polycentric legal landscape. Such complex landscape includes state-run Family Courts, the conservative men-dominated All Indian Muslim Personal Law

Board (AIMPLB) that claims to represent the entire Muslim community at the national level, and the equally male-dominated more recently formed All India Shia Personal Law Board. The goal of this urban anthropological research was to understand how the above-mentioned Muslim women's rights organisations, placed on the margins of the sociolegal landscape in the city of Lucknow, create space that allow for innovative grassroots articulations of justice in the area of marriage and the family beyond the Islam-citizenship dichotomy. In so doing, the book attempted to illustrate the heterogeneity and tensions at work among Muslims when engaging with questions of legal reform and gender in contemporary India. This is to show that Muslims' positioning within the law is neither uniform nor simple, but fragmented along lines of politics, class, race, and religious ideology.

Using multi sited research methods, my research intended to capture the manner in which discourses on gender justice and Islam 'circulate' (Abu-Lughod 2010) through the winding alleys of Lucknow's Shia quarter, the influential *Shariat*-courts, the local mosques, the outdoor offices of Lucknow's Family Court advocates, the over-crowded court rooms, the offices of women activists, media outlets, and people's home – and how they are understood and 'vernacularised' (Merry 2006) in these places. The result is an urban ethnography that weaves an intrinsic pattern of Muslim women's activism on the ground. This is structured by the activists' individual biographies, their creative and innovative use of formal and social legalities and institutions and their ability to interpret and represent different versions of religion and conjugal life. To this extent, this book revealed the means by which Muslim women's activists make use of the legal and institutional plurality so as to challenge the patriarchal-legal ideology of the orthodox religious clergy on the one hand, and that of the state on the other. I argue that these very contestations over the meaning of the family, gender relations, and religious membership evince the fluidity and the porosity of the categories of Islam and women's rights on the ground. To this end, my analysis challenges the widely accepted idea that patriarchal notions of the family and gender are rooted in a fixed, and hence unchangeable religious ideology. Rather, *Muslim Women's Quest for Justice* reveals that, in fact, Muslim women's activists contest and negotiate women's subjectivity within marriage and the family under Islamic laws by mixing and combining a variety of legal sources and discourse ranging from the Indian Constitution, the Islamic scripts, international human rights and women's rights conventions such as CEDAW, as well as social norms and values.

Pushing substantively for a more nuanced understanding of the categories of gender and justice within contested local and national settings and methodologically for more (and more rigorous) attention to the micro-level of institutional interaction, discursive complexity, and everyday understandings of justice and equality, this book – as outlined in the Introduction – sought to bring forward the following three arguments: *Firstly*, the production of ideas and discourses of women's rights is not restricted to the state and its legal system. *Secondly*, Muslim women's rights activists contribute to the pluralisation of the meaning of gender and sexuality in Islam within an increasingly politically, ideologically, and economically fragmented world. *Thirdly*, the ways in which Muslim women's activists themselves vigorously participate in debates, and struggles around women's rights, using Islamic history and ideology as an explanatory framework, shows that subjectivities predicated on a discursive Islamic tradition do not necessarily strip women of their agency. Rather, I suggested, it constitutes a different form thereof. In what follows, I will briefly elaborate on these arguments and state their theoretical importance before making several policy suggestion geared towards an integrated approach to gender justice in legally heterogeneous worlds.

Legal Pluralism and Muslim Women's Rights in Contemporary India

Like most postcolonial states, the Indian state acknowledges *de facto* the legal authority of non-state bodies ranging from caste and community mosque councils to neighbourhood associations and women's organisations. After independence, in an endeavour to accommodate the claim of minority groups for cultural pluralism and religious freedom through secular and democratic governance, the postcolonial Indian state adopted what Gopika Solanki (2011) calls a 'shared adjudication model'. Within such 'shared adjudication model' the contemporary Indian state shares its adjudicative power in the area of marriage and the family with a range of societal actors and organisations. Gopika Solanki's analysis of the highly heterogeneous, fragmented, and contested legal landscape constituting postcolonial India's religious family-law system in Mumbai is important as it offers important insights into the ways in which state/society interactions create spaces for legal actors from each side to 'rework cultural meanings of the family, gender relations in the family, and religious membership' (Solanki 2011, 30). It is these interactions, she compellingly argues, that create the possibility for gender-justice in postcolonial India. Legal, political, and feminist scholarship concerning legal pluralism in postcolonial India, however, tends to posit non-state law and accompanying social forums as diametrically opposed to the modern state-legal system and to stereotype Western liberal-legal ideology in general. From such a perspective, informal institutions, and informal laws are disparaged as illiberal obstacles to justice.

Such widespread mistrust toward community justice in academia is perhaps not surprising considering the highly misogynist and often cruel decisions made by men-dominated community councils such as rural *jati* (caste) and *Khap Panchayats*. For instance, in August 2015, a *khap panchayat* (an assembly of *khap* elders) in Meerut in the state of Uttar Pradesh ordered the rape of two *dalit* sisters and the parading of them naked through the village because their brother eloped with a woman from another caste.[1] In another recent case in 2016, a *Jati Panchayat* of the nomadic tribe of Gopal Samaj in Satara, Maharashtra, ordered the severe beating of a 10 to 14-year old girl for not having resisted the alleged rape by her father.[2] An example of communitarian approaches to cultural freedom in the area of law are a string of misogynist *fatwas* released by the clergy affiliated with the Deobandi school that restrict Muslim women's mobility within the public space and once again validate men's privilege of unilateral divorce (triple *talaq*).[3] So, given such harsh realities, state-centred feminists and legal scholars call on the Indian state to strengthen its authority so as to ensure women's citizenship rights as stipulated in the Constitution.

A focus on the state and its legal system as the sole dispenser for justice, however, tends to sideline the fact that the formal world of state courts and laws are not universally accessible (see Chapter 5). For instance, Indian feminists such as Ratna Kapur and Brenda Cossman (1996), Srimati Basu (2012, 2006), Veena Das (2008), and Nivedita Menon (2002a) have criticised the 'masculinist' state in the area of family law. They hold that state legal institutions and practices are inextricably bound up with the prerogatives of manhood in a men-dominated society. To this end, such scholarship criticises the state for reproducing, rather than tackling, male supremacy by casting the 'ideal' and 'justice-deserving' woman in terms of her dependency and powerlessness in the area of the family as well as politics. Such ontologisation of women in the area of law has far reaching consequences for women's rights on the ground: all too often, women who have the courage to speak up and seek legal remedies against abusive husbands and/or claim their rights for divorce, *mehar*, custody, or maintenance in the state-administrated family and criminal courts, find themselves in a scenario where the Indian state – represented by judges, the police, and advocates – seems more concerned with upholding and protecting 'traditional' ideals of womanhood rather than implementing a more inclusive civil rights framework in favour of women's rights. However, and despite such criticism, state-centred feminist scholarship tends to primarily focus on the nation state as the ultimate protector and harbinger of women's equality and justice. In so doing, I argue, this body of work overlooks the intricate interplay of state and non-state legal institutions, practice, and discourse in struggles for and the production of gender justice and women's rights on the ground. So, the *opportunities* such heterogeneity provides for local communities and civil actors to negotiate and frame justice within the penumbra of the Indian state remains by and large under-theorised.

Muslim Women's Quest for Justice sought to fill this gap. Throughout the book I made important links between various state and non-state institutional settings and presented a nuanced argument about the importance of legal and societal means of struggling for justice. As scholars of law and globalisation effectively illustrate, negotiations around and articulations of justice are not confined to the formal world of the courts, but they often take place in the penumbra of the state (Merry 2006; Wilson 2006). My research evinced that Muslim women's rights organisations in the city of Lucknow have taken advantage of India's 'shared adjudication model' (Solanki 2011) to challenge both the hegemony of the patriarchal state as well as the orthodox Muslim clergy in the area of family law. In fact, over the last decade, Muslim women's rights activists have considerably contributed to the fragmentation and pluralisation of the legal landscape in this North Indian city by carving out interactive sociolegal space from where to disseminate alternative versions of Islam, gender, and the family.

These women-friendly legal spaces, I hold, do not exist in a vacuum but they are an inherent feature of an interactive socio-political landscape characterised by complex and changing social and political dynamics of communication. For example, the presidents of the AIMWPLB, *Bazme Khawateen*, and the BMMA shape and contest institutional relations, equations of power, and precepts of Islam and gender through their growing visibility within the men-dominated political and legal landscape in Lucknow (see Chapter 3). They further challenge the legal authority of the powerful Sunni and Shia clergy in the city to design and adjudicate laws in the area of the family through the release of their own Islamic marriage contracts (*nikahnama*) (see Chapter 4). Moreover, the fact that Muslim women's rights activists and women litigants negotiate gender justice within marriage and the family across a broad spectrum of sociolegal discourse and institutions (see Chapter 5) illustrates the porosity and flexibility of legal and ideological boundaries in grassroots struggles for social and legal reform.

Theoretically and methodologically, such institutional interaction and flexibility can be best captured with the concept of interlegality, as theorised by the sociologist and legal scholar Boaventura de Sousa Santos (2002, 1987). The concept of interlegality defies legal centralistic approaches and stresses the porosity and fluidity of legal boundaries that results in the entanglement of legal codes and morals among the different legal systems (Santos 1987, 280–1). So from a perspective of interlegality, the legal landscape does not consist of parallel and unrelated state and societal legal institutions and authorities. Instead, interlegality urges us to think about the institutional plurality in the area of law as a highly dynamic process where the different legal spaces are non-synchronic and where legal authority, institutions, and knowledge are constantly negotiated amongst different state and societal actors (ibid, 298). Within such process, the epistemological boundaries of the state and society and of formal and informal law are constantly (un)done and blurred in current power struggles on deas of justice and equality. An understanding of legal institutions and discourse in terms of interlegality thus allows for a more inclusive approach to legal change and reform that takes into consideration the hidden places – located in the penumbra of the state – where law is produced and adjudicated.

Following such call, *Muslim Women's Quest for Justice* probed the tangled web of interrelationships between different normative orders as reflected in the discourses of women activists, the practices of state and non-state legal institutions in the city of Lucknow, as well as in the imaginaries of legal subjects. Leaning on critical and cosmopolitan approaches to legal pluralism (Kleinhans and Macdonald 1997; Merry 2006; Sousa Santos 2002 and 1987; Wilson 2006) my analysis rejected positivist ideas of law as a mere social fact. Instead, my goal was to advance an understanding of law as a form of knowledge that is given meaning within a larger context of intricate power relations – rather than institutional normativity. I will note that while I adhered to the analytical categories of state and non-state law to indicate their source of production, such distinction did at no point constitute my point of arrival. Instead, my analysis meant to break with such a hierarchising model of legal pluralism by focusing on the manner in which the boundaries between state and society and between state and non-state laws are constantly (un)done, disrupted, and imagined in current grassroots struggles on legal authority and justice.

For instance, my analysis of the different versions of the Muslim marriage contract (*nikahnama*) released by the AIMWPLB and the BMMA in Chapter 4 evinced how Muslim women's rights activists make sense and utilise different forms of legal knowledge in their own proposals of the Muslim marriage. So doing, these grassroots activists do not merely 'replicate' normative laws by either referring to and strengthen state or informal Islamic laws and authorities. Rather, as these documents show, they engage in processes of 'hybridisation' and 'vernacularisation'. This means to mix and merge human rights discourses and state-administered Muslim Personal Law with ideologically differing Islamic precepts on marriage and the family emanating from the city's elite spaces such as the *darul qazas* and the documents produced by both Shia and Sunni clergy as well as from people's very personal experience and practices. Similarly in Chapter 5, I analysed the manners in which the president of the AIMWPLB and *Bazme Khawateen* emerge as important 'brokers' (Merry 2006) between the formal worlds of state law, Muslim orthodoxy, and Muslim women's daily reality in their attempts to adjudicate cases of family law within their *own* mediation centres. Drawing on formal and informal institutions and law these Muslim women's rights activists manage to satisfy claims that often lie beyond the letters of formal law. These are the re-establishment of social relationships within marriage and/or the reinstatement of the social reputation of themselves and their natal family. My analysis of Muslim women's rights activism reveals the fact that the legal and the social constitute one another – they overlap and mix. The manner in which legal discourses are mixed, transformed, and carried across sites by Lucknow-based Muslim women's rights activists, I contended, facilitates the creation of a legal environment that benefits gender equality on the ground. In short, legal pluralism is not solely an obstacle to gender reform as proposed by state-centred feminist and legal scholarship, but provides room for women's rights activists to create space for bringing forward their own proposals of women's subjectivity within marriage and the family. Moreover, legal pluralism allows for activists and litigants alike to maximise chances for justice by deploying a variety of legal authorities and discourse.

Pluralisation of Islam, Gender, and Justice in Muslim Women's Quest

Assuming the boundaries between the state and society and thus between formal and informal laws as unstable and as constantly in flux allows for an analysis that renders visible the instability and unevenness of the categories of Islam, gender, and justice in current debates and negotiations on Muslim women's rights. Much of the political debate and scholarly work on Islam and women's rights in South Asia tends to subscribe to an idea of Islam as an archaic and unchangeable set of believes and practices that is irreconcilable with secular-Western notions of women's rights. Similar to the 'culture talk', as Mahmood Mamadani (2002) terms it, which, for instance, surrounds policies and political debates regarding the Global War on Terror, public and academic debates on women's rights and Islam in the subcontinent tend to subscribe to Samuel Huntington's problematic *Clash of Civilization* theory where Islam is cast in opposition to stereotype Western values of democracy and justice.

Within such discursive economy, Islam is portrayed as barbaric, backward, and as a hindrance to the realisation of women's rights. For example, the fierce national debate on a 'secular' Uniform Civil Code (UCC) provided an excellent platform for right-wing Hindu parties such as the *Bharatiya Janata Party* (BJP), *Hindutva* or the *Rashtriya Sevak Sangh* to further its Hindu-majoritarian agenda by painting a picture of the Muslim community as anti-national and as being especially discriminatory toward its women.[4] At the heart of such argument are the practices of polygamy and triple *talaq* – portrayed as especially detrimental to women's freedom and autonomy.[5] The Muslim clergy primarily represented by the AIMPLB, on the other hand, uses the same debate to strengthen their right to religious freedom in the area of the family. In so doing, the AIMPLB establishes the categories of Islam and Islamic culture as unchangeable and as incompatible with state legal discourse. A recent case from March 2016 illustrates such claim. There, a Muslim woman challenged the constitutionality of triple *talaq* under Muslim Personal Law in the Supreme Court. As a response, the AIMPLB contended that the 'foundational source of Muslim Personal Law are holy Quran and *Hadith* of the Prophet' and thus it can't fall within the preview of the Constitution.[6] To this end the debate around a UCC in contemporary India has been very successful in establishing the idea of a coherent and monolithic Muslim community in the subcontinent, neglecting internal fragmentations along lines of class, race, caste, and ethnicity. Moreover, such polarising debate considerably strengthened the idea of Islam as a closed and unchangeable belief system that rubs with secular ideas of women's rights.

In an effort to counter such simplified assumptions about Islam and the Muslim community in contemporary India, *Muslim Women's Quest for Justice* shed light on the diversity of voices within the Muslim community and the many ongoing innovative attempts at sociolegal reform from within it, which belie the widely prevalent stereotype of a homogeneous and conservative minority community resistant to change. So doing, the aim of this ethnography was to weave together an analysis of micro-level institutional and quotidian legal practices with macro-level ideas about gender justice and equality to challenge facile generalisations about the incompatibility of women's rights with Islam. Such pluralistic and anti-essentialist understanding of Islam and women's rights on the fashion of a 'discursive tradition' (Asad 2009 [1986]), allows for grasping the working of power dynamics that exist amongst institutions and diverse actors within competitive sociolegal worlds.

For example, in Chapter 3, I revealed the diverse sociolegal positions of Muslim women's rights activists in terms of religious ideology and institutional network in the area of Muslim family law. In so doing, I illustrated how the three different Muslim women's rights activists at the centre of this study upset hegemonic power relations within the sociolegal field through embodied representations of Islamic ideology and practice. Instead of complying with orthodox understandings of modesty that curtail women's access to the public sphere, these activists enter the public–political sphere by making their bodies seen and voices heard. Such actions, I hold, evince the plurality of understandings on women's subjectivity within an Islamic framework. They further render insight into a space of epistemological and discursive uncertainty and thus transformation – a 'third space' (Bhabha 1990) – within Lucknow's ideologically contested legal and political sites. In Chapter 4, I explored the pluralisation of legal and religious ideology in the context of the current politics surrounding the model-*nikahnama*. In it, I showed how the presidents affiliated with the AIMWPLB and the BMMA vernacularise and hybridise different legalities ranging from international human rights over state-administered laws such as Muslim Personal Law and/or the secular Special Marriage Act, 1954, to the religious script (*Quran, Hadith,* and *sunnah*) so as to re-articulate Muslim women's rights within marriage and the family. I argued that these women-friendly versions of the Muslim marriage contract illustrate elastic epistemological spaces of legal transformation and pluralisation within Lucknow's legal landscape.

The substantive Chapter 5 showed the pluralisation of law and religious discourse in the context of dispute settlement in the offices of the AIMWPLB and *Bazme Khawateen.* Analysing the way justice is expected and negotiated within these two sociolegal forums allowed me to draw conclusions on how, and to what extent, women's rights activists challenge the *status quo* of gender relations, and its inscribed forms of power, in people's everyday life. Such exploration rendered insight into the intricate ways in which women's identities as wife, mother, and/or daughter are reconfigured at the intersection of Islamic ideology, everyday experience, and different laws such as international human and women's rights and state-administered secular and religion-based personal laws. I have shown how in this context discourses and logics on Muslim women's rights get fragmented depending on litigants' social position as wife, co-wife, mother-in-law, daughter-in-law, sister, or mother. Understanding the categories of women's rights and Islam as epistemological constructs, rather than a social, political, or legal fact, means to pay closer attention to the narrative constructions by the subjects. In Chapter 5, I have thus given a voice to judges, advocates, women's rights activists, and Muslim women litigants who, for the large part, hailed from lower socioeconomic backgrounds. I have categorised the latter as the subaltern due to their all too often marginalised position within the sociolegal field. It was precisely by capturing the narratives and experiences of the subaltern that allowed me to analyse the situational meanings of women's rights and Islam on the ground. Leaning on critical legal and feminist approaches, my inquiry into the interstitial arrangements of the life of the law permitted to capture the situational knowledge configurations of law and religion that evinces the fluidity and the porousness of the meaning of Islam and women's rights on the ground.

Muslim Women's Legal Subjectivities and Agency

A critical approach to Islam and women's rights implies a shift toward the hermeneutical exploration of narratives, experiences, and knowledge that structure the question of women in Islam on the ground. Much of the feminist and political scholarship on the Muslim women's issue in India tends to portray the Muslim woman either as a victim of barbaric interpretations of Islam (Engineer 1999; Jeffrey 2000; Minault 1998a and 1998b; Mukhopadhyay 1998), or, as a victim of the patriarchal state that has little or no interest in the lives of especially poor (Muslim) women (Hasan and Menon 2005, 2004; Hasan 2000, 1999 and 1998; Patak and Sunder Rajan 1989). Such work that subscribes to the victimisation narrative of Muslim women either vis-à-vis the state or the community echoes an understanding of Muslim women as invisible, voiceless, and ultimately as stripped off agency. Interestingly, most of this work fails to actually give voice to those women (and men) who are at the centre of such analysis. Consequently, the experiences, histories, and circuits of power that exist amongst Muslim women remain under theorised.

In this book, I have given a voice to a broad range of Muslim women in the city of Lucknow, ranging from housewives, fruit-sellers, and seamstresses over teachers, university students, and doctors to activists, writers, and the clergy. These women live in different parts of the city, come from different educational, social, and political backgrounds, speak different Hindi/Urdu dialects, and have different understandings of religion, gender, and justice. Not surprisingly, the positionalities of these women in the city of Lucknow differ in terms of class, religious ideology, language, race, educational background, marital status, and family situation. This is reflected in the different manners in which they engage, think about, experience, narrate, and operate with the laws and legal institutions. For example, in Chapter 5, I examined the different strategies used by Muslim female litigants in the city to solve their marital dispute. This chapter evinced that even those Muslim women who are located on the very margin, socially and economically, und who are often portrayed as passive and without agency in feminist literature, are active agents within Lucknow's sociolegal landscape. In fact, my analysis shows that women litigants tend to 'shop' across a variety of state and non-state legal forums so as to maximise their chances for justice. These are the Family Court, the *Darul Qaza*, the mosque, or the doorsteps of Muslim women's rights offices. They did so simultaneously or in sequence. Thereby, these women actively contribute to the fragmentation of the legal landscape by blurring ideological and institutional boundaries.

Muslim women litigants turn to the Family Court, the *Darul Qaza,* and/or the office of a Muslim women's rights organisation for different reasons: some wish to opt out of an abusive marriage, others whose marriage is already broken want to get custody of their children and/or demand alimony for themselves and their children, yet others want to restore their broken marriages. The latter is quite common in a context where especially poor women find themselves alone with their children (if there are any) and with little possibilities to generate their own income after a marital breakdown. Divorced/rejected women often feel a financial burden to their natal family and a well-functioning welfare system does not exist in India. Yet other women address these forums to reinstate their and their family's lost/damaged honour – a claim that lies outside the purview of the law. So, analysing the way justice is expected and negotiated within these various legal forums renders insight into the intricate ways in which women's identities as wife, mother, and/or daughter structure their legal subjectivities in the process of dispute settlement. Very often, women's legal longings and thus choices derive from consideration of their own position within the family and the community and are often linked to their desire to uphold their security, respect, and honour. Consequently, their choices reflect their wishes to balance negotiations for women's rights and their social positionality within the constraint of patriarchy – revealing their fragmented and multi-layered legal subjectivities.

Feminists have grappled with the question whether or not 'choices' that are not entirely based on self-interest and hence are unencumbered by the weight of community norms, values, and traditions are actual choices since they seem to restrict women's negative freedom – as Isaiah Berlin (1969) termed it. This is a freedom that is free from restraints on one's ability to act as one wants. In short, women should be free to choose what they want regardless of their own embedment within social and familial ties. According to modern liberalism, freedom is a basic requirement for equal opportunity and personal dignity and in order for women to become full-fledged citizens their choices should not be impaired by patriarchal norms and values. However, as Gopika Solanki (2016) observed in the context of an informal Mumbai women's court run by the Muslim organisation *Awaaz-e-Niswan*, such reliance on a negative liberty framework of choice is too focused on women's autonomy as an individual. Solanki argues that an individualistic approach to freedom and autonomy puts forward the claim that agency is constitutive of free will and self-guided choice and action. Women who lack these criteria are thus not capable of agency. My data as well as Solanki's research show that such account on agency is not helpful to explain women's legal subjectivities that we find in the activities of Muslim women's litigants and activists. For instance, as Saba Mahmood (2005) in her study of a women's piety movement in Cairo has shown, subjectivities that are predicated on a non-stereotypical Western liberal framework do not necessarily strip women off their agency. Rather, it constitutes a different form thereof. Mahmood (2005, 188) argues in the women's piety movement context that simply because women adhere to a tradition of female piety or modesty does not automatically subordinate them. Rather, it is by understanding the working of discursive practices in the formation of subjects and their embedment within specific life situations 'that we become to understand the significance of that subordination to the women who embody it' (2005, 188). In other words, agency becomes visible not just in instances of resistance, but in the various practices, forms, and meanings of doing – in the interstices of pure resistance and compliance.

In Chapter 3, I substantiated such claim. There, I exposed the paradoxical means by which Muslim women's rights activists currently carve out semi-autonomous political and legal spaces in Lucknow. Referring to a discourse of Islamic piety, Shehnaz Sidrat (*Bazme Khawateen)*, Shaista Amber (AIMWPLB), and Naish Hasan (BMMA) consciously deploy their pious bodies, codified by modest dress and demeanour, as a means to legitimise their presence in the public sphere. One might be tempted to interpret these covered bodies and pious minds as a sign of patriarchal subjugation. However, in a context where women's entrance into the public sphere tends to be associated with the loss of their 'respectability', Islamic demeanour and dress does not strip them of their agency. Rather, such 'politics of piety', to use Saba Mahmood's (2005) words, account for a different form of political agency. This is to say that it is precisely the embodiment of an Islamic lifestyle and practice that allows for these activists to participate in struggles on legal and social reform without jeopardising their respectability, and without speaking condescendingly to the women and men they seek to target through their activism. These efforts, as I have explored throughout the book, implicates a constituent element of these three activists' practice to thwart orthodox readings and interpretations of the religious texts – contesting institutional relations, equations of power, and precepts of Islam and gender. The fact that their understanding of Islamic piety differs not only from hegemonic Islamic ideals, but also from one another, directly reflects the troubled legal landscape in which they operate, simultaneously negotiating constraints while still working to create legal spaces for ideological innovation.

So, a study on Islam and Muslim women in contemporary India necessarily needs to reflect on the burden of judgment the Western liberal tradition concerning Islam's patriarchal and misogynist qualities constitutes. While the women's question has been key in defending such position, this book further pushed for an understanding of Islam as a flexible discourse that is subject to contestation, translation, and hybridisation. The Muslim women's rights activists at the centre of this study have revisited the Muslim women's question within flexible epistemological spaces that allow for women's creative articulations of justice and equality that resonate with their everyday lives and practices.

Policy Suggestions for the Realisation of Muslim Women's Rights within Polycentric Legal Worlds

The findings and the arguments made in this study hold great relevance when one considers that not only in India, but also elsewhere in postcolonial states where gender equality is negotiated within a multiplicity of adjudicative sites. To this extent, the data set analysed and discussed in this book could be of interest and relevance to policymakers, legal advocates, and human and women's rights groups throughout the world. Women's rights activists and agencies active in postcolonial countries are most likely confronted with a legally and institutionally heterogeneous landscape. This is a landscape where the legal authority in the area of the family is decentred and shared amongst a variety of state and non-state legal institutions. In most postcolonial countries, the number of NGOs and community institutions that participate in negotiations around women's rights is on the rise. The arguments and insights presented in this study may serve as a good starting point to think about the realisation of women's rights and gender-justice more generally in situations where the state shares its legal authority with a variety of societal bodies and organisations.

The fact that legal pluralism in the area of family law is not about to vanish, as predicted by modernisation theorists, but is on the rise worldwide creates a great challenge to human and women's rights activists, practitioners, and policymakers. It is not enough to say that advocacy positions or policy options can be decided on the basis of local specificities, or simply recommend that plural legal orders must comply with international legal standards. Currently a number of international organisations such as the United Nations Program for Development (UNDP), the World Bank, UN Women, and the International Council on Human Rights, as well as governmental bodies, are engaged with the development of legal strategies and intervention mechanisms for the protection of social and gender equality apart from the state and state law. However, the complexity of legal pluralism on the practical level has so far remained under-researched. There is a need for scholarship that contributes toward the understanding of legal pluralism on a local, national, and global level in order for practitioners and organisations to develop effective tools and mechanisms. In practice, there is a dearth of frameworks, mechanisms, and tools that can guide human and women's rights advocates to grapple with the complex challenges of advocacy and policymaking.

The authors of a report published by the International Council on Human Rights Policy, Geneva, argue that it is necessary to acknowledge non-state legal orders as social and legal facts in the area of legal advocacy (International Council on Human Rights Policy 2009, 49–51). They hold that family laws are most likely to be adjudicated within a plurality of legal orders and hence remain relatively invisible in mainstream human rights discourse and practice with its focus on the state. However, this societal domain of law has so far been largely ignored by policymakers and rights advocates (2009, 71). The authors of the International Council's report hence call for research that contributes to a more nuanced understanding of how informal norms and ideas of law obstruct or enable progress with human rights on the grounds (2009, 140–142).

Yüksel Sezgin, the guest editor of the special issue of the *Journal of Legal Pluralism* (2010) entitled 'Human Rights and Legal Pluralism', took such a call seriously. Bringing together various scholars from across disciplines working in different regions in Africa, Asia, and Latin America, this issue addresses questions of human rights in legally pluralistic contexts through various empirical case studies. The objective was, according to Sezgin (2010, 3), 'to bring academic and programmatic communities close to one another by bridging the existing philosophical and methodological gaps'.[7] The studies reveal that there is a need for legal practitioners, development agencies, and policymakers to establish an interlegal and inter-juricultural dialogue with informal legal authorities and representatives in legally pluralistic societies. *Muslim Women's Quest for Gender Justice* is a direct contribution to this aspiration.

In conclusion, I would like to offer a number of policy-relevant recommendations. These could be helpful for legal practitioners, policymakers, and activists to develop useful strategies and intervention mechanisms to further a sensitive and context-conscious approach to women's rights and gender justice.

Firstly, it is necessary for legal practitioners, advocates, policymakers, and rights groups to adopt a perspective that acknowledges the plurality of legal orders and institutions. From such a perspective it quickly becomes apparent that universal standards of women's rights are just *one* amongst many formulations of gender justice that are currently validated in legal reality. The plurality of legal orders and ideas should not be viewed as limiting, but more as a possibility to engage in a process of reform that is more responsive to local specificities and needs. Those engaged in women's and human rights work need to understand the plurality of realities that shape relationships within marriage, family communities, and even between nation-states. Hence, taking as a premise the plurality of interpretations of gender justice as they exist on the ground allows for a more flexible engagement with legal reform, which avoids problems of taxonomies and discussions over the definition of law.

Secondly, it is important to question the dichotomy of state and non-state legal institutions, as well as the assumption of the state as being the only dispenser of justice. It is essential to acknowledge that postcolonial states share their adjudicative power with community courts and local authorities. The result is a thickly woven pluralistic institutional landscape of conflict, cooperation, and communication. In order for women's and human rights advocates to gain social and political legitimacy they should work in collaboration – rather than against – societal organisations. This means focusing on the potential role that non-state organisations – such as NGOs, mosques and temples, and community courts – can play in mediating between the national/transnational rights organisations and people at the grassroots. Moreover, the collaboration with activists, religious authorities, and community leaders could help lead to broader social acceptance by non-state legal actors (religious clergy, village heads, etc.). Without this, legal reform endeavours are most likely to fail. The plethora of institutions that exist in many postcolonial countries could hence serve human and women's rights advocates well. It allows them to work within and/or build upon already existing and well-established institutional networks.

Thirdly, policymakers and legal advocates have to be aware that although universal principles of social equality might seem the most effective tool available for the disenfranchised, the implementation of such concepts can be problematic. Women's and human rights groups need to understand the prejudice against autonomy and agency that are inherent in many liberal human and women's rights concepts. Couched in an abstract language of individual freedom, choice, individuality, bodily integrity, and autonomy, universal human and women's rights principles often find little application in the day-to-day realities of women at the grassroots level. To view women as individual subjects before the law makes little sense in a context where women's lives are deeply embedded and given meaning within ties of the family and the community. Hence, responding to gender injustice requires a deep and detailed reflection of how social relationships are shaped and autonomies constructed within families, communities, and societies.

Therefore, the introduction of women's rights from above is difficult if internal principles of equity and fairness are ignored. Gender reforms are more meaningful when linked to individuals' everyday experiences and expectations of the law. This means identifying women's needs and aspirations in their daily lives must serve as a basis for the formulation of a woman's rights agenda. It is not enough to hold workshops and discussions about ideas of women's and human rights. It is most important to first comprehend and understand women's everyday realities as the basis from which to initiate a meaningful dialogue on gender reforms. This does not mean to simply prioritise legal ideologies of specific religious ethnic communities or groups over liberal ideas of justice. Rather, in situations where notions of tradition and culture are used as tools to justify existing gender hierarchies, a critical approach to social and political forces that shape people's everyday interactions and relationships is important. In this regard, liberal women's and human rights discourse can be a very meaningful counter-narrative through which to challenge societal mechanisms that put women's social well-being and financial security at risk.

Fourthly, a lot can be learned from approaches to gender justice and rights from women's organisations and feminist networks. In order to find rights concepts that resonate well with substantive ideas of respect and fairness but do not interfere with Constitutional values and international rights standards, they engage in processes of vernacularisation and hybridisation. Within the last two decades, women's organisations and networks have become experts in walking the fine line between effecting a difference in a woman's life on one hand and securing the support of the local communities, as well as of national and international donor institutions on the other (Merry 2006). In so doing, they creatively merge and translate secular and non-secular state law with substantive idioms, ideologies, and experiences. As shown in this book, they offer novel interpretations and narratives of gender justice and produce new feminist norms within women's exclusive legal spaces. In this respect, I advise legal practitioners and advocates to not just 'mainstream' issues of gender justice but to take an active role in supporting and furthering the creation of women's legal spaces – and hence give women an active voice in the process of lawmaking. This asks for an approach to legal reform that appreciates novel and creative ideas of justice as formulated on the ground.

Lastly, I want to stress that putting non-state legal institutions into focus for the implementation of human and women's right does not mean to deny the state's responsibility to implement and monitor human and women's rights policies. Rather, the state has to assure and control the effective implementation of gender equality at a policy level even in areas where its influence is absent by working hand in hand with local NGOs. Therefore, these institutions need to be linked to the state as well as to local authorities in order to ensure the effective implementation and monitoring of national and international laws.

Given the relatively small institutional sample of this study, this book does not set out to propose definitive strategies that should be adopted by policymakers and human and women's rights groups. Rather, it provides thought-provoking material from which researchers, advocates, and policymakers can draw in furthering their understanding of the problems raised in regions where the majority of cases pertaining to marriage and family law never reach the formal courts and possible state-sanctioned solutions. In order to make more exhaustive suggestions for the future development of legal mechanisms and strategies, more empirical research that highlights individual's perspectives and expectations of and experiences with issues of justice and equality on the ground is necessary. For example, primary data on actors' legal epistemologies, felt needs, legal objectives, agendas, and experiences, as well as other micro-realities, would be a valuable contribution to further suggestions. In other words, women's legal subjectivities on the ground, which often coalesce with liberal ideas of individuality, freedom, and choice, are important for such a purpose. Also, it is advisable to study more in-depth the manners by which legal professionals such as the police, advocates, lawyers, and judges in formal and informal legal institutions frame and articulate gender justice. How is women's subjectivity within marriage and the family framed, constructed, and articulated? How do such articulations influence the outcome of adjudication in the state courts as well as in informal community courts? Ideally, such research is also concerned with the modalities by which larger legal agencies and networks, such as for example the UN or the World Bank, inform and influence macro-debates on gender justice. Such multinational organisations no longer just influence state actions and regulations, but also contribute to the rapidly growing non-state legal sector, especially in the Global South (Sezgin 2010, 2). In consideration of the increasing globalisation of local legal networks and agencies, scholarly perspectives that theorise local legal realities as a part of a larger national and transnational legal discourse have to be encouraged.

In sum, research that combines the micro-realities of individuals with the fractured reality of the legally pluralistic landscape contributes to a more contextualised and comprehensive understanding of women's actual rights on the ground. Such an approach is consistent with Santos' (2002, 269, 295–301) proposal of a multicultural approach to human and women's rights that takes into consideration the multiple dimensions of the legal landscape. I consider such an understanding of the working of law as especially valuable for further policy and legal advocacy work in the area of women's and human rights. In this respect, I challenge modernist ideas of justice where women's rights are conceptualised within an exclusively stereotype Western liberal rights framework. In spite of what is often stressed in modernist and liberal scholarship, (religious) non-state legal organisations and laws do not necessarily stand diametrically opposed to the idea of women's rights and gender justice. Nor are secular state laws, as associated with equality, citizenship rights, and progress, the only avenue for a fair and just society. This book proffered thus insight into the opportunities a legally pluralistic and ideologically heterogeneous landscape provides for alternative and novel formulations of women's rights and social justice at the grassroots.

Endnotes

1. See: http://timesofindia.indiatimes.com/india/Khap-panchayats-rape-order-of-2-UP-sisters-echoes-in-UK/articleshow/48737641.cms (accessed April 15, 2016).
2. See: http://www.youthkiawaaz.com/2016/03/satara-rape-of-minor-panchayat-punishment/ (accessed April 15, 2016).

3. Just recently in 2014, the Supreme Court confirmed the validity of such *fatwas* as long as they do not violate the rights of individuals guaranteed under the law (see Introduction) – a rather vague condition given the government's policy of non-interference in the area of marriage and the family.
4. See for example: http://www.theguardian.com/world/2014/apr/07/india-bjp-election-manifesto-uniform-civil-code-legislation (accessed April 23, 2016).
5. Such argument, however, neglects the fact that in reality, polygamy is not that widespread amongst Muslims. As recent statistics show, the polygamy rate amongst Hindus is slightly higher, 5.8 percent as compared to 5.7 percent amongst Muslims. http://scroll.in/article/669083/muslim-women-and-the-surprising-facts-about-polygamy-in-india (accessed May 8, 2016).
6. See: http://timesofindia.indiatimes.com/city/delhi/SC-seeks-panel-report-on-women-and-family-law/articleshow/51586887.cms (accessed April 25, 2016).
7. Sezgin (2010, 1) defines 'programmatic communities' as non-academic circles that have increasingly become interested in issues of legal pluralism.

Appendices

Appendix I: Model-*Nikahnama* of the AIMPLB

This version of the contract was translated from Urdu into English.

Nikahnama

1.	Place of *Nikah* .... post .... Block / mandal district .... State .... date .... time .... name of the nikah performer .... full address of the place	Signature
2.	Name of the groom .... father's name .... mother's name .... age .... nationality occupation .... Rank in occupation............... full address	Signature of groom
3.	Name of the bride .... father's name .... mothers name .... age .... nationality full address	Signature of bride
4.	Gaurdian of bride .... father's name .... age .... occupation .... Relation of bride .... full address..	Signature of guardian
5.	Name of *wakeel* .... father's name .. .. age .... occupation .... relation to bride .... full address	Signature of *wakeel*

6. Name of the withness (1) .... fathers' name .... age .... occupation .... full address .... — Signature of witness

7. Name of witness (2) .... father's name ....age .... occupation .... full address .... — Signature of witness

8. Amount of the Mehr .... in words .... in numbers .... given at the time of Nikah .... given after Nikaah .... — Signature of the *nikah* per-fomer with date

Signature of bride Signature of groom

Iqrarnama

The person performing the *nikah* has to ensure that the following criteria are met by the groom and the bride:

1. The man and woman agreeing to the marriage should not be related by direct blood relationship (sibling), nor should they be foster siblings or a close relative from the paternal or maternal side
2. The woman agreeing to the marriage must not be the sister, aunt (maternal or paternal), niece or a direct relative of the earlier divorcee of the man.
3. The woman cannot be married to another man at the time of this marriage.
4. The woman must not be in *iddat* either after a divorce or after death of the earlier husband at the tome of the *nikah*.
5. The woman must not be an earlier divorcee of the same man she is giving her consent to marry now.
6. The *Shariat* allows more than one spouse for the man given that all his wives are given equal rights and justice.
7. No demand for dowry can be made at the time of *nikah*.
8. The *mehar* should be paid at the time of the *nikah*.

I have been and have affirmed that there is no infringement on the *Shariat* laws and hence all the pre-marriage investigation/affirmation given above have been completed.

Hidayatnama

Marriage is a gif of God. It is mentioned in a *Hadith* that Rasulullah *sallallahu alayhi wa sallam* said: "Marry so that I can be proud of you." So, the one who is able to (fulfil the rights of a wife) should marry. By the grace of God, we are Muslims and we testify that we will follow the rules of *Shariat* as a service to God.

1. It is mentioned in a *Hadith* that when the husband and wife look at each other (with love), *Allah Taala* looks at both of them with mercy.
2. It is mentioned in a *Hadith* that Allah Taala has taken it upon Himself (i.e. out of His mercy, He as taken the responsibility) of helping the person who gets married in order to attain purity from that which Allah has made *haram*. In other words, the person who marries in order to save himself from adultery with the intention of obeying Allah Taala, Allah will help and assist him in his expenses and other affairs.
3. *Allah Taala* has given great rights to the husband and has attached a lot of virtue to him. Pleasing the husband and keeping him happy is a great act of *'ibadat* and displeasing him or keeping him unhappy is a major sin. Rasulullah sallallahu alayhi wa sallam said: "Were I to command anyone to prostrate to anyone other than *Allah*, I would have commanded the woman to prostrate to her husband. If the husband orders his wife to carry the boulders of one mountain to the next mountain, and the boulders of the next mountain to a third mountain, she will have to do this."
4. Rasulullah sallallahu alayhi wa sallam said: "When the husband calls his wife, she should go immediately to him even if she is busy at her stove." In other words, no matter how important a task she may be busy with, she should leave it and go to him.
5. A person asked: "Who is the best woman?" Rasulullah sallallahu alayhi wa sallam replied: "The best woman is one who pleases her husband when he looks at her, when he asks her to do something she obeys him, and she does not do anything that may displease him with regard to his wealth and honour."
6. Among the rights of the husband is that the wife should not remain in an untidy, dishevelled state. Instead, she should always remain clean and beautiful for her husband. In fact, if she remains untidy and dishevelled despite her husband ordering her to remain clean, he has the right of beating her (lightly) in order that she may obey him.

7. Another right of the husband is that she should not leave the house without his permission irrespective of whether it be the house of a friend, relative or anyone else.
8. It is mentioned in a *Hadith* that it is a major sin for a husband to be neglectful towards his wife and to have shortcomings in fulfilling her right to shelter and food.

We will fulfill the responsibilities we have towards each other. We will give our full efforts to make this a happy marriage. But, God forbid if any difference arise between us then the *Darul Qaza Nadwatul* – Ulama, Lucknow will be our mediator. We will follow the decision made by them.

Signature of Groom

Signature of Bride

Signature of Witness 1

Signature of Witness 2

Appendix II: Model-*Nikahnama* of AISPLB

This is an original translation from Urdu into English by the AISPLB

IN THE NAME OF ALLAH THE BENEFICENT AND THE MERCIFUL

NIKAHNAMA

(*Sanad-e-Nikah*)

Presented by: All India Shia Personal Law Board

PREFACE

All over the world marriage is regarded as the sacred social obligation. But Islam has not confined it to social values only but has explained its religious importance also.

Nikah is not only a tool to increase generation but it also helps in character building, protection from acts forbidden by Quran and formation of a family. The problem is that on the occasion of marriage people talk of religion, but the fact is that society has upper hand in every aspect. And when any issue takes a bad turn, then religion is always blamed for it.

In the Holy Quran importance and virtues of *Nikah* have been described in many occasions in very clear terms. In the *Hadith* (*hadees*) of Rasool-ul-lah and in the sermons of lmams importance and virtues of *Nikah* have repeatedly been told.

Both Quran and Sunnat have ordained better and kind behavior with wife and children.

The Quran has very explicitly explained the rights of husband and wife. In case of differences, the Quran has also suggested ways and means to solve the problem. When all the efforts of unity and reconciliation are exhausted, the Quran has advised *talaq* but still has condemned it.

The society has made marriage so difficult that today father of every daughter is perturbed.

Frivolous customs and rituals, *manjha, mehndi* and *chauthi* are nothing but wastage of lot of money. Demand of big sums of money as *Mehr* and huge dowry have devastated families. It is necessary that we should seek remedy of our problems in the light of Quran and *Hadith*. Emphasizing on the importance and need of the *Nikah* Quran says:

> *And this is one of the signs of his command that he created women for you of your own creed so that you live with them happily and developed love and compassion between you.*
>
> (*Sura-e-Rome at. 21*)

At another place the Quran says:

> *Perform Nikah of women who have no husband and your obedient slaves (male and female). If they would be hauper, the God by his mercy would made them rich. And the God is very knowledgeable and accommodation.*
>
> (*Sura-e-Noor at. 32*)

Rasool-e-lslam has said:

Nikah is my sunnat and anybody who goes against it is not from me.

Islam has given rights to husband against wife and to wife against husband and has declared them life partners, compliment to each other, source of prestige, secrecy and pride.

So in another *Ayat* the Quran says:

Hun Libas Lakum WaAntum Libas Lahan. Aurtein Goya Tumhari Choli Hain our Tum Goya Unka Daman Ho.

(Man is incomplete without woman and woman is incomplete without man).

(*Sura Baqar, Ayat 187*)

Prophet Mohammad has said that it is obligatory on wife to obey her husband. Never disobey him, keep watch on his house and not to give even 'Sadqa' from husband's money without his permission. Likewise, *Hadith* also ordains that it is imperative on husband to provide good food and clothes to wife and to forgive her if she commits any mistake unknowingly.

On another occasion the Prophet bas strongly admonished those who ignore the rights of their wives and children.

Discarded is the person who ignores the rights of his children.

(Wives should be kept with dignity, so the Prophet sold).

(*Wasail al Shia*)

Wives should be kept with dignity, so the Prophet said.

(Anybody who brings wife, he should give her due respect).

(*Wasail al Shia*)

As far as religion is concerned, it has ordered to keep women with dignity, provide them with basic necessities of life and protection of their rights.

Another evil of the society is that to show their superiority people fix big amounts as *Mahr* which in the eyes of religion is unpleasant. The Prophet said:

The best women in my 'Ummat' are those who are beautiful and their Mahr is very less.

(*Wasail al Shia*)

The Quran says:

Behave properly with your wives.

(*Sura-e-Nisa, Verse 19*)

Where on one hand against the teachings of Islam, huge amounts are fixed as *Mahr* on the other not to pay *Mahr* through the life, is an unpleasant act in the eyes of religion. So, *Imam* Jaffer Sadiq A. S. says:

There are three types of thieves, those who don't pay zakat, those who don't pay Maher of his wife and those to take debt with the intention not to repay it.

(*Behar-ul-Anwar*)

In this connection the biggest social evil is that people demand big amounts and huge dowry from bride's family. One cannot expect more un-Islamic, uncultured and inhuman thing than this evil. Though this ailment has nothing to do with the religion, this is an economic malady. But the sale of bridegroom for dowry is an inhuman act which has no parallel. It is the duty of every member of Muslim society to raise voice against this evil practice.

Since Islam is a practical religion, it has principles to solve issues even in difficult times. If all efforts of reconciliation have failed and there is no possibility of agreement and the mutual trust has finished, the divorce is the last resort. *Talaq* in Islam is valid but it has been condemned and has been permitted only as a last resort. Imam Jaffer Sadiq says, "Solemnize marriage but don't give divorce because Arsh-eKhuda shakes when a *talaq* takes place."

On another occasion it is said God loves that house where marriage takes place and dislikes that house where divorce is given. In the presence of these specific instructions it is the duty of every pious Muslim to make utmost effort to cleanse the society from the scrouge of divorce.

CONDITIONS BY THE BRIDE

1. Within the bounds of the Shariah, the bridegroom will not impose unwarranted restrictions upon me.
2. Without any proper reason, he will not refuse me to meet my parents, my siblings and my near relatives.
3. He will not force me to do anything in violation of the Shariah or which may cause me embarrassment in the society.
4. Without authentic evidence he will never make any allegation against me.
5. In case of domestic dispute, I too will have full freedom to present my cause.
6. To fulfill domestic obligations, within the bounds of the Shariah and to improve the economic situation if I wish to work anywhere, he shall not stop me.
7. In matters of upbringing of children and in domestic affairs my opinion shall carry weight too.
8. After marriage, the groom shall never demand from my parents or me or members of my family any more gifts or cash.
9. The groom shall provide all essential and lively needs.
10. The groom shall be responsible for the maintenance of the children.
11. If the groom disappears for two consecutive years and does not provide essentials to me, I shall have the right to refer to Hakim-e-Shar'a for divorce the groom should delegate power to divorce to me in this regard.
12. (a) If the groom constantly disappears and does not inquire about me for months together and does not provide for the essential needs and if this state continues for four consecutive years.
    (b) Or, if the husband uses physical force and if his action causes danger to my life or limbs, or if the forces me to have sexual relations with other men, under these circumstances the husband will delegate to me the right to divorce him so as to be relieved of physical and mental torture.
13. After consummation takes place, in case of divorce, I shall retain full rights over my *Mahr*. Besides, it being obligatory upon him to return to me all my belongings.
14. If any of the groom's relatives excessively troubles me, I shall have the right to ask my husband for a separate living arrangement. If this demand is not fulfilled, I shall have the right to refer to the Hakim-e-Sahr'a and his decision shall be binding upon both of us.

15. The groom shall have no right to ask for anything in cash or kind. He will also make no demands as far as reception of *barat* is concerned.
16. These days the demand for bridal gifts exceeds those given to the daughter of The Prophet SAWW, hence, the *Mahr* should also be more than that of Hazrat Fatima AS and there shall be no insistence upon limiting the amount of *Mahr* equivalent to the *Mahr* of Hazrat Fatima A. S.
17. If the groom divorces me at his own will and at that time if I have no other means of maintaining myself and to provide for my necessities, till the time the means of livelihood are acquired by me, the groom shall, as an unrelated helper, provide for my essential needs. Let it be made clear that with this condition I do not intend to interfere with the provisions of the Shariah, rather, this condition is based on humanitarian grounds that a helpless woman instead of having to beg from strangers, why she should not impose this condition binding the person to whom for a long time she had served as spouse.
18. If the groom has any complaints against me, he shall first present them before the arbitrators mentioned in this *Nikahnama* and shall not directly approach the court.
19. If he agrees to the conditions mentioned above, I consent to marry him.

I hereby declare that I shall not act upon conditions 11 and 12 until I procure five witnesses and have consulted a religious scholar to whose erudite opinion I shall give due weight age.

Signature of the Groom .... Signature of the Bride ....

Date ....

Witnesses:

1.
2.
3.
4.
5.

CONDITIONS BY THE GROOM

1. The bride shall support me in all matters according to Shariah and social norms.
2. After fulfilling the lawful needs of the bride if I expend my money on my parents or relatives, the bride shall have no right to object.
3. The bride shall not by wasteful expenditure which is beyond my means, land me in debt.
4. The bride shall not have the right to do anything that would cause a disgrace to me or my relatives in the society.
5. The bride shall not have the right to make any allegations against me without investigation and authentic evidence.
6. If my financial position deteriorates and the bride's financial condition improves then until such time my economic situation improves, she shall by way of *qarz-e-hasana* (soft loan) support me, which shall include the maintenance of children also.
7. If the bride has any complaint against me, she will first refer the matter to the arbitrators mentioned in this *Nikahnama* and shall not directly approach the court.

If the bride accepts the above conditions, I consent to marry her.

Signature of the Groom .... Signature of the Bride ....

Date ....

Witnesses:

1.
2.
3.
4.
5.

It is not mandatory for both parties to accept the conditions laid down for the bride and the groom in this *Nikahnama*. However, any condition(s) can be deleted, cancelled or narrowed and on a separate sheet of paper, shall be described in detail and signatures of all concerned affixed.

Similarly, if any conditions are to be added, for example, if the bride works to support her aging parents and minor siblings and she wishes to continue working even after the marriage so that they are not remained unsupported, or the groom immediately wishes to take his bride outside the country or the city or any other conditions can also be included, provided two religious scholars scrutinize them and approve that the conditions do not go against the Shariah.

DECLARATION

I, ... son of ....,
residing at ....
on this date .... corresponding to ....
declare that there does not exist a wife by any previous temporary or permanent marriage/ there exists a wife by previous temporary or permanent marriage.

I have/do not have/child(ren) ....
My monthly income is ....and the maintenance of .... family members are my responsibility.

My educational qualifications are ....
My means of income are (with designation) ....

Signature ....

Signatures of witnesses ....

I ...., daughter of ....,
residing at ....,
on this date.................................. corresponding to ....,
after reading the above declaration, am consenting to accept Mr. ....
.... son of .... as my husband.

However, if any of the provisions of the declaration are proven false, I shall have the delegated authority to divorce, and if I do not want to live with him, I shall exercise my delegated authority to divorce. However, I will not exercise this right without consulting a religious scholar and my witnesses.

Signature ....

Signature of witnesses: ....

If any of the provisions of this declaration are proven false, then Mrs. .... daughter of .... will have the delegated authority to divorce me.

Signature ....

Appendix III: *Shariat Nikahnama*: Model-*Nikahnama* of the AIMWPLB

This contract was translated from Hindi into English.

Promote goodness and bring an end to bad habits

Brothers and sisters! Our aim is not to prove us or prove others wrong, but to provide the correct information about Islamic *Shariat* to families.

For this purpose, I make the following requirements:

1. I request my brothers and sisters to read the translation of *Quran.*
2. I request parents to make their sons/daughters read the translations before their children's marriage so as to make them aware of the rights and regulations and to prevent problems in future. If the spouses are not aware about the dos/don'ts they may unknowingly commit some mistake, which might disperse their families forever. Every person dreams about his/her prosperous and loving marriage and in case the spouses are not aware of their rights written in the holy *Quran*, their dream would remain a dream.
3. I deeply believe that once every one is aware of their duties and rights bestowed upon them by God the almighty there will be no mistrust between family members. This will save the families from the tragedy of a marital break-up.
4. You all are aware that every Muslim's soul lies in the *Shariat* because the *Shariat* makes every Muslim a complete believer. On the basis of *Shariat* a Muslim checks his attitude and behaviour and decides whether he is going right or wrong. If a believer always keeps these *Shariat* in mind than there is no way that he can go wrong in his behaviour, conduct and working. It will always stop him from taking any wrong step. If every Muslim properly follows the *Shariat* than I can vouch and say that there would be no dispute between husband or wife, or family or in the society. Even in case of some dispute the people would come together peacefully and talk together to find a solution.

Therefore, we recommend that every Muslim must be aware of the *Shariat.* The All India Muslim Women Personnel Law Board has created this *Shariat Nikahamah,* which will hopefully be useful for creating a happy married life.

Iqrarnama

1. Whoever listened and obeyed prophet they have in fact obeyed Allah, the almighty God. And the person who doesn't obey you then you are not responsible for them – From the *Quran*.

Surah Nisa – Verse 80

2. The life and actions of Prophet Muhammad (P.B.U.H.) is a very good example for the people.
3. O believers! You have no right to take the right and property of women without their agreement.

Surah Nisa – Verse 19

4. Pay your wives *mehr* to the best of your abilities.

Surah Nisa – Verse 4

5. If you cannot do justice to all then marry only one (in respect to marriages).

Surah Nisa – Verse 3

6. If differences arise between the husband and wife then bring just and honest family members of both the sides, sit together and solve the problem, verily Allah is aware of everything.

Surah Nisa – Verse 35

7. The women whom you agree to give divorce must be treated nicely and fairly.

Surah Nisa – Verse 24

8. Do not throw out the women from you homes while they are in their period of *iddat*. Woman too must not leave her house.

Surah Nisa – Verse 1

Shaista Amber
President
All India Muslim Women's Personal Law Board

Nikahnama

For the Marriage Bureau
Place of Marriage .... & Country

1. Post Office .... Address ....
   City / Town .... Date ....
   Acc. to Islamic Calendar .... Day ....
   Time ....
   Name of Groom ....
   Name of father (Groom) ....
   Name of mother (Groom) ....
   Date of Birth .... Nationality ....
   Occupation ....
   Permanent & Registered Address ....

Signature of Groom

If marriage done in court by lawyer then name of lawyer ....
....
Age .... post .... Address
....

Signature of Lawyer

2. Name of bride ....
   Name of father (Bride) ....
   Name of mother (Bride) ....
   Date of Birth .... Nationality ....
   Occupation ....
   Permanent & Registered Address ....
   Signature of Bride
   Name of bride's guardian ....
   Age .... Occupation ....
   Relation to the bride .... Address ....
   ....

Signature of the guardian

If there is no witness from the bride's side at the time of the ceremony, two people present at that time have to sign the contract as witnesses to the marriage.

Witness to the marriage

3. Name of witness (1) ....
Age .... Occupation ....
Address. ....
Name of Witness (2) ....
Age .... Occupation ....
Address. ....

Signature of *Mullah*

Signature of Bride

Signature of Groom

With *Allah*, the almighty, as our witness we agree to be married to each other. We will try our best to remain happily married to each other. I pledge that to the best of my ability I will support my husband through the good and the bad, and will follow the *Shariat*. I too, pledge that I will follow the *Shariat* and will support my wife through good and bad times to the best of my ability. We will follow the *Shariat* in case of any problem and god forbid in case of divorce too we will seek the guidance of the holy *Quran*. We will keep faithful to each other.

Prayer

O the giver of sustenance! Bestow your blessings, love, prosperity and patience on them and give them beautiful children and your blessing.

Shariat-e-Islam is a pure and established set of rules. The marriage ceremony is not only considered as an event but also as a service to God.

Hidayatnama

The bride and groom are expected to lead a happy and peaceful life. The marital bond cannot be broken without a valid reason.

1. The person reading out the *nikahnama* should be an adult, having a sound mind. He must be Muslim by faith and should have the complete knowledge of the *Shariat*.
2. He / she should clearly tell the rights and duties obligatory on the husband and wife.
3. The name of the bride and groom to be registered should be properly written without any mistake. Either of them cannot be forced to marry the other as such a marriage would be considered void. The guardians of both the side should take care that they must not marry their children if they are still in the juvenile ages. It is best for the sides, that the bride and groom should on their own free will agree to merry each other.
4. Forcing the bride's family to pay dowry is against Allah's wishes and contrary prophet Muhammad (P.B.U.H.) *dunnah*. We must follow our prophet's *sunnah*. Hazrat Ali at the time of his marriage to Fatima (RTA) gave her *mehr*, which were to the best of his abilities at the time.
5. If the wife decides to forego her *mehr* then it should be checked that she did it on her own decision and not under pressure.
6. *Mehr* is a compulsory obligation on the husband, which he must give to his wife at the time of marriage. If due to circumstances he isn't able give it at the time of marriage, then he must do so whenever it becomes possible for him and be attains the means.
7. Husband and wife are supposed to respect and support each other. The husband cannot take his wife as a housekeeper because, she like him, is also the master of the house and thus he must not overburden her with work. She too deserves respect. Likewise, the wife must also give respect and honour to her husband. Both should be loyal to each other and must not cheat the other partner.
8. It is duty of the husband to look after the welfare of his wife. He is to provide for her shelter, food, clothes etc. He is to do so to the best of his abilities.
9. Both of then must treat each other well and happily. It is not right that when wife goes out she dresses to her best but when the husband returns she meets him in her dirty cloths.
10. The women who loves her husband, and is more ready to solve problems rather than creating them and can apologies when she commits some mistake is surely someone who deserves paradise.
11. The wife must not demand more than the husband can afford.
12. The couple should take care that the close relatives of their spouse must not interfere or cause a rift between them.

13. The relatives of the spouses must be given equal respect as they give their own parents.
14. The Holy Prophet Mohammad (PBUH) has strictly forbidden the husbands from hurting their wives in any way either physical or mental.
15. It is better for the in-laws to consider their daughter-in-law as their own daughter. Both the sides must give respect to the family members of their son's/daughter's spouse.
17. All the intelligent and balanced people follow the straight path and never confuse the right with the wrong.

Talaq when followed as according to the _Shariat_ irrevocably ends a marriage

1. *Talaq* is not something to be said in anger or retaliation, but instead, *talaq* is only given in dire need or when no other way is left.
2. From all the things Allah despises, he despises *talaq* most.
3. Despite His strong dislike, *Allah* legalised *talaq* for Muslims.
4. The husband must treat the woman who was earlier his wife properly. He should not throw her out of the house, but instead give her means that she can live her life in peace.
5. At the time of giving *talaq* to his wife the husband must follow all the *Shariat* and should take this step after seeking guidance from a religious scholar. It may be that after sometime both, the husband and wife, are able to bury the hatchet and come to an understanding. In case the decision is final there should be a mullah or scholar who would read out the *talaq* and there should also be two witnesses who should be firm in their faith and would not waver in what they witnessed.
6. All the gifts which the wife received in the time between the marriage and *talaq* from her husband's family, or his relations or his friends are now hers and must not be taken back from her.
7. According to *sunnah talaq* can only be given when the woman is not menstruating. This way she can count her period of *iddat*.
8. Neither the husband should nor should the wife leave her husband's house, before the period of *iddat* is complete because it may be that they both come to an understanding.
9. *Talaq* is not considered when the husband is drunk, asleep, ailing from some disease in which when he cannot think straight. It is also not considered via e-mail, S.M.S. or via phone. Sometimes the husband doesn't give his wife *talaq* but tortures her endlessly. In such a case she herself can take *khul* from her husband.

10. Whatever the husband and wife decide in *khul* is acceptable but the wife cannot demand more than the *mehr* she received.

The marriage is naturally ended if the husband

1. is missing from four years or more.
2. refuses to give the wife her right.
3. behaves in a cruel manner to his wife.
   These are:
   (a) If the husband has an illicit relationship with other wife.
   (b) Makes her life miserable.
   (c) The husband hides that he carries the HI virus even before they were married. This is valid because hiding such a serious condition is equal to cheating.

Appendix IV: Model-*Nikahnama* of the BMMA

This is an original translation from Hindi into English by the BMMA

نکاح نامہ

اور

اقرار نامہ

منجانب بھارتیہ مسلم مہیلا

آندولن

نومبر ۲۰۰۸

भारतीय मुस्लिम महिला आंदोलन
द्वारा बनाया गया

निक़ाहनामा
और
इक़रारनामा

NIKAAHNAMA
AND
IQRAARNAMA

Prepared by
BHARATIYA MUSLIM MAHILA ANDOLAN

NIKAAHNAMA

1. This Nikaahnama is in consonance with the Holy Quran and entered into at ________________(city/state), this________________ of________________ between________________(A) hereafter referred to as they BRIDEGROOM AND________________ (B) hereafter referred to as the BRIDE.
2. This Nikaahnama is subject to the exclusive jurisdiction of the court where the bride ordinarily resides at any future date.

Personal particulars of parties A and B are given below :

1. Name of the bridegroom (Full Name) ____________

   ____

   Date of birth :________________________________

   Address :____________________________________

   ____

   ____

   Martial status (single, widower, married, divorcee) :

   ____

2. Name of the bridegroom (Full Name) ____________

   ____

   Date of birth :________________________________

   Address :____________________________________

   ____

   ____

   Martial status (single, widower, married, divorcee) :

   ____

3. Date of Nikaah : ____________________
4. Islamic date : ____________________
5. English Date : ____________________
6. Place of Nikaah (full address) : ____________________

____

____

7. Time of Nikaah ____________________
8. Name of Witness No. 1 from the bridegroom's side :

____

9. Age : ____________________
10. Address : ____________________

____

____

11. Name of Witness No. 2 from the bride's side : ____________________

____

12. Age : ____________________
13. Address : ____________________

____

____

14. Permanent address of Bride's Family :

____

____

____

15. Permanent address of Bridegroom's family :

____

____

____

13

16. The amount of Rs.__________________in cash or kind has been fixed as Mahr in this Nikaah.

I, the above named bridegroom do hereby agree to give Rs.________________ or ______________ as Mehr (Prompt (Mujjal) / Deferred (Muwajjal}) for this marriage to the bride and the same has been approved by her.

No.	Item	Quantity
1	Cash	
2	Gold	
3	Silver	
4	Fixed Deposits	
5	Land	
6	Cheque / DD	
7	Any other	

Annexure to this Nikaahnama are original lists duly signed by both the parties. The list is as given below :

- Articles received by bride from the bride parents and relatives.
- Articles received by bride from the bridegroom parents and relatives.
- Articles given by bride to the bridegroom and his relatives and friends.

Other details about the bridegroom :

- Present occupation :________________________
- Address of the place of employment : __________

____

____

- Income per month : ____________________
- Particulars of property (self acquired and share in inherited property)

  ____

  ____

  ____

The following documents are enclosed with this Nikaahnama

- Passport size photos of the bride and the groom
- Wedding invitation card (if there is one)
- Copy of the passport/PAN card/voter I-care/IT Identity card attached.
- Copy of the ration card.
- Proof of employment.
- In case of divorce documents related to the divorcee from first spouse.
- In case of widower/widow death certificate of spouse.

But the bride and bridegroom do hereby confirm that each of them have read the Nikaahnama, understood its contents and given their consent to abide by all the conditions and nothing has been concealed or suppressed by either of them.

****

- Signed by the bridegroom

  Mr.____________________

  In the presence of Witness No. 1 and Witness No. 2

  Name : ____________________

  Sign : ____________________

15

- Signed by the bride

  Ms.______________________________

  In the presence of Witness No. 1 and Witness No. 2

  Name : ______________________________

  Sign : ______________________________

- Signed and delivered by Marriage Solemnizer

  Name :______________________________

  Sign : ______________________________

Three (3) original copies of the nikaahnamas have been prepared and given to the bridegroom, bride and the Marriage Solemnizer

IQRARNAMA

MEHR :

Since mehr is the right of the bride at the time of nikaah, the amount has to be paid at the time of the solemnization of the nikaah. The groom has agreed to pay the mentioned amount at the time of nikaah. However, since the mehr amount can also be deferred to later date, the bridegroom has agreed to pay the deferred amount on____________________

In case of any imperative reason the full amount of Mahr agreed upon has not been paid at the time of the Nikaah then the bridegroom undertakes through this Nikaahnama that he or his relatives or any one on his behalf, shall not in any manner apply any physical, social, emotional, psychological, or economic pressure on the bride to forego the Mahr or to decrease the Mahr amount.

The bridegroom also undertakes that in the event of his untimely death, his family members/relatives shall be responsible for payment of Mahr and acknowledges that Mahr is the right of the wife which cannot be compromised. Further, it is non-refundable and non-negotiable and shall be the absolute property of the bride and under her exclusive control and power.

DISPUTE :

The bride and bridegroom agree that in case of marital discord neither party has the right to terminate the marriage unilaterally.

The husband shall not resort to, under any circumstances, unilateral oral triple divorce in one sitting. The right to divorce is shared equally by both the bride and the groom in keeping with the spirit of justice in Islam.

If matrimonial discord occurs, then the parties shall appoint a representative each from their respective family who will constitute the Arbitration Council along with NGO's representatives and other individuals having knowledge and integrity. No dissolution shall take place while the arbitration process is ongoing and until it is finally concluded.

While neither party will have the right to unilateral divorce, in the event of talaak initiated by either party the husband shall be bound to comply with the following financial rights of the wife.

- Mehr (if deferred and not yet paid)
- Gifts received by her at the time of and during the subsistence of the marriage.
- Right to reside in the matrimonial home.
- Equal share of all property acquired during subsistence of the marriage.
- A reasonable and fair provision (mattaa) for the future sustenance which shall be equivalent to maintenance for a period of 10 years according to the standard of life which she is accustomed to during her marriage.

Either party can go to the secular court to settle their dispute.

If the dispute has been settled outside the court then the couple are advised to validate the decisions of the Arbitration Council in the court of law.

AGE

The age of the bride shall be 18 years and that of the groom 21 years.

POLYGAMY

The husband shall not be entitled to and shall not enter into a second marriage during the subsistence of this first marriage as monogamy is the stated ideal in the Quran.

The bride and the bridegroom may insert any other provision provided it does not violate the provisions of this Nikaahnama.

The bride and bridegroom undertake to follow these terms and conditions and respect each other from this day on.

18

THE NIKAAHNAMA IS BASED ON THE FOLLOWING QURANIC VERSE

"The rights of wives (with regard to their husband) are equal to the (husband's) rights with regard to them" (HQ 2:228)

"They are apparel for you and you are apparel for them" (HQ 2:187)

"Men shall benefit from what they earn and women shall benefit from what they earn" (HQ 4:32)

"If you fear a breach between the two, appoint an arbiter from his people and an arbiter from her people. If they both desire an agreement, Allah will effect harmony between them" (HQ 4:35)

"For divorced women maintenance should be provided on a reasonable scale. This is the duty of the righteous" (HQ 2:241)

"Lo! Men who surrender unto Allah and women who surrender, and men who believe and women who believe, and men who obey and women who obey, and men who speak the truth and women who speak the truth, patient men and patient women, and humble men and humble women, and the charitable men and charitable women, and the fasting men and fasting women, and men who guard their chastity and women who guard their chastity, and men who remember Allah and women who remember Allah, Allah has prepared for them forgiveness and a mighty reward" (HQ 33:35)

"Oh! Mankind, be conscious of your Sustainer, who has created you out of one living entity, and out of it created its mate, and out of the two spread abroad a multitude of men and women" (HQ 4:1)

"And if you have reason to fear that you might not be able to act equitably towards orphans, then marry from among other

19

women such as are lawful to you – two or three or four; but if you have a reason to fear that you may not be able to treat them with equal fairness then only one or from among those who you rightfully possess. This will make it more likely that you will not deviate from the right course." (HQ 4:2)

"Even if it is your ardent desire you cannot do justice in between your wives" (HQ 4:129)

"…..even if you have given a heap of gold….." (HQ 2:20)

"And give women dowries as free gifts. But if they of themselves be pleased to give you a portion thereof, consume it with enjoyment and pleasure" (HQ 4:4)

"Let him who has abundance spend on his wife out of his abundance and let him whose means of subsistence are scanty spend in accordance with what God has given him" (HQ 2:236)

Glossary

Alima	Female religious scholar
Ashraf	Noble caste
Ayat	Verse in the *Quran*
Azan	Muslim summon to prayer
Baradari	Garden pavilion
Basti	Slum
Bazme Khawateen	Women's club
Brahman	A Hindu of the highest caste, also the ultimate essence of material phenomena
Burqa	Robe that covers a woman's body from head to toe
Chador	Full-length open cloak worn by Persian women and Shia women in India
Dahej	Dowry
Dalit	Term to describe the category of untouchables
Darul Qaza	literally, house of adjudication
Darul Uloom Nadwatul	Is a large Islamic institution at Lucknow that draws students from all over the world
Dawa Rukhsati	Uncodified equivalent for Muslims to the restitution of conjugal rights (Section 9 of the Hindu Marriage Act, 1955)
Deobandi	Revivalist movement in Sunni Islam
Dupatta	Long shawl
Faisla	Decision
Faskh	Nullification of marriage by the *qazi* and without the consent of the husband. In this case, a man admits that he mistreats his wife but he does not want to divorce her, so the *qazi* can end the marriage. Whether or not the woman gets her *mehar* and the maintenance during *iddat* depends upon the husband.

Fatwa	Legal opinion
Fiqh	The product of human understanding that sought to interpret and implement the *Shariat*
Firangi Mahal	Famous religious centre for Sunni Muslims in Lucknow
Gunnah	Religious sin
Hadith	The oral tradition regarding the Prophet Muhammad's statements and his endorsement of actions
Halal	Allowed
Halala	Practice that requires the woman to consummate the marriage with another man and go through *iddat* before she can go back to her former husband
Hanafi	One of the four schools in jurisprudence in Sunni Islam. It is said to be the oldest school in jurisprudence. The Barelvi and Deobandi are both *Hanafi*.
Hanbali	One of the schools of *fiqh* or religious law within Sunni Islam
Haram	Forbidden
Hidayatnama	Section of the marriage contract that lists the guidelines for marriage
Hijab	Headscarf covering the hair and leaving the face open
Hindutva	Hindu nationalist group
Hizanat	The Islamic right of the mother to child custody – this right is not absolute
Ibadat	Religious/spiritual act – relationship between God and the worshipper
Iddat	Waiting period of four months and ten days. This is the period a woman must observe after the death of her husband or after a divorce. During that time a woman cannot marry another man. This period stands for three menstrual periods and is intended to determine whether or not the woman is pregnant with her ex-husband's baby.
Ijma	Agreement among legal scholars. This was supported by the *Hanafi* doctrine that the law must change with changing times, and the *Maliki* doctrine that new facts require new laws. Based on *ijma,* the doctrine of *ijtihad* was developed.
Ijtihad	Interpretive science of juridical reasoning
Imam	Male prayer leader in a mosque

Iqrarnama	Part of the marriage contract that stipulates the agreement
Jamaat	Assembly, council
Jati	Caste
Kafir	Non-believer
Khairat	Optional charity
Khul	*Khul* is an extra-judicial initiated divorce by the woman, in which she asks her husband to release her from the marriage in return for some 'payment'. In most cases, a woman has to forfeit the *mehar* or whatever portion of its payment is outstanding, and her right to maintenance during the time of *iddat*. Additionally, the husband may urge her to waive her rights to retain custody of the children if they are over four years of age. The negotiations over whether or not the wife is granted the right to *khul* usually take place in the presence of a *qazi* as per example in the *Shariat*-court.
Khuli Adalat	Open court or assembly
Lakh	Hundred thousand
Lok Adalat	People's Court
Lok Sabha	The lower house of the Parliament in India
Madrasa	Muslim school, university or college that is often a part of a mosque
Mahila Adalat	Women's court
Mahila Panchayat	Women's court
Maliki	One of the schools of *fiqh* in Sunni Islam
Manusmriti	Ancient Hindu texts
Martam	The congregation of men and women for the ceremonial chest beating in Shia Islam
Mattaa	One-time payment of maintenance paid by the husband to his wife after a divorce.
Maulana	Muslim religious scholar
Mehar	An important right of the wife in Islam, where the husband is responsible to pay his wife's dower at the time of the marriage
Mubarat	Divorce on mutual agreement. All rights and mutual agreements between husband and wife come to an end.
Mufti	Muslim scholar, juriconsultant
Muharram	The first month of the Islamic calendar

Mujtahid	A person accepted as an original authority in Islamic law. Such authorities continue to be recognised in the Shia tradition, but Sunni Muslims accord this status only to the great lawmakers of early Islam
Mullah	Religious teacher or leader
Muta	Temporary marriage contracted under Shia law. This marriage does not create the right of inheritance between the spouses. The children, however, are legitimate and can inherit from both parents.
Muamalat	Realm of the private; relationship between humans in the private sphere
Nafaqa	A man's obligation to provide shelter, food, and clothes to his wife and children. This obligation toward the wife is terminated by death or divorce. In the latter case, the husband has to maintain his wife during the time of *iddat*.
Namaz	Prayer
Nawabi	Nawabi refers to the Nawab of Avadh, the title of rulers who governed the state of Oudh (Avadh) in the eighteenth and nineteenth century – Lucknow's golden cultural era
Niqab	A veil covering a woman's face but leaving her eyes open
Nari Adalat	Women's court
Nikah	Marriage. In Islam, marriage is a contract between a man and a woman to live as husband and wife.
Nikahnama	Marriage contract. A formal binding contract is considered as an integral part of an Islamic marriage. The *nikahnama* often stipulates the conjugal rights and duties of the wife and husband.
Panchayat	Assembly, council
Purdah	lit. Curtain or screen used to keep women separate from, and invisible to, men. In South Asia, the term has a visual, spatial, and moral dimension. These are as follows: veiling of women, segregation of sexes, and a set of norms and attitudes that sets the boundaries for women's moral conduct. *Purdah* is, therefore, commonly used as equivalent to female modesty.
Qazi	Muslim judge, officiating officer representing religious authority

Qiyas	A rule of legal interpretation based on the idea of reasoning by analogy. It became a source of law as a sort of compromise by the Shafii and *Maliki* schools.
Quran	Sacred text of Islam divided into 114 chapters or *Surahs*. Revered to as the word of God, dictated to Muhammed, and accepted as the foundation of Islamic law, religion, culture, and politics.
Rajya Mahila Ayog Adhiniyam	Uttar Pradesh State Commission for Women
Ramadan	The ninth month of the Islam calendar; Muslims worldwide observe this as a month of fasting
Rukhsati	lit. Consummation of the marriage. *Rukhsati* takes place after the wedding and marks the moment when husband and wife start living together as spouses. In India, *rukhsati* commonly refers to the ceremony where the bride moves to the groom's house.
Salwaar Kameez	Indian dress comprised of loose-fitting pants and a long top
Sadqa	Voluntary charity
Sati	A widow's self-immolation by burning on her husband's funeral pyre
Shadi	Wedding
Shaafi	One of the schools of thought and jurisprudence in Sunni Islam
Shareef	Good, correct
Shariat	The moral guidelines and the code of law derived from the *Quran*, and teachings and examples of Muhammed
Stridhan	Gifts given to a woman at the time of her marriage or during the course of her marriage
Sunnah	The way of life described as normative for Muslims on the basis of Muhammed's deeds and teachings and the *Quran*.
Surah	Chapter or division of the *Quran*
Talaq	Divorce. Divorce in Islam has three steps: initiation, reconciliation, and completion. During the period of initiation (*talaq-e-rajai*) the couple do not have to publicise the *talaq*. After the second pronunciation (*talaq-e-bain*) the couple has to involve family members to help

	to reconcile. After the third pronunciation (*talaq moghul*) the divorce is valid and irrevocable. The husband is no longer responsible for the expenses of his wife who is now *haram* to him.
Talaq-e-bain	A term delineating that if the husband has pronounced *talaq* twice only before deciding to remain in the marriage the couple can be remarried in the presence of a *maulana*
Talaq-e-tafweez	A delegated right to divorce vested in the wife where the wife can exercise herself the right to end the marriage. In India, this right is little-known and hardly implemented.
Talaqnama	Divorce decree
Tarawih	Extra congregational prayers performed by Muslims at night in the month of *Ramadan*
Taziya	The re-enactment of the battle of Karbala
Triple talaq	Three pronouncements made usually in one sitting clearly dissolving the marriage irrevocably and followed by *iddat*. This practice is prevalent among Sunnis where men can divorce their wife in one sitting and without the presence of a witness. Shia Islam considers such methods of divorce as illegal. Shia practice requires two witnesses and a waiting period between each pronouncement of *talaq* where the couple is supposed to try to reconcile with the help of mediators from each family.
Ulema	Community that consists of eminent religious authorities
Wakeel	Lawyer
Walimah	Wedding banquet. The *walimah* is performed right after the wedding ceremony (*nikah*) to publicly announce the marriage.
Waqf	A charitable Islamic trust for the welfare of needy and poor people
Zakat	Obligatory charity; constitutes one of the five pillars of Islam
Zenana	Woman
Zina	Extramarital affair. *Zina* is considered one of the greatest sins in Islam.

Bibliography

Abu-Lughod, Lila (1998a) 'Introduction.' In Lila Abu-Lughod (ed.), *Remaking Women: Feminism and Modernity in the Middle East*. Princeton: Princeton University Press, 3–31.

______ (1998b) 'The Marriage of Feminism and Islam in Egypt: Selective Repudiation as a Dynamic of Postcolonial Cultural Politics.' In Lila Abu-Lughod (ed.), *Remaking Women: Feminism and Modernity in the Middle East*. Princeton: Princeton University Press, 243–69.

______ (2002) 'Do Muslim Women Really Need Saving? Anthropological Reflections on Cultural Relativism and its Others.' *American Anthropologist, New Series* 104 (3): 783–90.

______ (2010) 'The Active Social Life of 'Muslim Women's Rights': A Plea for Ethnography, not Polemic, with Cases from Egypt and Palestine.' *Journal of Middle-East Women's Studies* 6 (1): 1–45.

Agnes, Flavia (1992) 'Protecting Women against Violence? Review of a Decade of Legislation, 1980-89.' *Economic and Political Weekly*, WS19–WS33.

______ (1999) *The Politics of Women's Rights in India*. Oxford/York: Oxford University Press.

Agosin, Marjorie (2001) 'Introduction.' In Marjorie Agosìn (ed.), *Women, Gender and Human Rights*. New Brunswick: Rutgers University Press, 1–11.

Ahmad, Imtiaz (1976) *Family, Kinship and Marriage among Muslims in India*. New Delhi: Manohar Book Service.

Ahmad, Jalal Al-I (2002) 'Westoxication.' In Mansoor Moaddel and Karman Talattof (eds.), *Modernist and Fundamentalist Debates in Islam*. New York: Palgrave Macmillan, 243–57.

Ahmed, Leila (1992) *Women and Gender in Islam: Historical Roots of a Modern Debate*. New Haven/London: Yale University Press.

Al-Ali, Nadje (2012) 'Gendering the Arab Spring.' *Middle East Journal of Culture and Communication* 5 (1): 26–31.

Ali, Kecia (2003) 'Progressive Muslims and Islamic Jurisprudence: The Necessity for Critical Engagement with Marriage and Divorce Law.' In Omid Safi (ed.), *Progressive Muslims: on Justice, Gender and Pluralism*. Oxford: Oneworld Publications, 162–89.

Amman, Ludwig (2006) 'Private and Public in Muslim Civilization.' In Nilüfer Göle and Ludwig Ammann (eds.), *Islam in Public: Turkey, Iran, and Europe*. Istanbul: Istanbul Bilgi University Press, 77–125.

Appadurai, Arjun (1996) *Modernity at Large: Cultural Dimensions of Globalization*. Minneapolis/London: University of Minneapolis Press.

Asad, Talal (2009[1986]) 'The Idea of an Anthropology of Islam.' *Qui Parle* 17 (2): 1–30.

______ (1992) 'Religion and Politics: An Introduction.' *Social Research* 59 (1): 3–16.

______ (2003) *Formations of the Secular: Christianity, Islam, Modernity*. Stanford: Stanford University Press.

Badran, Margot (1991) 'Competing Agenda: Feminists, Islam and the State in Nineteenth- and Twentieth-Century Egypt.' In Deniz Kandiyoti (ed.), *Women, Islam and the State*. Houndmills/Basingstoke/Hampshire/London: Macmillan Press Ltd., 201–36.

______ (1994) 'Gender Activism: Feminists and Islamists in Egypt.' In Valentine M. Moghadam (ed.), *Identity Politics and Women: Cultural Reassertions and Feminisms in International Perspective*. Boulder/San/Francisco/Oxford: Westview Press, 202–27.

______ (1995) *Feminists, Islam and the Nation: Gender and the Making of Modern Egypt*. Princeton: Princeton University Press.

______ (2013) *Feminism in Islam: Secular and Religious Convergences*. Oxford: Oneworld Press.

Baird, Robert D. (2001) 'Gender Implications for a Uniform Civil Code.' In Gerald James Larson (ed.), *Religion and Personal Law in Secular India: A Call to Judgment*. Bloomington/Indianapolis: Indiana University Press, 145–83.

______ (2005) 'Religion and Law in India: Adjusting to the Sacred as Secular.' In Robert D Baird (ed.), *Religion and Law in Independent India*. New Delhi: Manohar Publishers, 7–34.

Balchin, Cassandra (2002) 'The Network 'Women Living Under Muslim Law': Strengthening Local Struggles Through Cross-Boundary Working.' *Development* 45 (1): 126–31.

Barlas, Asma (2004) 'The Qu'ran, Sexual Equality and Feminism.' Talk given at University of Toronto. Available at: http://www.asmabarlas.com/TALKS/20040112_UToronto.pdf (accessed June 10, 2013).

Bartelink, Brenda and Marjo Buitelaar (2006) 'The Challenges of Incorporating Muslim Women's Views into Development Policy: Analysis of a Dutch Research Project in Yemen.' *Gender and Development* 14 (3): 351–62.

Basu, Srimati (2001) *She Comes To Take Her Rights: Indian Women, Property, and Propriety*. New Delhi: Kali for Women.

______ (2006) 'Playing off Courts: The Negotiation of Divorce and Violence in Plural Legal Settings in Kolkata.' *Journal of Legal Pluralism* 38 (52): 41–75.

______ (2012) 'Judges of Normality: Mediating Marriage in the Family Courts of Kolkata, India.' *Signs* 37 (2): 469–92.

______ (2015) *The Trouble with Marriage: Feminists Confront Law and Violence in India*, Volume 1. University of California Press.

Baxi, Upendra (2009) 'Voices of Suffering and the Future of Women's Rights.' In William Twinning (ed.), *Human Rights Southern Voices*. Cambridge: Cambridge University Press, 162–204.

Beck, Ulrich, Wolfgang Bonss and Christoph Lau (2001) 'Theorie Reflexiver Modernisierung–Fragestellungen, Hypothesen, Forschungsprogramme.' In Ulrich Beck and Wolfgang Bonss (ed.) *Die Modernisierung der Moderne*. Frankfurt am Main: Suhrkamp, 11–59.

Benda-Beckmann, Franz von (2002) 'Who's Afraid of Legal Pluralism?' *Journal of Legal Pluralism* 34 (47): 37–82.

______ (2003) 'Rechtsethnologie.' In Bettina Beer and Hans Fischer (eds.), *Ethnologie: Einführung und Überblick*. Berlin: Reimer, 179–95.

Benda-Beckmann, Keebet von (1981) 'Forum Shopping and Shopping Forums: Dispute Processing in Minangkabau Village.' *Journal of Legal Pluralism* 13 (19): 117–59.

______ (2001) 'Legal Pluralism.' In *Tai Culture: International Review on Tai Cultural Studies* 4 (1 and 2): 18–40.

Bennett, Linda Rae (2005) *Women Islam and Modernity: Single Women, Sexuality and Reproductive Health in Contemporary Indonesia*. London/New York: Routledge.

Berlin, Isaiah (1969) 'Two Concepts of Liberty.' *Berlin* I: 118–72.

Bhabha, Homi (1990) 'The Third Space.' In Jonathan Rutherford (ed.), *Identity: Community, Culture, Difference*. London: Lawrence and Wishart.

Bhagwati, P. N. (2005) 'Religion and Secularism Under the Indian Constitution.' In Robert D. Baird (ed.), *Religion and Law in Independent India*. New Delhi: Manohar Publishers, 35–50.

Bhargava, Rajeev (2004) 'Die Demokratische Vision Vision einer neuen Republik: Indien 1950.' In Shalini Randeria, Martin Fuchs and Antje Linkenbach (eds.), *Soziale Welt. Sonderband 15. Konfigurationen der Moderne. Diskurse zu Indien*. Baden–Baden: Nomos Verlagsgesellschaft, 115–36.

______ (2007) 'The Distinctiveness of Indian Secularism.' *The Future of Secularism*, 20-53.

Bhattacharya, Nandini (1996) 'Behind the Veil: The Many Masks of Subaltern Sexuality.' *Women's Studies International Forum* 19 (3): 277–92. Pergamon.

Bose, Brinda (2002) 'Introduction.' In Brinda Bose (ed.), *Translating Desire: The Politics of Gender and Culture in India*. New Delhi: Katha, ix–xxix.

Brass, Paul R. (1998) 'Secularism Out of its Place.' *Contributions to Indian Sociology* 32 (2): 485–505.

Brown, Wendy (1992) 'Finding the Man in the State.' *Feminist Studies* 18 (1): 7–34.

Bullock, Katherine (2002) *Rethinking Muslim and the Veil: Challenging Historical and Modern Stereotypes*. London: The International Institute of Islamic Thought.

Bunch, Charlotte (1990) 'Women's Rights as Human Rights: Toward a Re-Vision of Human Rights.' *Human Rights Quarterly* 12: 486–98.

Burawoy, Michael (1998) 'The Extended Case Method.' *Sociological Theory* 16 (1): 4–33.

Butler, Judith (1988) 'Performative Acts and Gender Constitution: An Essay in Phenomenology and Feminist Theory.' *Theatre Journal* 40 (4): 519–31.

______ (2006) 'Gender Trouble'. *Feminism and the Subversion of Identity*. New York/London: Routledge.

Cain, Patricia A. (1991) 'Feminist Jurisprudence: Grounding the Theories.' In Katherine T. Bartlett and Rosanne Kennedy (eds.), *Feminist Legal Theory: Readings in Law and Gender*. Boulder: Westview Press, 263–80.

Carroll, Lucy (1982) 'Talaq-i-Tafwid and Stipulations in a Muslim Marriage Contract: Important Means of Protecting the Position of the South Asian Muslim Wife.' *Modern Asian Studies* 16 (2): 277–309.

Chhachhi, Amrita (1991) 'Forced Identities: The State, Communalism, Fundamentalism and Women in India.' In Deniz Kandoiyoti (ed.), *Women, Islam and the State*. Philadelphia: Temple University Press, 144–75.

——— (2005) 'The State, Communalism, Fundamentalism and Women in India.' In Mala Khullar (ed.), *Writing the Women's Movement: A Reader*. New Delhi: Zubaan, an Imprint of Kali for Women, 218–42.

Chatterjee, Partha (1989) 'Colonialism, Nationalism, and Colonialized Women: The Contest in India.' *American Ethnologist* 16 (4): 622–33.

——— (1993) *The Nation and its Fragments: Colonial and Postcolonial Histories*. Princeton: Princeton University Press.

——— ([1999] 2006) 'The Nation and it's Women.' In Partha Chatterjee (ed.), *The Partha Chatterjee Omnibus*. New Delhi: Oxford University Press, 116–34.

Cinar, Alev (2005) *Modernity, Islam and Secularism in Turkey: Bodies, Places and Time*. Minneapolis: University of Minnesota Press.

Code, Lorraine (2000) 'How to Think Globally: Stretching the Limits of Imagination.' In Uma Narayan and Sandra Harding (eds.), *Decentering the Center: Philosophy for a Multicultural, Postcolonial, and Feminist World*. Bloomington: Indiana University Press, 67–79.

Collier, Jane (1975) 'Legal Processes.' *Annual Review of Anthropology*, 121–44.

Collins, Patricia Hill (2000) 'It's All in the Family: Intersections of Gender, Race, and the Nation.' In Uma Narayan and Sandra Harding (eds.), *Decentering the Center: Philosophy for a Multicultural, Postcolonial, and Feminist World*. Bloomington: Indiana University Press, 62–82.

Comaroff, John L. and Simon Roberts (1981) *Rules and Process: The Cultural Logic of Dispute in An African Context*. Chicago: The University of Chicago Press.

Comaroff, Jean and John L. Comaroff (1980) 'Introduction.' In Jean and John L. Comaroff (eds.), *The Meaning of Marriage Payments*. London: Academic Press, 1–44.

Crenshaw, Kimberle (1991) 'Mapping the Margins: Intersectionality, Identity Politics, and Violence against Women of Color.' *Stanford Law Review*, 1241–99.

Das, Veena (2008) 'Violence, Gender, and Subjectivity.' *Annual Review of Anthropology* 37: 283–99.

Dennerlein, Bettina (1999) 'Changing Conceptions of Marriage in Algerian Personal Status of Law.' In R. S. Khare (ed.), *Perspectives on Islamic Law, Justice and Society*. New York: Rowman and Littlefield Publishers, INC, 123–41.

——— (2001) 'Legalizing the Family: Disputes about Marriage, Paternity and Divorce in Algerian Courts (1963–1990).' *Continuity and Change* 16 (2): 243–62.

Dequen, Jean-Philippe (2012) 'Justice for Muslim Women in India: The Sinuous Path of the All India Muslim Women's Personal Law Board.' *Journal of Law and Social Research* 3: 81–95.

Doezema, Jo (2001) 'Ouch! Western Feminist's 'Wounded Attachment' to the Third World Prostitute.' *Feminist Review* 67 (1): 16–38.

Eickelmann, Dale and James Piscatori (1996) *Muslim Politics*. Princeton: Princeton University Press.

Eisenstadt, Shmuel Noah (2000) 'Multiple Modernities.' *Daedalus* 129 (1): 1–29.

Engineer, Asghar Ali (1999) *Contemporary Politics of Identity, Religion and Secularism*. New Delhi: Ajanta Books International.

_____ (2001) 'Islam, Women and Gender Justice.' In Asghar Ali Engineer (ed.), *Islam Women and Gender*. New Delhi: Gyan Publishing House, 23–42.

Esposito, John L. (1998) 'Women in Islam and Muslim Societies.' In Yvonne Yazbeck Haddad and John L. Esposito (eds.), *Islam, Gender, and Social Change*. New York and Oxford: Oxford University Press, x–xxviii.

Ewick, P. and S. S. Silbey (1991) 'Conformity, Contestation, and Resistance: An Account of Legal Consciousness.' *New England Law Review* 26: 731–49.

Ezeilo, Joy Ngozi (2005) 'Feminism and Human Rights at a Crossroads in Africa: Reconciling Universalism and Cultural Relativism.' In Marguerite Waller and Sylvia Marcos (eds.), *Dialogue and Difference: Feminism Challenge Globalization*. New York. Palgrave Macmillan, 231–52.

Foley, Rebecca (2004) 'Muslim Women's Challenges to Islamic Law.' *International Feminist Journal of Politics* 6 (1): 53–84.

Forbes, Geraldine H. (1982) 'From Purdah to Politics: The Social Feminism of the All-India Women's Organization.' In Hannah Papanek and Gail Minault (eds.), *Seperate Worlds: Studies of Purdah in South Asia*. Delhi: Chanakya Publications, 219–44.

Foucault, Michel (2010) 'Practices and Knowledge.' In Paul Rabinow (ed.) *The Foucault Reader*. New York: Vintage Books (A Division of Random House, Inc.), 121–239.

Freitag, Sandria (1989) *Collective Action and Community: Public Arenas and the Emergence of Communalism in North India*. Berkley, Los Angeles and Oxford: University of California Press.

_____ (2014) 'A Visual History of Three Lucknows.' *South Asia* 37 (3): 431–45.

Fyzee, Asaf A. A. ([1949] 1964) *Outlines of Muhammadan Law*. London: Oxford University Press.

Galanter, Marc (1981) 'Justice in Many Rooms: Courts, Private Ordering and Indigenous Law.' *Journal of Legal Pluralism* 13 (19): 1–47.

Gayer, L. and Christophe Jaffrelot (2012) *Muslims in Indian Cities: Trajectories of Marginalisation*. Columbia University Press.

Giddens, Anthony (1985) *Nation State and Violence: Volume Two of a Contemporary Critique of Historical Materialism*. Berkley and Los Angeles: University of California Press.

Glaser, Barney G. and Anselm L. Strauss (1980) *The Discovery of Grounded Theory: Strategies for Qualitative Research*. New York: Aldine Publishing Company.

Göle, Nilüfer (1996) *The Forbidden Modern: Civilization and Veiling*. Ann Arbor: The University of Michigan Press.

_____ (2000) 'Snapshots of Islamic Modernities.' *Daedalus* 29 (1): 91–117.

_____ (2006) 'Islamic Visibilities and Public Sphere.' In Nilüfer Göle and Ludwig Ammann (eds.), *Islam in Public. Turkey, Iran, and Europe*. Istanbul: Istanbul Bilgi University Press, 3–43.

Graff, Violette, Narayan Gupta and Mushirul Hasan (1997) 'Introduction.' In Violette Graff (ed.), *Lucknow: Memories of a City*. New Delhi: Oxford University Press, 1–15.

Greenhouse, Carol J. (1998) 'Legal Pluralism and Cultural Difference: What is the Difference? A Response to Professor Woodman.' *Journal of Legal Pluralism* 30 (42): 61–72.

Grewal, Inderpal and Caren Kaplan (1994) *Scattered Hegemonies: Postmodernity and Transnational Feminist Practice*. Minneapolis/London: University of Minnesota Press.

Haddad, Yvonne Yazbeck (1998) 'Islam Gender: Dilemmas in the Changing Arab World.' In Yvonne Yazbeck Haddad and John L. Esposito (eds.), *Islam, Gender, and Social Change*. New York/Oxford: Oxford University Press, 3–29.

Hasan, Mushirul (1997) *Legacy of a Divided Nation: India's Muslims since Independence*. London: Hurst and Company.

______ (1998) 'Introduction.' In Mushirul Hasan (ed.), *Islam, Communities and the Nation. Muslim Identities in South Asia and Beyond*. New Delhi: Manohar Publishers, 7–24.

Hasan, Zoya and Ritu Menon (2004) *Unequal Citizens: A Study of Muslim Women in India*. New Delhi: Oxford University Press.

______ (2005) *In a Minority: Essays on Muslim Women in India*. New Delhi: Oxford University Press.

Hasan, Zoya (1998) 'Gender Politics, Legal Reform, and the Muslim Community in India.' In Patricia Jeffrey and Amrita Basu (eds.), *Appropriating Gender: Women's Activism in Politicized Religion in South Asia*. New York/London: Routledge, 71–88.

______ (1999) 'Muslim Women and the Debate on Legal Reforms.' In Bharati Ray and Aparnu Basu (eds.), *From Independence towards Freedom: Indian Women since 1947*. New Delhi: Oxford University Press, 120–34

Hassan, Riffat (1995) 'Rights of Women within Islamic Communities.' In *Canadian Woman's Studies/Les Cahiers de la Femme*. Available at: http://pi.library.yorku.ca/ojs/index.php/cws/article/viewFile/9462/8579 (accessed May 16, 2012).

Hatem, Mervat F. (1998) 'Secularists and Islamist Discourses on Modernity in Egypt and the Evolution of the Postcolonial Nation-State.' In Yvonne Yazbeck Haddad and John L. Esposito (eds.), *Islam, Gender, and Social Change*. New York/Oxford: Oxford University Press, 85–99.

Héli-Lucas, Marie-Aimée (1994) 'The Preferential Symbol for Islamic Identity: Women in Muslim Personal Laws.' In Valentine M. Moghadam (ed.), *Identity Politics and Women: Cultural Reassertions and Feminisms in International Perspective*. Boulder/San Francisco/Oxford: Westview Press, 391–407.

Hijab, Nadia (1998) 'Islam, Social Change, and the Reality of Arab Women's Lives.' In Yvonne Yazbeck Haddad and John L. Esposito (eds.), *Islam, Gender, and Social Change*. New York/Oxford: Oxford University Press, 45–55.

Hirsch, Susan (1998) *Pronouncing and Preserving: Gender and the Discourse of Disputing in an African Islamic Court*. Chicago: The University of Chicago Press.

Holden, Livia (2004) 'Official Policies for (un)official Customs: The Hegemonic Treatment of Hindu Divorce Customs by Dominant Legal Discourses.' *Journal of Legal Pluralism* 36 (49): 47-74.

______ (2008) *Hindu Divorce: A Legal Anthropology*. Hampshire and Burlington: Ashgate Publishing Limited.

Hong Tschalaer, Mengia (2010) 'Women Entering the Legal Landscape: Negotiating Legal Gender Reforms in a Tribal Women's Court.' *Journal of Legal Pluralism* 42 (60): 41–72.

______ (2012) 'Competing Model-Nikahnamas: Muslim Women's Spaces within the Legal Landscape in Lucknow.' *Journal of Law and Social Research* 3: 65–80.

______ (2015) 'Muslim Women's Rights Activists' Visibility: Stretching the Gendered Boundaries of the Public Space in the City of Lucknow.' *South Asia Multidisciplinary Academic Journal* 11: 1–18.

Hoodfar, Homa (1991) 'Return to the Veil: Personal Strategies and Public Participation in Egypt.' In Nanneke Redclift and M. Thea Sinclair (eds.), *Working Women: International Perspectives on Labour and Gender Ideology*. London: Routledge, 320–3.

Hossain, Rokeya Sakhawat (2005) *Sultana's Dream: And Padmarag: Two Feminist Utopias*. New Delhi: Penguin Books India.

Hussain, Sabiha (2001) 'Mobilisation of Muslim Women for Gender Justice.' In Asghar Ali Engineer (ed.), *Islam Women and Gender*. New Delhi: Gyan Publishing House, 143–68.

______ (2006) 'Shariat Courts and Women's Rights in India.' *Occasional Paper Series*. Delhi: Center for Women's Development Studies, 1–40.

______ (2007) 'Reflections on Islamic Identity, Citizenship Rights and Women's Struggle For Gender Justice: Illustration from India.' *Journal of International Women's Studies* 9 (1): 63–79.

International Council on Human Rights Policy (2009) *When Legal Orders Overlap: Human Rights, State and Non-State Law*. Vernier, Switzerland: ATAR Roto Press SA.

Iyengar, Sushma (2007) 'A Study of Nari Adalats (Women's Courts) and Caste Panchayats in Gujarat.' *UNDP*. Available at: http://regionalcentrebangkok.undp.or.th/practices/governance/a2j/docs/CaseStudy-05-India-NariAdalat.pdf (accessed May 6, 2013).

Jeffery, Patricia, and Amrita Basu (eds.) (2012) *Appropriating Gender: Women's activism and Politicized Religion in South Asia*. New York: Routledge.

Jeffrey, Patricia (2000) 'Identifying Differences: Gender Politics and Religious Community in Rural Uttar Pradesh.' In Julia Leslie and Mary McGee (eds.), *Invented Identities: The Interplay of Gender, Religion and Politics in India*. New Delhi: Oxford University Press, 286–309.

Justin, Jones (2010) '"Signs of Churning": Muslim Personal Law and Public Contestation in Twenty First Century India.' *Modern Asian Studies* 44: 175–200.

Kandiyoti, Deniz (1991a) 'Introduction.' In Deniz Kandoiyoti (ed.), *Women, Islam and the State*. Philadelphia: Temple University Press. 1–21.

______ (1991b) 'Bargaining with Patriarchy.' In Judith Lorber and Susann A. Farrell (eds.), *The Social Construction of Gender*. Newbury Park, CA: Sage Publications, 104–18.

______ (1998) 'Some Akward Questions on Women and Modernity in Turkey.' In Lila Abu-Lughod (ed.), *Remaking Women: Feminism and Modernity in the Middle East*. Princeton: Princeton University Press, 270–87.

Kapur, Ratna (2006) 'Normalizing Violence: Transitional Justice and the Gujarat Riots.' *Colum. J. Gender and L.* 15: 885–927.

______ (2013) 'Gender, Sovereignty and the Rise of Sexual Security Regime in International Law and Postcolonial India.' *Melbourne Journal of International Law* 14 (2): 1–29.

——— (2014a) 'In the Aftermath of Critique We are not in Epistemic Free Fall: Human Rights, the Subaltern Subject, and Non-Liberal Search for Freedom and Happiness.' *Law and Critique* 25 (1): 25–45.

——— (2014b) 'A Leap of Faith: The Construction of Hindu Majoritarianism through Secular Law.' *South Atlantic Quarterly* 113 (1): 109–28.

Kapur, Ratna and Brenda Cossman (1996) *Subversive Sites: Feminist Engagements with Law in India.* New Delhi: Sage Publications India Pvt Ltd.

——— (1997) 'Secularism's Last Sigh: The Hindu Right, the Courts, and India's Stuggle for Democracy.' *Harvard International Law Journal* 38: 113–70.

Kaviraj, Sudipta (2004) 'Religion, Politik und Moderne.' In Shalini Randeria, Martin Fuchs and Antje Linkenbach (eds.), *Soziale Welt. Sonderband 15. Konfigurationen der Moderne. Diskurse zu Indien*. Baden–Baden: Nomos Verlagsgesellschaft, 199-214.

Khan, Sameera (2007) 'Negotiating the Mohalla: Exclusion, Identity and Muslim Women in Mumbai.' *Economic and Political Weekly* 42 (17): 1527–33.

Khan, Shahnaz (2002) 'Muslim Women: Negotiations in the Third Space.' In Therese Saliba, Judith A. Howard and Carolyn Allen (eds.), *Gender, Politics, and Islam*. Chicago and London: The University of Chicago Press, 305–36.

——— (2003) 'Zina and the Moral Regulation of Pakistani Women.' *Feminist Review* 75: 75–100.

Khory, Kavita R. (2005) 'The Shah Bano Case: Some Political Implications.' In Robert D. Baird (ed.), *Religion and Law in Independent India*. New Delhi: Manohar Publishers, 149–65.

Khundmiri, Alam (2009) 'Religion and its Application to Modern Life: The Islamic Problem.' In Mushirul Hasan (ed.), *Islam in South Asia: The Realm of the Secular, Volume IV.* New Delhi: Manohar, 171–78.

Kidwai, Sabina (2005) 'Images and Representations of Muslim Women in the Media, 1990–2001.' In Zoya Hasan and Ritu Menon (eds.), *In a Minority. Essays on Muslim Women in India*. New Delhi: Oxford University Press, 370–98.

Kymlicka, Will and Wayne Norman (1994) 'Return of the Citizen: A Survey of Recent Work on Citizenship Theory.' *Ethics* 104 (2): 352–81.

Kirmani, Nida (2009) 'Claiming Their Space: Muslim Women-led Networks and the Women's Movement in India.' *Journal of International Women's Studies* 11 (1): 72–85.

——— (2011a) 'Beyond the Impasse: 'Muslim Feminism(s)' and the Indian Women's Movement.' *Contributions to Indian Sociology* 45 (1): 1–26.

——— (2011b) 'Re-thinking the Promotion of Women's Rights through Islam in India.' *IDS Bulletin* 42 (1): 56–66.

——— (2013) *Questioning the Muslim Woman: Identity and Insecurity in an Urban Indian Locality*. New Delhi: Routledge.

Kleinhans, Martha-Marie, and Roderick A. Macdonald (1997) 'What is a Critical Legal Pluralism?' *Canadian Journal of Law and Society* 12 (2): 25–46.

Kozloski, Gregory C. (2005) 'Muslim Personal Law and Political Identity in Independent India.' In Robert D. Baird (ed.), *Religion and Law in Independent India*. New Delhi: Manohar Publishers, 103–20.

Kumar, Radha. (1993) *The History of Doing: An Illustrated Account of Movements for Women's Rights and Feminism in India, 1800–1990.* New Delhi: Zubaan.

Lateef, Shahida (1973) 'Separate Worlds and Symbolic Shelter.' *Comparative Studies in Society and History* 15 (3): 289–325.

______ (1990) *Muslim Women in India: Political and Private Realities.* London and New Jersey: Zed Books Ltd.

______ (1998) 'Muslim Women in India: A Minority within a Minority.' In Herbert L. Bodman and Nayereh Esfahlani Tohidi (eds.), *Women in Muslim Societies: Diversity within Unity.* Boulder. Colorado: Lynne Rienner Publisher, 251–73.

______ (2008) 'From Shahbano to Sachar.' *Seminar* 583: 46–50.

Lazarus-Black, Mindie (1997) 'The Rites of Domination: Practice, Process, and Structure in Lower Courts.' *American Ethnologist* 24 (3): 628–51.

______ (2008) 'Vanishing Complaints: The Place of Violence in Family, Gender, Work, and Law.' *Carribean Studies* 25 (1): 25–51.

Lemons, Katherine (2010) *At the Margins of Law: Adjudicating Muslim Families in Contemporary Delhi.* Unpublished Dissertation.

______ (2014) 'When Marriage Breaks Down, How Do Contracts Matter? Marriage Contracts and Divorce in Contemporary North India.' In Ravinder Kaur and Rajni Palriwala (eds.), *Marrying in South Asia: Shifting Concepts, Changing Practices in a Globalising World.* Delhi: Orient Blackswan, 371–88.

MacKinnon, Catharine A. (1987) *Feminism Unmodified: Discourses on Life and Law.* Cambridge/Massachusetts: Harvard University Press.

Mahmood, Saba (2005) *Politics of Piety: The Islamic Revival and the Feminist Subject.* Princeton: Princeton University Press.

Mahmood, Tahir (2001) *The Shari'at Courts in Modern India: A study of Working and Contribution in Comparison with State Courts.* Delhi: Unpublished paper.

______ (2005) 'Interaction of Islam and Public Law in Independent India.' In Robert D. Baird (ed.), *Religion and Law in Independent India.* New Delhi: Manohar Publishers, 121–48.

Majid, Anouar (2002) 'The Politics of Feminism in Islam.' In Therese Saliba, Carolyn Allen and Judith A. Howard (eds.), *Gender, Politics, and Islam.* Chicago/London: The University of Chicago Press, 53–93.

Mamdani, Mahmood (2002) 'Good Muslim, Bad Muslim: A Political Perspective on Culture and Terrorism.' *American Anthropologist*, 104 (3): 766–75.

Mani, Lata (1987) 'Contentious Traditions: The Debate on Sati in Colonial India.' *Cultural Critique* 7: 119–56.

Marcus, George E. (1995) 'Ethnography in/of the World System: The Emergence of Multi-Sited Ethnography.' *Annual Review of Anthropology* 24: 95–117.

Meghissi, Haideh (1999) *Feminism and Islamic Fundamentalism: The Limits of Postmodern Analysis.* London/New York: Zed Books.

Mehra, Madhu (1998) 'Exploring the Boundaries of Law, Gender and Social Reform.' *Feminist Legal Studies* 6 (1): 59–83.

Menon, Nivedita (1998) 'State/Gender/Community: Citizenship in Contemporary India.' *Economic and Political Weekly*, PE3–PE10.

______ (2002a) 'Embodying the Self: Feminism, Sexual Violence and the Law.' In Brinda Bose (ed.), *Translating Desire: The Politics of Gender and Culture in India*. New Delhi: Katha, 200–37.

______ (2002b) 'Surviving Gujarat 2002'. *Economic and Political Weekly* 37 (27): 2676–78.

Menski, Werner, 2001. 'Postmodern Hindu Law.' SOAS Law Department Occasional Papers, 1-42.

Mernissi, Fatima ([1975] 1987) *Beyond the Veil: Male-Female Dynamics in Modern Muslim Society*. Bloomington Indiana: Indiana University Press.

______ ([1987] 1991) *The Veil and the Male Elite: A Feminist Interpretation of Women's Rights in Islam*. New York: Basic Books.

Merry, Sally Engle (1986) 'Everyday Understandings of the Law in Working-Class America.' *American Ethnologist* 13 (2): 253–70.

______ (1988) 'Legal Pluralism.' *Law and Society Review* 22: 869–96.

______ (1990) *Getting Justice and Getting Even: Legal Consciousness among Working-Class Americans*. Chicago: The University of Chicago Press.

______ (2001) 'Women, Violence, and the Human Rights System.' In Marjorie Agosìn (ed.), *Women, Gender and Human Rights*. New Brunswick: Rutgers University Press, 83–97.

______ (2003) 'Rights Talk and the Experience of Law: Implementing Women's Human Rights to Protection from Violence.' *Human Rights Quarterly* 25 (2): 343–81.

______ (2002) 'Global Human Rights and Local Social Movements in a Legally Plural World.' In Martha Mundy (ed.), *Law and Anthropology*. Dartmouth: British Library Cataloguing in Publication Data, 95–115.

______ (2006) 'Transnational Human Rights and Local Activism: Mapping the Middle.' *American Anthropologist* 108 (1): 38–51.

Metcalf, Barbara D. (1996) 'Islam and Women: The Case of the Tablīghī Jamā'at.' *Stanford Electronic Humanities Review* 5 (1).

______ (2004) *Islamic Contestations: Essays on Muslims in India and Pakistan*. New Delhi: Oxford University Press.

Minault, Gail (1982a) 'Purdah Politics: The Role of Muslim Women in Indian Nationalism, 1911-1924.' In Hannah Papanek and Gail Minault (eds.), *Seperate Worlds: Studies of Purdah in South Asia*. New Delhi: Chanakya Publications, 245–61.

______ (1982b) *The Khilafat Movement: Religious Symbolism and Political Mobilization in India*. New York: Columbia University Press.

______ (1998a) 'Women, Legal Reform and Muslim Identity.' In Mushirul Hasan (ed.), *Islam, Communities and the Nation: Muslim Identities in South Asia and Beyond*. New Delhi: Manohar, 139–58.

______ (1998b) *Secluded Scholars: Women's Education and Muslim Social Reform in Colonial India*. New Delhi: Oxford University Press.

Mir-Hosseini, Ziba (1999) *Islam and Gender: The Religious Debate in Contemporary Iran*. Princeton: Princeton University Press.

______ (2000) *Marriage on Trial: A Study of Islamic Family Law*. London/New York: I.B. Tauris Publishers.

______ (2003) 'The Construction of Gender in Islamic Legal Thought and Strategies for Reform.' *Hawwa* 1 (1): 1–28.

______ (2006) 'Muslim Women's Quest for Equality: Between Islamic Law and Feminism.' *Critical Inquiry* 32 (4): 629–45.

Mirza, Qudsia (2008) 'Islamic Feminism and Gender Equality.' *Isim Review* 21: 30–31.

Moghadam, Valentine M. (2002a) 'Islamic Feminism and its Discontents: Towards a Resolution of the Debate.' In Therese Saliba, Judith A. Howard and Carolyn Allen (eds.), *Gender, Politics, and Islam*. Chicago/London: The University of Chicago Press, 15-51.

______ (2002b) 'Islamic Feminism and its Discontents: Toward a Resolution of the Debate.' *Signs* 27 (4): 1135–71.

______ (2005) *Globalizing Women: Transnational Feminist Networks*. Baltimore/London: The Johns Hopkins University Press.

______ (1994) 'Introduction: Women and Identity Politics in Theoretical and Comparative Perspective.' In Valentine M. Moghadam (ed.), *Identity Politics and Women: Cultural Reassertions and Feminisms in International Perspective*. Boulder/San Francisco/Oxford: Westview Press, 3–26.

Mohnati, Chandra Talpade (1988) 'Under Western Eyes: Feminist Scholarship and Colonial Discourses.' *Feminist Review* 30: 61–88.

______ (2002) '"Under Western Eyes" Revisited: Feminist Solidarity through Anti-Capitalist Struggles.' *Signs* 28 (2): 499–535.

Moore, Erin P. (2002) 'Gender, Power and Legal Pluralism: Rajasthan, India.' In Martha Mundy (ed.), *Law and Anthropology*. Dartmouth: British Library Cataloguing in Publication Data, 522–42.

Moore, Sally Falk (1973) 'Law and Social Change: The Semi-Autonomous Social Field as an Appropriate Subject of Study.' *Law and Society Review* 7: 719–46.

______ (2001) 'Certainities Undone: Fifty Turbulent Years of Legal Anthropology, 1949–1999.' *Journal of the Royal Anthropological Institute* 7 (1): 95–116.

Mukhopadhyay, Maitrayee (1998) *Legally Dispossessed: Gender, Identity and the Process of Law*. Calcutta: Stree.

Nader, Laura (1969) 'Introduction.' In Laura Nader (ed.), *Law in Culture and Society*. Chicago: Aldine Publishing Company, 1–10.

Nandy, Ashis (1990) 'The Politics of Secularism and the Recovery of Religious Tolerance.' In Veena Das (ed.), *Mirrors of Violence: Communities, Riots and Survivors in South Asia*. New Delhi: Oxford University Press.

Narayan, Uma (2000) 'Essence of Culture and a Sense of History: A Feminist Critique of Cultural Esssentialism.' In Uma Narayan and Sandra Harding (eds.), *Decentering the Center: Philosophy for a Multicultural, Postcolonial, and Feminist World*. Bloomington: Indiana University Press, 80–100.

Narain, Vrinda (1998) 'Women's Rights and the Accommodation of Difference: Muslim Women in India.' *Southern California Review of Law and Women's Studies* 8: 43–72.

______ (2013) 'Muslim Women's Equality in India: Applying a Human Rights Framework.' *Human Rights Quarterly* 35 (1): 91–115.

Narain, Vrinda (2014) 'Taking 'Culture' out of Multiculturalism.' *Canadian Journal of Women and the Law* 26 (1): 116-152.

Najmabadi, Afsaneh (1993) 'Veiled Discourse-Unveiled Bodies.' *Feminist Studies* 19 (3): 487–518.

Naqvi, Farah (2006) 'Constructing Community.' *Seminar* 557. Available at: http://www.india-seminar.com/2006/557/557%20farah%20naqvi.htm (accessed December 30, 2016).

Needham Anuradha Dingwaney and Rajeswari Sunder Rajan (2007) *The Crisis of Secularism in India.* Durham/London: Duke University Press.

Nussbaum, Martha (1999) *Sex and Social Justice.* New York: Oxford University Press.

______ (2009) *The Clash Within: Democracy, Religious Violence, and India's Future.* Cambridge: Harvard University Press.

Okin, Susan Moller (1994) 'Gender Inequality and Cultural Differences.' *Political Theory* 22 (1): 5–24.

______ (1999) 'Is Multiculturalism Bad for Women?' In Joshua Cohen, Matthew Howard and Martha C. Nussbaum (eds.), *Is Multiculturalism Bad for Women?* Princeton: Princeton University Press, 9-24.

Oldenburg, Veena Talwar (2007) 'Nawabi Lucknow: Through Western Eyes.' In Veena Talwar Oldenburg (ed.), *Writings on Lucknow: Shaam-e-Awadh.* New Delhi: Penguin Books, 12–16.

Omvedt, Gail (2004) 'Women's Movement: Some Ideological Debates.' In Maitrayee Chaudhuri (ed.), *Feminism in India.* New Delhi: Kali for Women and Women Unlimited, 177–186.

Ong, Ahiwa (1990) 'State versus Islam: Malay Families, Women's Bodies, and the Body Politic in Malaysia.' *American Ethnologist* 17 (2): 258–76.

Papanaek, Hanna (1982) 'Purdah: Separate Worlds and Symbolic Shelter.' In Hannah Papanek and Gail Minault (eds.), *Separate Worlds: Studies of Purdah in South Asia.* New Delhi: Chanakya Publications, 3–53.

______ (1990) 'The Ideal Woman and the Ideal Society: Control Autonomy in the Construction of Identity.' In Valentine M. Moghadam (ed.), *Identity Politics and Women: Cultural Reassertions and Feminisms in International Perspective.* Boulder/San Francisco/Oxford: Westview Press, 42–75.

Phadke, Shilpa, Shilpa Ranade, and Sameera Khan (2009) 'Why loiter? Radical Possibilities for Gendered Dissent.' In Melissa Butcher et.al. (eds.), *Dissent and Cultural Resistance in Asia's Cities.* New York: Routledge, 185-203.

Pathak, Zakia and Rajeswari Sunder Rajan (1989) 'Shabano.' *Signs* 14 (3): 558–82.

Pateman, Carole (1988) *The Sexual Contract.* Stanford, California: Stanford University Press.

Pearl, David and Werner Menski (1998) *Muslim Family Law* (Third Edition). London: Sweet and Maxwell.

Quraishi, Asifa and Frank E. Vogel (2008) *The Islamic Marriage Contract: Case Studies in Islamic Family Law.* Cambridge/Massachusetts: Islamic Legal Studies Program, Harvard Law School, 195–200.

Rabinow, Paul (2008) 'Midst Anthropology's Problems.' In Ahiwa Ong and Stephen J. Collier (eds.), *Global Assemblages: Technology, Politics, and Ethics as Anthropological Problems*. Malden/Oxford/Victoria: Blackwell Publishing, 40–53.

Rajagopal, Balakrishnan (2005) 'The Role of Law in Counter-Hegemonic Globalization and Global Legal Pluralism: Lessons from the Narmada Valley Struggle in India.' *Leiden Journal of International Law* 18 (3): 345–87.

Randeria, Shalini (2002) 'Entangled Histories of Uneven Modernities: Civil Society, Caste Solidarities and Legal Pluralism in Post-Colonial India.' In Yehuda Elkana, Ivan Krastev, Elisio Macamo and Shalini Randeria (ed.), *Unraveling Ties: From Social Cohesion to New Practices of Connectedness*. Frankfurt am Main/New York: Campus, 284–211.

_____ (2003) 'Between Cunning States and Unaccountable International Institutions: Social Movements and Rights of Local Communities to Common Property Resources.' *Discussion Paper Nr. SP IV* 2003-502. ISSN 1612-1643, 1–30.

_____ (2004) 'Verwobene Moderne: Zivilgesellschaft, Kastenbindungen und nicht-staatliches Familienrecht im (post)kolonialen Indien.' In Shalini Randeria, Martin Fuchs and Antje Linkenbach (eds.), *Soziale Welt. Sonderband 15. Konfigurationen der Moderne. Diskurse zu Indien*. Baden–Baden: Nomos Verlagsgesellschaft, 155–78.

_____ (2007) 'Civil Society and Legal Pluralism in the Shadow of the Caste: Entangled Modernities in Postcolonial India.' In Dominique Schirmer, Gernot Saalmann and Christl Kessler (eds.), *Hybridising East and West: Tales Beyond Westernisation. Empirical Contributions to the Debates on Hybridity*. Berlin: LIT Verlag, 97–124.

Redding, Jeffrey A. (2010) 'The Case of Ayesha, Muslim 'Courts', and the Rule of Law: Some Ethnographic Lessons for Legal Theory.' Unpublished Paper.

Relis, Tamara (2011) 'Human Rights and Southern Realities.' *Human Rights Quarterly* 33 (2): 509–51.

Riles, Annelise (2005) 'A New Agenda for the Cultural Study of Law: Taking on the Technicalities.' *Buffalo Law Review* 53: 973–1033.

Robinson, Francis (2001) *The Ulama of Firangi Mahall and Islamic Culture in South Asia*. New Delhi: Permanent Black.

_____ (2008) 'Islamic Reform and Modernities in South Asia.' *Modern Asian Studies* 42 (2–3): 259–81.

Rouse, Shahnaz (1996) 'Gender Nationalism(s) and Cultural Identity: Discursive Strategies and Exclusivities.' In Ritu Menon and Kamla Bhasin (eds.), *Borders and Boundaries: Women in India's Partition*. New Delhi: Kali for Women, 42–70.

Roychowdhury, Poulami (2016) 'Over the Law Rape and the Seduction of Popular Politics.' *Gender and Society* 30 (1): 80–94.

Rubin, Gayle (1975) 'The Traffic in Women: Notes on the Political Economy of Sex.' In Rayna R. Reiter (ed.), *Toward an Anthropology of Women*. New York: Monthly Review Press, 157–200.

_____ (1984). 'Thinking sex: Notes for a radical Theory of the Politics of Sexuality.' Social Perspectives in Lesbian and Gay Studies; A Reader, 100-33.

Rudolph, Susanne Hoeber and Lloyd I. Rudolph (2001) 'Living with Difference in India. Legal Pluralism and Legal Universalism in Historical Context.' In Gerald James Larson (eds.), *Religion and Personal Law in Secular India. A Call to Judgment.* Bloomington: Indiana University Press, 36–65.

Said, Edward W. (2003 [1978]) *Orientalism*. New York: Random House, Inc.

Saliba, Therese (2002) 'Introduction: Gender, Politics and Islam.' In Therese Saliba, Carolyn Allen and Judith A. Howard (eds.), *Gender, Politics, and Islam*. Chicago/London: The University of Chicago Press, 1–13.

Sangari, Kumkum (1999) 'Gender Lines: Personal Laws, Uniform Laws, Conversion.' *Social Scientist* 27 (5/6): 17–61.

Sarkar, Tanika (2004) 'Frau, Gemeinschaft und Nation. Eine historische Entwicklungslinie hinduistischer Identitätspolitik.' In Shalini Randeria, Martin Fuchs and Antje Linkenbach (eds.), *Soziale Welt Sonderband 15. Konfigurationen der Moderne. Diskurse zu Indien*. Baden–Baden: Nomos Verlagsgesellschaft, 231–47.

Schneider, Nadja-Christina (2009) 'Islamic Feminism and Muslim Women's Rights Activism in India: From Transnational Discourse to Local Movement – or Vice Versa?' *Journal of International Women's Studies* 11 (1): 56–71.

Scott, David (1995) 'Colonial Governmentality.' *Social Text* 43: 191–220.

Sen, Ilina (2004) 'Women's Politics in India.' In Maitrayee Chaudhuri (ed.), *Feminism in India*. New Delhi: Kali for Women and Women Unlimited, 187–210.

Sezgin, Yüksel (2010) 'Introduction to the Special Issue.' *Journal of Legal Pluralism* 42 (60): 1–4.

_____ (2013) *Human Rights under State-Enforced Religious Laws in Israel, Egypt and India*. New York: Cambridge University Press.

Shackelford, S. (2008) 'In The Name of Efficiency: The Role of Permanent Lok Adalats in the Indian Justice System and Power Infrastructure.' In Manoj Kumar Sinha (ed.), Global Governance, Development and Human Rights.

Shah, Prakash A. (2003) 'Attitudes to Polygamy in English Law.' *International and Comparative Law Quarterly* 52 (2): 369–400.

Shaikh, Sa'diyya (2003) 'Transforming Feminisms: Islam, Women, and Gender Justice.' In Omid Safi (ed.), *Progressive Muslims: On Justice, Gender and Pluralism*. Oxford: Oneworld Publications, 147–62.

Shohat, Ella (2001) 'Area Studies, Transnationalism, and the Feminist Production of Knowledge.' *Globalization and Gender* 26 (4): 1269–72.

Solanki, Gopika (2011) *Adjudication in Religious Family Laws: Cultural Acommodation, Legal Pluralism, and Gender Equality in India*. Cambridge: Cambridge University Press.

_____ (2013) The Retelling of Tales: Disentangling the Feminist Evolutionary Analytic Approach, Legal Pluralism, and Gender Justice.' *Politics and Gender* 9 (1): 105–10.

_____ (2016) 'A Court of Her Own: Autonomy, Gender, and Women's Courts in India.' In Samia Bano and Jennifer Pierce (eds.), *Gender Equality and Justice in Family Law Disputes: Women, Mediation and Religious Arbitration*. New England: University of New England Press.

Sousa Santos, Boaventura de (1987) 'Law: A Map of Misreading. Toward a Postmodern Conception of Law.' *Journal of Law and Society* 14 (3): 279–302.

_____ (2002) *Toward a New Legal Common Sense: Law, Globalization, and Emancipation*. London: Butterworths Lexis Nexis.

______ (2006) 'The Heterogenous State and Legal Pluralism in Mozambique.' *Law and Society Review* 40 (1): 39–75.

Sousa Santos, Boaventura de and César A. Rodriguez-Caravito (2005) 'Law, Politics, and the Subaltern in Counter-Hegemonic Globalization.' In Boaventura Sosa Santos and César A. Rodriguez-Caravito (eds.), *Law and Globalization from Below: Towards a Cosmopolitan Legality*. Cambridge: Cambridge University Press, 1–26.

Spivak, Gayatri Chakravorty (1988) *Can the Subaltern Speak?*. UK: Macmillan Education.

______ (2000) 'The New Subaltern: A Silent Interview.' In Vinayak Chaturvedi (ed.), *Mapping Subaltern Studies and the Postcolonial*. New York: Verso, 324–40.

Starr, June and Mark Goodale (2002) 'Introduction: Legal Ethnography: New Dialogues, Enduring Methods.' *In Practicing Ethnography of Law: New Dialogues, Enduring Methods*. New York: Palgrave Macmillan, 1–10.

Stowasser, Barbara (1998) 'Gender Issues and Contemporary Quran Interpretation.' In Yvonne Yazbeck Haddad and John L. Esposito (eds.), *Islam, Gender, and Social Change*. New York/Oxford: Oxford University Press, 30–44.

Strathern, Marilyn (1984) 'Marriage Exchanges: A Melanesian Comment.' *Annual Review of Anthropology* 13: 41–73.

______ (2004) 'Loosing (out on) Intellectual Resources.' In Alain Pottage and Martha Mundy (eds.), *Law, Anthropology and the Constitution of the Social: Making Persons and Things*. Cambridge: Cambridge University Press, 201–33.

Strauss, Claude Lévi ([1949] 1969) *The Elementary Structures of Kinship*. Beacon Press.

Subramaniam, Mangala (2004) 'The Indian Women's Movement.' *Contemporary Sociology:* 33 (6): 635–9.

Subramaniam, Narendra (2008) 'Legal Change and Gender Inequality: Changes in Muslim Family Law in India.' *Law and Social Enquiry* 33 (3): 631–72.

______ (2014) *Nation and the Family: Personal Law, Cultural Pluralism, and Gendered Citizenship in India*. Stanford: Stanford University Press.

Sullivan, Zohren T. (1998) 'Eluding the Feminist, Overthrowing the Modern? Transformation in Twentieth-Century Iran.' In Lila Abu-Lughod (ed.), *Remaking Women: Feminism and Modernity in the Middle East*. Princeton: Princeton University Press, 215–42.

Sunder Rajan, Rajeswari and Needham, Anuradha Dingwaney (2007) 'Introduction.' In Anuradha Dingwaney Needham and Rajeswari Sunder Rajan (eds.), *The Crisis of Secularism in India*. Durham/London: Duke University Press, 1–42.

Sunder Rajan, Rajeswari (2003) *The Scandal of the State. Women, Law, and Citizenship in Postcolonial India*. Durham/London: Duke University Press.

Suneetha, A. (2011) 'Indian Secularism and Personal Law: The Story of Model-Nikahnama.' *Social Difference-Online* 1: 54–62.

Susewind, Raphael and Christopher B. Taylor (2015) 'Introduction: Islamicate Lucknow Today: Historical Legacy and Urban Aspirations.' *South Asia Multidisciplinary Academic Journal* 11: 1–24.

Tamanaha, Brian Z. (2008) 'Understanding Legal Pluralism: Past to Present, Local to Global.' *Sidney Law Review* 30: 375–411.

Tavakoli-Targhi, Mohammad (1994) 'Women of the West Imagined: The Farangi Other and the Emergence of the Woman Question in Iran.' In Valentine M. Moghadam (ed.), *Identity Politics and Women. Cultural Reassertions and Feminisms in International Perspective*. Boulder/San Francisco/Oxford: Westview Press, 98–120.

Therborn, Göran (1995) 'Routes to/through Modernity.' In Mike Featherstone, Scott Lash and Roland Roberton (eds.), *Global Modernities*. London: Sage, 124–37.

Tripp, Aili Mary (2003) 'Women in Movement Transformations in African Political Landscapes.' *International Feminist Journal of Politics* 5 (2): 233–55.

Vatuk, Sylvia (2005) 'Muslim Women and Personal Law.' In Zoya Hasan and Ritu Menon (eds.), *In a Minority. Essays on Muslim Women in India*. New Delhi: Oxford University Press, 18–68.

______ (2008) 'Islamic Feminism in India: Indian Muslim Women Activists and the Reform of Muslim Personal Law.' *Modern Asian Studies* 42 (2–3): 489–518.

______ (2013) 'Islamic Feminism in India: Indian Muslim Women Activists and the Reform of Muslim Personal Law.' In Filippo Osella and Caroline Osella (eds.), *Islamic Reform in South Asia*. Cambridge: Cambridge University Press, 346–82.

Verniers, Gilles (2012) 'A Minority within a Minority: The Shias of Kashmiri Mohalla, Lucknow'. In Laurent Gayer and Christoph Jaffrelot (eds.), *Muslims in Indian Cities: Trajectories of Marginalisation*. New York: Columbia University Press, 105–28.

Volpp, Leti (2001) 'Feminism versus Multiculturalism.' *Columbia Law Review*: 1181–218.

Wadud, Amina (2009) 'Islam Beyond Patriarchy through Gender Inclusive Qur'anic Analysis.' *Wanted: Equality and Justice in the Muslim Family*. 95–112.

Weiss, Anita M. (1998) 'The Slow Yet Steady Path to Women's Empowerment in Pakistan.' In Yvonne Yazbeck Haddad and John L. Esposito (eds.), *Islam, Gender, and Social Change*. New York/Oxford: Oxford University Press, 124–43.

Wilson, Richard Ashby (2006) 'Afterword to 'Anthropology and Human Rights in a new Key': The Social Life of Human Rights.' *American Anthropologist* 108 (1): 77–83.

Young, Iris Marion (1990) *Justice and the Politics of Difference*. Princeton, N. J.: Princeton University Press.

Yuval-Davis, Nira (1997) 'Women, Citizenship and Difference.' *Feminist Review* 57 (1): 4–27.

______ (2006) 'Human/Women's Rights and Feminist Transversal Politics.' In Myra Marx Ferree and Aili Mari Tripp (eds.), *Global Feminism: Transnational Women's Activism, Organizing, and Human Rights*. New York/London: New York University Press, 275–95.

Index